The Wrong Country

The Wrong Country

ESSAYS ON MODERN IRISH WRITING

Gerald Dawe

IRISH ACADEMIC PRESS

First published in 2018 by
Irish Academic Press
10 George's Street
Newbridge
Co. Kildare
Ireland
www.iap.ie

9781788550284 (Cloth)
9781788550291 (Kindle)
9781788550307 (Epub)
9781788550314 (PDF)

British Library Cataloguing in Publication Data
An entry can be found on request

Library of Congress Cataloging in Publication Data
An entry can be found on request

Interior design by www.jminfotechindia.com
Typeset in Bembo 11.5/14.5 pt

Jacket design by River Design
Jacket front: Colin Middleton, *The Holy Land*, 1945 (oil on canvas),
© Estate of Colin Middleton, IVARO Dublin, 2018.
Printed by TJ International Ltd. Padstow Cornwall

CONTENTS

'You can't be afraid of saying the opposite, even if you look like a fool and everybody thinks you're in the wrong country, speaking the wrong language.'

Hugo Hamilton, *The Speckled People*

ACKNOWLEDGEMENTS

The book was completed in Pembroke College, Cambridge, thanks to the good offices of Dr Mark Wormald, to whom kind acknowledgement is made for his hospitality and the opportunity to think things over in the serene environment of Pembroke College Library; and to the staff there, particularly Ms Patricia Aske, and for the home from home at Botolph Lane. Acknowledgements also to the organisers of several academic conferences/literary gatherings where many of the issues and subjects explored in *The Wrong Country* were first aired: Paul Delaney, School of English, Trinity College Dublin for a symposium on 'Identity and Cultural Diversity' (Hugo Hamilton); 'Reading the Fifties', with Darryl Jones, School of English and Trinity Long Room Hub, as well as lectures given to the John McGahern Conference, Carrick-on-Shannon (John Kenny); Stewart Parker Commemorative Conference, School of Drama, Queen's University Belfast (Mark Phelan); Trinity College Samuel Beckett Summer School (Sam Slote); 'Imagination in the Classroom', Royal Irish Academy, Dublin (Anne Fogarty, Éilís Ní Dhuibhne and Eibhear Walshe); Goldsmith Literary Weekend, Longford (Seamus McCormack and Clare Butler); 'One City One Book: *Strumpet City*', Dublin and Dún Laoghaire Libraries (Marian Keyes and Jane Alger); John Hewitt Summer School, Armagh (Cathal Dallat and Anthony Kennedy); 'From *Dusty Bluebells* to *Parallax*: reading and writing poetry from Northern Ireland', Ulster Poetry Project, Ulster University (Kathryn White and Frank Ferguson), 'George Reavey Commemoration' Trinity College Dublin (Sandra O'Connell); 'The North Began? Ulster and the Irish Revolution, 1900–1925', Trinity College Dublin (Marnie Hay and Eunan O'Halpin). 'History Lessons' is based upon two lectures on Derek Mahon delivered at ISAIL Japan and on Seamus Deane at Pembroke College, Cambridge.

I would particularly like to thank Dorothea Melvin for her advice and insight into much of the social and cultural background covered in this book and also to my late friend Gerard Fanning, and to Seona Mac Réamoinn, who answered queries about UCD and Dublin during the 1970s. To Conor Linnie, who helped out when the formatting was beyond me, and Jonathan Williams, first responder, many and lasting thanks. Earlier versions of some of the chapters appeared in the following publications, to whom kind acknowledgement is made: Paul Delaney (ed.), *Reading Colm Tóibín* (Dublin: Liffey Press, 2008); Gerald Dawe, Darryl Jones and Nora Pellazi (eds), *Beautiful Strangers: Ireland and the World of the 1950s* (Bern: Peter Lang AG, 2012); Anne Fogarty, Éilís Ní Dhuibhne and Eibhear Walshe (eds), *Imagination in the Classroom: Teaching and Learning Creative Writing in Ireland* (Dublin: Four Courts Press, 2013); Siobhan Campbell and Nessa O'Mahony (eds), *Eavan Boland: Inside History* (Dublin: Arlen House, 2016); Aileen Douglas (ed.), *Trinity Writers Portal* (School of English, Trinity College Dublin, 2016); and Eamon Maher (ed.), *The Reimagining Ireland Reader: Examining Our Past, Shaping Our Future* (Oxford: Peter Lang, 2018). Extracts appeared in *The Irish Times* (Dublin), *Irish Pages* (Belfast), *Journal of Irish Studies* (Tokyo), *Irish University Review* (Dublin), *Poetry Ireland Review* (Dublin) and online in the *Dublin Review of Books* and RTÉ.

CHAPTER ONE

HEARING THINGS

'All life', W.B. Yeats remarked in *Reveries over Childhood and Youth*, 'weighed in the scales of my own life seems to me a preparation for something that never happens.'[1] It is tempting to take this as an epigraph to the comparative lives of Yeats and Samuel Beckett and trace how their distinctive biographies and literary work intersected. Indeed, reading around the lives they knew in Ireland, what looms large alongside their upbringing, their families, their education and what Terence Brown, Yeats's biographer, describes as the Butler 'caste, obsessively alert to gradations of calling and breeding',[2] is the inner world and crucial influence of Irish Protestantism which the writers shared. The social customs associated with both men's families, their religious and educational backgrounds seem so strikingly similar at one level and yet so utterly different at another. (In passing, there is also the curious fact – given this relatively small if variable 'Protestant' group – that it should produce three Nobel Prize laureates in literature. This is quite exceptional when one thinks about the global context and the likelihood of such a thing happening elsewhere.)

From the opening chapter of James Knowlson's *Damned to Fame: The Life of Samuel Beckett*, 'Images of Childhood 1906–1915', the stability of Beckett's childhood and youth in his south County Dublin home is as clear as day:

> On Sunday mornings, the bell of Tullow Church called all good local Protestants to worship. May Beckett was an assiduous attender at the church and ensured that, from an early age, her two sons accompanied her regularly. They had, Beckett remembered, a pew close to the pulpit, which they shared with a market gardener called Matt Tyler, and across the aisle from another well-known Foxrock family, the Orpens. Beckett was never happy to go to church and hated wearing the hard, chaffing collars that 'Sunday-best' entailed. So he used to sit scowling at Beatrice Orpen and at the world in general. His father never came with them to Tullow Church. Instead he used to say 'that he'd go to Church with the birds up the mountains' and take himself off into the Dublin hills … Later on, Beckett used to accompany him on these Sunday walks.[3]

Thirty and more years earlier, Yeats's family had started well into the peripatetic roving from their south County Dublin origins, as father John Butler Yeats, Yeats's 'profoundly unhappy mother', Susan, sisters and brothers, moved back and forth to England, living with difficulty in and out of homes there and also back in Dublin and Sligo. The contrast in the start in life from which both writers emerged is striking. Yet the more one reads Beckett with Yeats in mind, the more compelling and lasting is Yeats's presence felt and heard. In what follows I am going to rehearse some of these points of contact before ending with an unlikely parallel between both men and the wider reaches of the culture from which they came.

As several scholars in the past, such as D.E.S. Maxwell,[4] Katharine Worth,[5] Gordon Armstrong[6] and Enoch Brater in his essay, 'Intertextuality',[7] have identified, the intertextual play between Beckett and Yeats runs deeply through Beckett's poetry, his fiction and his drama. In a sense, Beckett's reading of Yeats's *plays* reworked the latter's drama and revivified scholarly (if not artistic) interest in Yeats's ideas about theatre and the dramatic image. From Beckett's earliest fiction and literary criticism, Yeats surfaces as a critical and/or parodic point of order or departure. As Enoch Brater puts it, Beckett's ambivalence in dealing with Yeats 'begins in parody and ends as eloquence'.[8]

Yeats provides the in-joke from *Dream of Fair to Middling Women* with its 'fat June butterfly' about 'to pern in a gyre', to Beckett's signature play, *Waiting for Godot*, as Estragon discusses Vladimir's cue: 'I thought it was he.'

> E: Who?
> V: Godot.
> E: Pah! The wind in the reeds.[9]

Between the unpublished *Dream of Fair to Middling Women* of 1931–2 to *Waiting for Godot* (1954), it is possible to list the Yeatsian references that clearly sparked off Beckett's needs.

He had, after all, watched Yeats's plays as a young man as they were performed in Dublin in 1926 and subsequently, and he wasn't greatly impressed; although it has been repeatedly identified that *At the Hawk's Well* and *Purgatory* mattered significantly to Beckett in his search for a theatrical experience fundamentally physical and spoken but without the encumbrances of plot or 'design'. As Maxwell has it, Beckett's stage characters brought 'Yeats's heroic figures down in the world. Formally, he parodies Yeats's Noh-business ... and burlesques Yeats's stage.'[10] Think perhaps of Winnie in *Happy Days* (1963):

> One loses one's classics (*Pause*). Oh not all (*Pause*). A part
> (*Pause*). A part remains (*Pause*). That is what I find so wonderful,
> a part remains, of one's classics, to help one through the day
> (*Pause*). Oh yes, many mercies. Many mercies (*Pause*). And
> now? (*Pause*). And now, Willie? (*Long pause*). I call to the eye
> of the mind ...[11]

Of the opening of (Willie) Yeats's *At the Hawk's Well*, that is:

> I call to the eye of the mind
> A well long choked up and dry
> And boughs long stripped by the wind,
> And I call to the mind's eye
> Pallor of an ivory face,
> A man climbing up to a place
> The salt sea wind has swept bare.[12]

Beckett would create in his later drama testimonials to Yeats and ultimately, in ... *but the clouds* ...[13] (1976), channel one of Yeats's greatest poems from *The Tower*. By which time Beckett was entering his seventies and looking back as Yeats's senior, so to speak, on how in 1928 Yeats had grappled with age in *his* sixties. It is all about sustaining examples, for along with much else, *The Tower* as a collection of poems, as much as the individual sequence of poems called 'The Tower', is obsessed with the verifiability of memory, the landscapes of home reimagined and the meaning, or meaninglessness, of artistic achievement and of what remains post-event, post-experience. As the final stanza of part II of 'The Tower' enquires:

4

Does the imagination dwell the most
Upon a woman won or woman lost?
If on the lost, admit you turned aside
From a great labyrinth out of pride,
Cowardice, some silly over-subtle thought
Or anything called Conscience once;
And that if memory recur, the sun's
Under eclipse and the day blotted out.[14]

Clearly Yeats's clerical inheritance did not completely evaporate in the occult.

So whether we cite Beckett's Yeats from the beginning, in references in the early stories such as 'Walking Out',[15] in the literary polemical crossfire of 'Recent Irish Poetry'[16] where Yeats's 'A Coat' is quoted, as well as 'The Tower', and the 'attar of far off, most secret and inviolate rose' from 'The Secret Rose' (*The Wind Among the Reeds*, 1899) or in one of his most important early letters – to Axel Kaun in 1937, which John Pilling[17] glosses as a Yeatsian riff – the 'idea of the "trembling of the veil", no doubt familiar to Beckett by way of Yeats's prose', Yeats is a crucial *defining* presence:

> It is indeed getting more and more difficult [Beckett writes], even pointless, for me to write in formal English. And more and more my language appears to me like a veil which one has to tear apart in order to get to those things (or the nothingness) lying behind it.[18]

It is important to state the obvious here: that Beckett's engagement with Yeats was public, published and contemporaneous. Yeats was, after all, still very much alive during the writing of these early flourishes of Beckett.

So too the private correspondences contain further passing remarks, jokes, avoidances, notes, recommendations – all of which connect with Yeats. One could name each and every one contained in those amazing volumes of Beckett's *Letters* and it would make for a very long list indeed – along with the extensive citing of Yeatsian echoes, reverberations and allusions that critics have heard or seen in Beckett, such as W.J. McCormack's spotting of possible typographical links in County Clare between Yeats's *Dreaming of the Bones* and *Watt*.[19]

On a more basic level, some of the younger Beckett's spleen – that which produced 'Recent Irish Poetry', say – can be heard in a letter he wrote from his Foxrock fastness to his pal Thomas MacGreevy in 1936. The letter is full of gossip and is rich pickings for the social historian, but it is the following extract that caught my eye: 'I was down at the mailboat last Monday week meeting Frank [his brother] returning from Anglesea [*sic*] and WB stalked off with his bodyguard, Lennox, Dolly, Gogarty, Walter Starkie, O'Connor, Hayes, Higgins, all twined together.'[20] This is 7 July 1936 to be exact. Yeats was actually recovering from a heart condition and finishing off work on the *Oxford Book of Modern Verse 1892–1935*,[21] a publication that was to cause all kinds of controversy, much to Yeats's delight. Incidentally, in a letter written a few weeks after Beckett's, Yeats writes to Dorothy Wellesley on 26 July from 'Riversdale', his home in Dublin: 'I get up every morning about 4, work at proof sheets until about 5.30, then go to bed again, breakfast at 7.30, and then write poetry, with interruption for rest, till 12'[22] – not bad working habits for a 71-year-old!

According to W.J. McCormack,[23] in a further letter to Dorothy Wellesley the following year, May 1937, and only partially republished, Yeats relates in the original the story of a libel case in which Beckett had appeared against Yeats's friend Oliver St John Gogarty and his autobiography, *As I was Going Down Sackville Street* (1936):

> In his book [Yeats is quoted as writing to Dorothy Wellesley] Gogarty has called a certain man a 'chicken butcher' meaning that he makes love to the immature. The informant, the man who swears that he recognised the victim[,] is a racketeer of a Dublin poet or imatative [*sic*] poet of the new school. He hates us all – his review of the Anthology was so violent the *Irish Times* refused to publish it.
>
> He & the 'chicken butcher' are Jews ... Two or three weeks ago Gogarty & the chicken butcher were drinking in our 'poet's pub' laughing at the work.

There is no corroboration that I know of but if the 'imitative poet of the new school' is (if I read McCormack's suggestion correctly) Beckett and not, say, Leslie Daiken, an important Dublin Jewish left-wing radical poet and anthologist of the time, Yeats clearly had Beckett in his sights. Yet it is curious that Yeats did not recall Beckett's name, if, that is, we take it that the two men had met only a few years previously. Lots of 'ifs'. But it also depends on which story one takes as fact.

Anthony Cronin's biography of Samuel Beckett emphatically states that while Beckett had both opportunities and a network of mutual connections (Alan Duncan for one), 'there is no evidence that [he] met any of [the prominent Dublin literary figures] who attended soirées such as Walter Starkie's' and 'in fact [Beckett] was never to meet [Yeats] the greatest poet of the age, there or anywhere else'.[24] Deirdre Bair's biography of two decades earlier tells it differently:[25]

Just as he sought Jack B's company, Beckett avoided introduction to his brother, whom he regarded as pompous and posturing, fatuously slobbering over all the wrong aspects of Ireland and Irish society.

But she continues:[26]

> Beckett actually met W. B. Yeats only once, during a brief encounter in Killiney, where he was disgusted with the way W. B. Yeats simpered over his wife and made an inordinate fuss with his children.

For her sources, Bair cites A.J. Leventhal, John Montague, John Kobler, the papers of Thomas MacGreevy and a letter to H.O. White (15 April 1957)[27] – both in TCD library – and an anonymous source. Following suit, in his lively *Contemporary Irish Drama from Beckett to McGuinness* (1994), Anthony Roche confidently identifies Killiney and 1932 as the place and year of the meeting, set up through Thomas MacGreevy, and remarks that 'the young Beckett could find little to identify with in the persona Yeats was then projecting, of a family man with wife and children'. However, according to Roche, Beckett was 'taken aback when the older poet praised a passage from Beckett's "Whoroscope", his first published poem of two years earlier [1930]'.[28]

Roche's sources include Richard Ellmann, who in *Four Dubliners* (1986) elaborates a little further: 'Beckett and Yeats met only once, at Killiney, south of Dublin … At this single meeting Yeats astonished Beckett by quoting a passage from "Whoroscope"':[29]

> A wind of evil flung my despair of ease
> against the sharp spires of the one
> lady.

And yet, unless I have simply missed it, I cannot see any mention of the encounter in Beckett's *published* correspondence of the time, although he was, as it happens, in Killiney in 1932, dining with the Hones in December of that year. Calling up H.O. White's letter will probably solve it all. But what does it matter, anyway? Far more important is that the following year, 1933, was to be an extremely difficult and tragic year for Beckett, with a permanent effect upon his life, as well as marking perhaps the real beginnings of his life as a writer.[30]

First there was the loss through tuberculosis of his cousin Peggy Sinclair in May, and then the heart attack that led to his father's death in June. These tragedies were followed by (at last) a publishing contract for *More Pricks Than Kicks*, published the following year, and the writing of the story 'Echo's Bones', originally to cap the collection of stories but rejected and unpublished until 2015 with the impressive edition of Mark Nixon, who notes possible Yeatsian inflections here and there, particularly Beckett's 'nod' to Yeats's *A Vision* (1927, revd. 1934).[31] Of those who knew Beckett, it is clear that like so many of his generation in Ireland and subsequently until the late 1960s or 1970s, poetry was considered a 'spoken' art. As such, Beckett would have been schooled from an early age to remember poems (hymns, songs) by reciting them. Testimonials record his great ability, 'even in delirium',[32] to recite poetry.

In *Four Dubliners*, Richard Ellmann remarks, 'among Yeats's poems Beckett had distinct preferences'[33] and it is clear from the recollections of John Montague in both his memoirs,[34] along with other anecdotal evidence, that Beckett identified with Yeats's poetry the processes of his own maturity and ageing as a man *and* as a writer. He 'singled out unerringly', Ellmann notes, 'the one [of Yeats's early poems] that was most extraordinary … "He Wishes His Beloved Were Dead"'.[35]

We know from several sources that Beckett would quote from memory lines from *The Countess Cathleen* and, as Ellmann tells it, so much else was quick to Beckett's mind, even towards the very end of his own life. Anne Atik movingly reveals this ability in her poignant memoir, and Gerry Dukes relates the time when he and the critic Hugh Kenner called upon Beckett 'at the cheerless nursing home' the month after his wife's funeral in July 1989:[36]

> Just before we left, Beckett recited, in a quavering voice, the last verse paragraph of W. B. Yeats's poem 'The Tower' … [It] had first appeared in book form in 1928, the very year that Beckett had first arrived in Paris. It made a most moving valedictory.

Between both Ellmann and Atik, a cluster of poems emerges. Indeed to quote Ellmann, 'There were bundles of memories':[37] 'The Old Men Admiring Themselves in the Water' (*In the Seven Woods*, 1904), 'A Drinking Song' (*The Green Helmet*, 1910), 'Girl's Song' (*The Winding Stair*, 1933), 'Why Should Old Men Not Be Mad' (*On the Boiler*, 1939), 'Crazy Jane', 'Mad Tom', as well as the Swift play, *The Words Upon the Window Pane*, Yeats's *Oedipus*, *At the Hawk's Well*, *Purgatory*, of course, and Yeats's Byzantium poems, constructed as artifice, yet contained within that lonely solo voice's rhetoric which so captivated Beckett:

> An aged man is but a paltry thing,
> A tattered coat upon a stick, unless
> Soul clap its hands and sing, and louder sing
> For every tatter in its mortal dress[.][38]

Beckett's mother had kept him informed back in 1948 with an account in the *Irish Times* of Yeats's reburial in Ireland;[39] four years later, in 1952, Beckett is recommending to a friend that he should look out Yeats's and Synge's Deirdre plays, pointing to Yeatsian references when the subject of Ireland comes up with his correspondents; responding to requests, such as Cyril Cusack's, for a Beckett response to a Shaw festival with the famous line: 'What I would do is give the whole unupsettable apple-cart for a sup of the Hawk's well, or the Saints', or a whiff of Juno, to go no further.'[40] A little later, in July 1956, he writes to the Irish novelist Aidan Higgins:

> The Yanks want the Proust but I hesitate. Shall be sending you Malone. Suppose you are glad to be getting shut of London. Queer the way you all go to Ireland when you get a holiday. Piss on the White Rock for me and cast a cold eye on the granite beginning on the cliff face.[41]

It is from a little later again, 1959, that Anne Atik's memoir shows the full force of Yeats breaking through Beckett's own imaginative contact with others that will last until the very end of his life. Indeed, Deirdre Bair has Beckett only a couple of years later, in 1961, absorbed in reading W.B. Yeats's *Collected Poems*.[42] In Atik's recollections, Yeats's poetry features prominently in conversation.[43] Beckett also refers Atik to 'the correspondence between Yeats and Dorothy Wellesley,[44] saying he thought it would interest me'. 'Each time he came back to Yeats's last poems, and each time would urge me to read them again. A standard of comparison.'[45]

This may be why James Mays hears in Beckett's *Lessness* (1970), 'an extended meditation on the line from Yeats's poem "The Black Tower"'.[46] Atik's memoir revisits Beckett's recitation in 1983, as Beckett 'wobbling on his legs … from ageing'[47] talks about Synge, Lady Gregory and Yeats and incidentally writes from memory and without error a Synge poem – 'Epitaph':[48]

> A silent sinner, nights and days,
> No human heart to him drew nigh,
> Alone he would his wanton ways,
> Alone and little loved did die.
>
> And autumn Death for him did choose,
> A season dank with mists and rain,
> And took him, while the evening dews
> Were settling o'er the fields again.

Later still, towards the end, Beckett is retelling stories about 'Yeats, and Yeats's father who stayed in New York for seventeen years'.[49] Atik's final recollection of Beckett I repeat without comment; it is about 'Joyce's admiration for Yeats, the showy wreath he sent to his [friend's] funeral': '"He liked to make that sort of gesture," says Beckett, who then continues to recite poems of Yeats, who "had written some great poems", including "The Tower" – a poem Beckett had read after his friend's Con Leventhal's cremation.'[50]

> The death of friends, or death
> Of every brilliant eye
> That made a catch in the breath –
> Seem but the clouds in the sky.[51]

Beckett is also reported to have told his friend Eoin O'Brien that the lines on the poet 'making his soul' were Yeats's greatest – the concluding third part of 'The Tower':

Till the wreck of body,
Slow decay of blood,
Testy delirium
Or dull decrepitude,
Or what worse evil come –

'About old people,' Beckett remarked, 'Yeats has written a good poem about old age, "a tattered thing".'[52] Ten days after making this comment, Beckett himself had passed away.

During this final stretch, in John Montague's recollection Beckett had been reading Keats's 'Ode to a Nightingale': 'It's very beautiful,' Beckett said. Montague suggests he had 'gone back to the pleasant discoveries of boyhood', and Montague reflects that he had not heard Beckett 'use the word "beautiful" before, except in connection with Yeats. I mention that to him, and he nods. "Ah, yes, yes, beautiful, too."'[53]

It is therefore apt that Nicholas Grene should summon Beckett's Molloy to his side to act as the epigraphic opening to his subtle and restorative study, *Yeats's Poetic Codes*:[54] 'All I know is what the words know.'[55] And thinking of what we all now know it is precious wonder that Beckett should deem it fitting in … *but the clouds* … to rewrite Yeats's great concluding lines of 'The Tower' with a piece of theatre all his own – a teleplay that Yeats would surely have understood as the act of praise it is. But also as an acknowledgement that Terence Brown, in concluding his Yeats biography, sees as much an act of 'creative appropriation' as it is 'fitting', more:

> that Beckett's ghost play for television … *but the clouds* … (first televised 1977) should salute Yeats, one great twentieth-century writer recognizing another, in employing the final lines of 'The Tower' as a haunting conclusion to a haunted work. In this work

a man in old age seeks to recall the image of a lost love ... only to have the words she inaudibly speaks, at last come fully to his own mind, like a communication from the dead; 'but the clouds of the sky ... when the horizon fades ... or a bird's sleepy cry ... among the deepening shades'.[56]

And so the ghostliness of ... *but the clouds* ... brings us to one abiding element in both writers since, in the words of Katharine Worth, 'Beckett's are ghost plays too in Yeats's sense of a ghost as a clinging presence, an emanation from some obscure region of consciousness or a mysterious continuation of mind outside the body: "An earth-bound shell, fading and whimpering in the places it loved."'[57] But for one addendum – a final curious, random, utterly unexpected and probably unconnected piece in this sketch of Beckett's Yeats.

In his contribution to a centenary celebration, *Reflections on Beckett* (2009), Terence Brown wrote about how Beckett was 'wonderfully alert to how modern media with their machines were altering the ways in which human beings would experience selfhood' and, what is more, that 'Beckett hints at an irreducible ghostlike presence of the human in his late works for television.'[58] Brown contrasts this with Yeats's obsession with the spirit world, something that started early in his life and lasted until the very end.

Brown goes on to mention that in the 1930s Beckett would visit Thomas MacGreevy in his London lodgings at 15 Cheyne Walk Gardens, a house owned by Hester Dowden. Miss Dowden was a famous spiritualist, and while there is no evidence that Beckett had anything to do, or would have had anything to do, with such a carry-on, he did occasionally play duets with Dowden and, according to Brown, 'enjoyed the musical evenings she arranged'. Quoting Knowlson's biography, it seems clear that Beckett 'got terribly tired of all the psychic evidence [and wondered] what it has to [do] with the psyche as I experience that old bastard'.[59] Unlike Yeats then in every way, one would think; the Yeats fascinated by spiritualism, automatic writing, spirit guides, absent healing, and all the rest of it. Beckett never travelled down that strange path although I can't help thinking that some of his characters might 'dabble' a bit.

Clearing out my late mother's books, I came across *This is Spiritualism* by Maurice Barbanell (1959). I remember the book from my childhood – a rather transgressive feeling of dabbling in the dark arts pervaded the book, and remarkably still does. The book, like its subject, belonged to a time between the wars she and her family had lived in London and, by all accounts, spiritualism was quite fashionable. Flicking through the pages of this book, in which Hester Dowden and W.B. Yeats feature, along with information on clairvoyance, ectoplasm, materialisation, mediums, psychic eye and faculties, psychosomatic disease, reincarnation, spirit bodies, spirit clothing, spirit healing, trance, vibrations, and umbilical cords, I chanced upon an image of the clairvoyant Jack Webber, one of several dealing with séances, ghostly presences, afterlives, self-communing with the past, voices from beyond the grave.

Notwithstanding his understandable scepticism and impatience with Yeats's fantastic flights of fancy, did Beckett happen in upon one such session in Hester Dowden's Cheyne Walk Gardens, hearing things, imagining what was going on elsewhere in the house? Were similar books lying about the place or descriptions circulated to his displeased if curious mind – who can tell? Did Beckett retain Hester in his novel *Murphy* as Miss Dew ('no ordinary hack medium, her methods were original and eclectic')[60] while for the image of Murphy in his 'medium-sized cage' in 'his rocking-chair of undressed teak'[61] the entranced medium Jack Webber, bound hand and foot in his chair, looks unerringly like Beckett's anti-hero – or is it just that I am beginning to see things?

❧

CHAPTER TWO

PLUNKETT'S CITY

The selection of *Strumpet City* as the 'Dublin: One City, One Book' choice in 2013 brought back into public view a great novel. In what follows I would like to consider the novel from a particular angle as mediation between poetry and the city of Dublin. It will come as little surprise when I say that *Strumpet City* is itself full of poetry. For not only is James Plunkett's writing charged with a poetic lyricism from the beginning to the end of the novel's almost 550 pages, but different kinds of poetry pervade the text as well. For all the realistic detail and historical sweep of the story, there is a great sense of the physical and natural world, which is captivating, even when the focus is disturbing and grotesque, such as poor Rasher's death scene. The streetscapes and civic spaces of two urban environments (Dublin and Kingstown) are the twin-tracks along which run the parallel, if at times intersecting, lives of Plunkett's unforgettable characters. The journey between both these dramatized worlds is rendered swiftly but tellingly in Plunkett's attentive descriptiveness:

Yearling, back in the city for the first time in six weeks, remarked anew its characteristic odours; the smell of soot and hot metal

in Westland Row station, the dust-laden air in streets, the strong
tang of horse urine where the cabbies had their stand, the waft
of beer and stale sawdust when a public house door swung
open. If the fishing in Connemara had been poor this season, at
least the open spaces had given him back his nose.[1]

While there is movement between Dublin and Kingstown, and
an awareness of the coastline of Dublin and its southern shores,
Strumpet City is also characterised by numerous walks in and
around the city and jaunts out to the seafronts. These walks
– as characters talk to one another, but also observe the city
around them – are part of a long tradition of perambulation
in Irish writing.[2] Certainly in terms of twentieth-century Irish
writing, Dublin is a greatly *walked* city. Out of this journeying
the experience of what is seen – from the gardens and houses
of the middle class to the inner-city tenements of the working
class, to the public parks, available spaces and greens, intimacies
of the snug pub life, canal ways and urban villages – are
translated by the writer's mind into fiction and poetry.

Strumpet City is rooted in a particular time as much as
the characters are formed by the lives they lead in particular
places: Chandlers Court, the Catholic Presbytery, and the
houses of upper-middle-class Kingstown. The novel begins in
1907 and concludes in 1914 with a troop ship leaving Dublin
Bay for the battlefields of the First World War. The centrepiece
of these seven years is the 1913 Lockout and the struggle for
social justice and democracy in Ireland, with Dublin as the
cockpit.

Swirling around this intensifying period of political and
economic conflict, *Strumpet City* embodies, with an understated
yet revealing intelligence, the cultural world of the time. A
little like Joyce in 'The Dead', Plunkett points to the kind of

poetic life of the streets in the cultural preoccupations of the drawing room, with a tragic and, at times, tragi-comic intensity contrasted with the fraught propriety of manners. In the middle of this contradictory world there is, as a fixed point of reference, Rashers Tierney, like a figure out of mid-nineteenth-century post-famine Ireland.

A Raftery-like figure, Rashers can turn his hand to writing ballads, songs and street rhymes, playing his tin whistle and making recitals at the drop of a hat, or more likely, a penny. On the other hand, the Bradshaws, Yearlings and Father O'Connor entertain themselves somewhat differently:

> Mr Yearling suggested the introduction to the second act which contained a sombre opening for the 'cello, but little else that the company could manage satisfactorily, because of the disposition of the voices and the fact that it required a chorus too. Father O'Connor came out best, with a moving interpretation of 'Is Life a Boon?' Mr Bradshaw remained silent but Mr Yearling supplied an obbligato on the 'cello. Then Mrs Bradshaw, knowing how much her husband enjoyed singing and not wishing him to feel neglected, closed the score and produced a volume of Moore's Melodies which contained duets which occupied everybody, the priest and Mr Bradshaw on the voice parts, accompanied by piano and Mr Yearling's clever 'cello improvisations. Then she asked if it was time for soup.[3]

The singing of 'Life is a Boon' sentimentally brings to Yearling's mind a Joycean-like epiphany, similar to those of Joyce's masterly story 'The Dead'. And a little like the argument between Gabriel and Miss Ivors in the same story, there runs throughout Plunkett's novel an under-acknowledged narrative concerning the *intellectual* arguments of the time. As he heads into town to meet Father O'Connor, we are told that Yearling 'liked travelling by train especially on the Kingstown line':

> He liked the yachts with coloured sails in the harbour, the blue shape of Howth Hill across the waters of the bay, the bathers and the children digging sandcastles. These were pleasant to look at in the last hours of an August evening [1912]. Yearling loved his city, her soft salt-like air, the peace of her evenings, the easy conversation of her people. He liked the quiet crossings at Sydney Parade and Lansdowne Road, simply because he had swung on them as a schoolboy. The gasometers near Westland Row were friends of his. He could remember passing them many a time as a young man making amorous expeditions to the city. When he looked at these things they in some way kept the presence of loved people who were now dead or in exile ... .[4]

The idyll of the moment is soon to be shattered, however, and who is associated with this pivotal change of tone, but none other than William Butler Yeats:

> 'I hope Mr and Mrs Bradshaw are enjoying the theatre,' Father O'Connor offered. They had gone to the Abbey to see Mr Yeats's *Kathleen ni Houlihan* and a play called *The Eloquent Dempsey* by a Mr Boyle. Later they would call to the Imperial for a light supper with Yearling and Father O'Connor. Father O'Connor's cloth forbade him to enter a playhouse. Yearling had been disinclined.
>
> 'They're welcome to my share of Mr Yeats,' he said, rising to look more closely at the street ... What he saw drove the thought from his mind. There was no traffic to be seen in the

street below. At the end near the bridge a cordon of police stood with batons drawn.

'Come and look,' he said to Father O'Connor. They both stood and watched. Yearling opened the window a little. From the streets to their right came the sounds of people shouting and glass breaking.

'My God,' Yearling said, 'a riot.'[5]

As the riot unfolds, with looting and 'a bombardment of stones', Yearling 'opening the windows wider, drew Father O'Connor with him as he stepped out onto the balcony. "Bradshaw should have come here," he remarked, pointing to the milling crowd below. "There's the real Kathleen ni Houlihan for you."'[6]

History has literally broken into Yearling's reverie of his past life as both he and O'Connor are confronted with the reality of their city's poor attacking the forces of law and order. It is an important juncture in the novel, roughly halfway through. A little later, Yeats comes back into the frame. It is the following year on St Patrick's Day. Yearling and O'Connor have spent the evening in the drawing room of the Bradshaw's Kingstown home where they have been singing some of Moore's *Melodies*:

On the way home Yearling and Father O'Connor spoke of Ireland in a sentimental way, of her sad history, of her hopes of nationhood so often and so bloodily thwarted, of the theatre of Mr Yeats and Mr Synge. Father O'Connor confessed that he had not seen any of the plays, but he had heard that they were in tone and language somewhat immoral. How much better Tom Moore had served Ireland through the medium of music and literature. He quoted:

'Dear Harp of my country in darkness I found thee
The cold chain of silence had hung o'er thee long.
When proudly, my own Island Harp I unbound thee
And gave all thy chords to light Freedom and Song.'

Yearling agreed. He said he wished often that he could have been present when the brave Tom was bringing tears to the eyes of pretty ladies in early nineteenth-century London drawing rooms by singing them songs that were sweetly seditious.[7]

What follows is a short discussion between the two men about what will happen. Home Rule is 'a mirage' Yearling states, 'Carson will stop it', before both he and Father O'Connor leave and Yearling drops off the priest at his church where the 'railings were black and forbidding, and the bulk of the church rose darkly against the sky'. The sense of imminent catastrophe deepens from this point onwards as the Lockout begins. The political heat is turned up and local disaster comes to Bradshaw's Kingstown door with the collapse of tenements Bradshaw owns and the death of several of the occupants.[8]

'We live in terrible times,' Mrs Bradshaw said. The ambulance bells, the gusting wind, filled her with foreboding. Outside the cosy circle of lamplight lay all the uncertainty and hardship of the world.

'I went shopping in town last week,' she told them. 'It was terrifying. There were little children everywhere and they were begging for pennies.'[9]

The priest will have none of this, though. Speaking 'directly to Mrs Bradshaw', he remarks, '"I know how cold and even cruel it must all sound to a nature that is tender and maternal, we must harden our hearts." Her husband set his mouth and nodded approvingly. She lowered her eyes.'[10] But it is Yearling who reacts, and it is telling to see how:

> He found his sympathy to be completely on Larkin's side. The discovery filled him with good humour. In future he would help them whenever he could. He would not be the only one of his class to do so. George Bernard Shaw had spoken for them. George Russell, the mad mystic, had written a scathing letter against the employers. William Orpen, the painter, and several highly respectable intellectuals were denouncing William Martin Murphy and his policy of starvation.[11]

Yearling does indeed follow this path. He meets the 'poet William Mathews', a 'follower of Jim Larkin' and is inducted into Larkinism:

> the fashion among the writers and the intellectuals. Moran in *The Leader* has suggested that Liberty Hall ought to form a Poet's Branch. Russell had written a moving letter in the *Irish Times* on the strikers' behalf. Shaw had championed them at a meeting in London. 'You should write them a marching song,' Yearling suggests, 'something bloodthirsty', to which Mathews replies, 'I've done a little more than that ... I've helped in Liberty Hall.'[12]

Outside of those drawing-room lyrics that are sung to accompanying piano and cello, and the regaling of the songs of the streets and political ballads of which *Strumpet City* has its share, there is the allusive presence of the great founding fathers of Irish cultural nationalism – Yeats, Synge and George Russell – set alongside the hard-core political and trade union activists, based around the all-embracing figure of Larkin. However, we should not forget the somewhat curious figure of the visiting German Jesuit, Reverend Father Boehm, 'a Gaelic scholar of distinction' who is to lead the Rosary during St Patrick's Day and deliver the sermon (in Irish) on devotions at St Brigid's.

At supper, the German priest discusses early Irish monasticism and Kuno Meyer's *Ancient Irish Poetry*, reciting 'The Hermit's Song', a ninth-century poem on which the unctuous Father O'Connor remarks: '"What a pity we cannot all follow the poet", regretting the need to be involved with the world.'[13] Bearing in mind what is actually happening in their world, the Dublin he is living in, the yearning to escape has its own kind of sad story attached. For Father O'Connor's 'involvement' is going to get much more torturously *present* as he is called away from the supper and the 'amicable and talkative' Father Boehm by the news that 'Someone has been killed – or has been found dead, I cannot be sure which – in Chandlers Court.'[14] Once again, the poetry of the moment – in this instance, literally the poetry of the Irish monastic tradition – is interrupted by the reality of the lives or the appalling death of the poor Rashers Tierney. The revelatory moment that awaits Father O'Connor has its own poetic intention which, in deference to those who haven't yet read the novel, I will pass over.

For all his high talk to the contrary, Yeats – a shadowy presence throughout *Strumpet City* – was emotionally and intellectually 'involved with the world'. While he swung like a pendulum throughout his writing life between engagement such as Yearling's, and rejection, like Bradshaw's or O'Connor's, his sense of ordinary working lives was not based on the urban poor but of the idealised rural labourer – the peasant. That said,

Yeats was aware of 'the great hardship' – his words – that the Lockout of 1913 had caused and several of the poems written during the time in which *Strumpet City* is set are in themselves distinctly *political* statements. As Terence Brown remarked in his critical biography *The Life of W.B. Yeats*, 'the poet in his mid-forties remained a passionate man who could be overcome with intense feelings of anger, perhaps the most eruptive emotion in his psychological make-up. Not all was mask and studied performance.'[15]

Yeats's distaste for the materialistic-minded business class who orchestrated the Lockout is well-documented, including, to quote Yeats, 'an old foul mouth', William Martin Murphy. Murphy had attacked Yeats and in the *Irish Independent*, which Murphy owned, had disapproved of the proposals of Hugh Lane, Lady Gregory's nephew, for a Dublin Municipal Gallery of Art. The cultural politics surrounding 1913 – from the symbolic visit of the British monarchy in 1907, with which *Strumpet City* opens, to the shuttering up of Yearling's house in Kingstown and his return to London ('It was time to go. There was nothing to stay for any longer')[16] – the sense of weighing up history at a critical point of change is recorded in Yeats's poems of the time as the beginnings of the end of imperial rule in Ireland. In part, at least, Yeats's poetry gives voice to this process as one of cultural change.

Written over fifty years *after* the events of 1913 and what 1913 ultimately led to, Plunkett's novel had of course the benefit of hindsight. Yeats worked instead on contemporaneous instinct and immediate reaction. It was some achievement. One need look no further than his poem 'September 1913', written in August 1913 and published in *The Irish Times* on 8 September 1913 as 'Romance in Ireland: On reading much of the correspondence against the Arts Gallery'. The poem was published in an interim collection before appearing in *Responsibilities*, Yeats's breakthrough volume of 1914.

As a poem of its time, 'September 1913' sets down a marker about what Plunkett refers to as 'the stricken city' and its likely future. 'September 1913' is full of subdued anger and dismissiveness directed at those with money and business solely on their minds who demonstrate little genuine feeling for the integrity of the country and its idealistic past and use nationalist sentiment for their own gain. The disdain that Yeats expresses here and in other poems written at the same time – 'lethal broadsides' as they have been called – such as 'Paudeen' and 'To a Shade' – are explicitly connected to events taking place in what he calls, in 'To a Shade', 'the town': Dublin.

Indeed, 'To a Shade' locates the city topographically in *almost* the same way that Yeats name-checked the rivers, hills and townlands of his beloved west of Ireland. The references here, though, are to the 'monument' – Parnell's monument at the top of O'Connell Street, the 'gaunt' houses of Dublin that anticipate those 'grey eighteenth-century houses' out of which the leaders of the Rising will appear in 'Easter 1916', and to Glasnevin, the resting place of the great Irish leader, Parnell, another of Yeats's spirited anti-heroes, who had been buried in Glasnevin a generation before in 1891.

Over thirty years ago, Terence Brown noted in a landmark essay on 'Dublin in Twentieth-Century Writing: Metaphor and Subject' that, for Yeats, 'Irish reality, at its most authentic, is rural, anti-industrial, spiritually remote from the life of the town or city.'[17] Yet it is possible to discern a change taking place in 'To a Shade' as the city is 'momentarily transformed by the evening light and by a purgative wind from the sea, allowing for a moment of austere drama and possibly an earnest of the future'.[18] Brown goes on to suggest that in Yeats's talismanic poem 'Easter 1916', which is set in Dublin (Yeats called the Rising in a published note to an expanded trade edition of *Responsibilities* published in 1916, 'the Late *Dublin Rebellion*'), though suffused with images of the countryside, Yeats's 'transformation of the city is no momentary trick of evening light'.[19]

For the future Senator, Yeats had discovered in 'Easter 1916' a way to celebrate – along with much else – 'an absolute transformation of a city from apparent comic irrelevance to a tragic centrality in the drama of a nation's regeneration'. The 'greasy till', 'shivering prayer', 'old Paudeen in his shop' of the poems of 1913–14 had been redeemed.[20]

And this is basically where *Strumpet City* leaves us too, in the knowledge of what would happen in the intervening years between the outbreak of the First World War, the Easter Rising, the War of Independence and the Civil War to the beginnings, forty-five years later, of the Northern 'Troubles' which were just unfolding at the time James Plunkett's novel was first published in 1969.

CHAPTER THREE

BORDER CROSSINGS

*I*n John Hewitt's *A North Light*, his memoir of twenty-five years in a municipal art gallery,[1] there is a wonderfully revealing moment when he recalls attending, as a delegate from Northern PEN, the re-interment of W.B. Yeats's remains in Drumcliff cemetery in County Sligo on 17 September 1948. Yeats had died on 28 January 1939 in south-eastern France and had been buried there, according to his own wishes: 'If I die here bury me up there [at Roquebrune] and then in a year's time when the newspapers have forgotten me, dig me up and plant me in Sligo.'[2] The delay was attributable to the intervening war.

Behind the scenes, various Irish writers, including Thomas MacGreevy, diplomats and Yeats's family and friends, were involved in arranging the re-interment and the occasion itself was by all accounts a neatly staged, poignant and dignified one, attended by many of the leading figures of the time, including Louis MacNeice, Austin Clarke ('that scrupulous poet' as Hewitt calls him),[3] Frank O'Connor, Lennox Robinson, Maurice James Craig and Maud Gonne's son, Seán MacBride. Maud Gonne, Yeats's muse light, was absent, 'afflicted with arthritis' and 'remained in Dublin', according to Roy Foster.[4] Seán MacBride was the Irish government's Minister for External Affairs, and one-time Chief of Staff of the IRA.

Hewitt's setting of the scene shows a keen eye for detail and also a sense of uncertainty about what to expect as the cortege approaches Sligo town on its short journey to the Church of Ireland burial ground, five miles north-west of the city so much identified with Yeats, his poetry and his family connections:

> Newspapers were folded away, like two waves of breaking foam, as the feeling of an approach ran down the street. Children were hoisted on shoulders. In the stillness, for the first time, I could hear far away the cry of pipes, wild and sad, and the slow distant thump of drums. Soon they rounded the corner and came down the hill towards us.[5]

Ever-vigilant for the telling moment or hint of tension in the air, or possible indiscretion, Hewitt remarks on the accompanying music as 'the pipe band of local lads in their blue serge Sunday suits, tense and tall with dignity ... came forward slowly step by step, the drums crepe-wrapped and anonymous'. The choice of 'Oft in the Stilly Night', in spite of 'what Yeats had written of Tom Moore' ['merely an incarnate social ambition' and 'never a poet of the people'][6] is praised by Hewitt, along with the band: 'it seemed', he writes, 'decorous and just, a tune we could all share'.[7] So the sense of community underpinning the commemorative moment is in Hewitt's mind as Yeats is finally laid to rest in his own home. Hewitt's gloss on the occasion is worth quoting in full:

> And somehow, I was glad that it was the local civilian band and not the brass and braided uniforms of the state. It was

enough that the old poet's body had been brought back from the Mediterranean sunshine in an Irish gunboat called Macha, for he had been, maybe chief among them who had made that gesture possible.

Hewitt then quotes the (in)famous lines from Yeats's poem, 'Man and the Echo' (1938): 'Did that play of mine send out/ Certain men the English shot?'[8] reflecting Yeats's extended obsession with 1916, inscribing his 1902 *Cathleen ni Houlihan* ('that play') into the narrative of what had happened after the Rising and its immediate aftermath; a kind of 'get the commemoration in first' ploy, not unknown in Irish political circles to this day. The story continues with the sighting of the hearse itself:

> a very bright coffin, the largest I have ever seen, half-covered by the Irish flag, next, followed on foot, by the Mayor of Sligo, public representatives, cabinet ministers, men from Galway university [the frigate bearing Yeats's coffin had docked in Galway harbour] capped and gowned in their degree ... [and then] a long file of creeping cars, with, here and there, a profile behind glass and its passing reflections, that I could recognize.[9]

Hewitt goes through the choreography of the event with the crowds, the ceremony outside Sligo Town Hall where Irish defence forces stand 'with bowed heads and arms reversed in a guard of honour', before the 'whole cortege moved slowly to Drumcliff'. Hewitt spots 'de Valera, head and shoulders above the rest', and runs into Austin Clarke again who 'inquired if one might smoke at a Protestant funeral'.[10] As an observer, maybe even with the hint of being the outsider, Hewitt 'could only look around' and, as he recounts, 'peer up at the tower which seemed too high for the Church, and watch men with a movie-camera recording the scene, look at the rain, slanting through the trees, and find names celebrated in twentieth-century Ireland for the backs – and the backs of heads, the actor, the poet, the man of letters, the politicians.'[11]

Yeats's reburial was an act of repatriation. It was also, crucially, a statement of the shortly renamed Republic's efforts to identify Yeats, the internationally renowned poet, Nobel laureate and one-time Irish senator, with the relatively young state's being open and, in some form or other, inclusive of its Protestant minority, personified by the First Inter-Party government minister's attendance. It was a commemorative act, one can say, although in the years immediately after his death, Yeats's legacy was hotly debated in Ireland and became ensnared in some dreadful invective and, as Roy Foster notes in his biography, 'predictably violent attacks by the *Catholic Bulletin* and – from an incensed Aodh de Blácam [a journalist and political activist who supported Franco] – in the *Irish Monthly*, describing [Yeats] as satanic, atheistical and, above all, unIrish.'[12] 'I could hear the sound of spaded earth,' Hewitt concludes, as 'the mourners round the grave dispersed and others pushed forward to look. There was a general loosening of tension, an easy standing around.'

According to Foster's account, 'the [Yeats] family held out against a state funeral' and, though Frank O'Connor had been asked by them to 'make a graveside oration ... this was vetoed by Jack [B. Yeats, the poet's artist brother] who disapproved of O'Connor's politics'. So Reverend James Wilson, the local rector, conducted the Church of Ireland service, though Bishop Hughes (Bishop of Kilmore, Elphin and Armagh) privately 'felt a little doubtful as to Yeats's claim to Christian burial'.[13]

What happens next is astonishing. In Hewitt's account, written fifteen years later in 1963–4, fellow poet and diplomat

Valentin Iremonger 'came over and said that Seán MacBride would like to meet me'.[14] In 1948 Hewitt was in his early forties (born in 1907), roughly the same age, give or take a few years, as Seán MacBride (born in 1904 in Paris). Hewitt was about to see in print *No Rebel Word*, his first substantial single collection of poetry, published in November 1948 by Frederick Muller in London. Hewitt had been politically active as a left-winger throughout the 1930s and during the Second World War and into the post-war era of the divided states of Ireland, north and south. As W.J. McCormack's study of Hewitt makes abundantly clear, both John Hewitt and his wife, Roberta, were no strangers to the arts and literary world of the Irish state, and kept themselves well informed on social and political developments south of the border too. In the soon-to-be-looming crisis over the 'Mother and Child' welfare project of 1951, Roberta's journal of 12 April 1951 notes 'the great stir' when the Catholic Church 'denounced' the Noel Browne-inspired scheme of health care. According to McCormack, 'She and John thought the Minister [Browne] "very courageous", and felt that his party leader, Seán MacBride, had been shown up as a bogus radical. "I am becoming more and more afraid of the R.C. Church".'[15]

But back barely three years to that encounter in the thronged Church of Ireland churchyard in County Sligo, as 'small boys and girls threaded through the groups, autograph books open and pens tilted forward butt foremost'. This is how Hewitt retells what happens next:

> I was introduced to the Minister, a pale intense man with light hair, son of Maud Gonne, he had a right to be there. But while I was explaining that the only hope for a united country was in federation with firm guarantees for the north in regard to

censorship, divorce, birth control and the place of organised religion in the constitution, I could see a few feet away Micheál Mac Liammóir, the actor, walking past …

The scene closes, neatly enough, with 'people gathering or making small circles round us, other folk who wished obviously to shake the Minister's hand, so we drifted to the waiting cars.

Under bare Ben Bulben's head
In Drumcliffe Churchyard Yeats is laid.'[16]

Let us pause here and rewind this scene. Hewitt is standing in the churchyard of a small, somewhat remote Church of Ireland church and, undoubtedly tactfully but nevertheless, forthrightly, identifying four key matters that the Irish Republic should rectify before the possibility of a 'federal' Ireland could be considered! It is 1948, remember. Debate and schism has been ongoing regarding the constitutional changes to the Irish state, which would leave the Commonwealth of Nations and declare itself a Republic in 1949. So this conversation was wedded to current hot-wired political realities and issues. Look at the wish list Hewitt 'shares' with the pale and intense young(ish) Minister for External Affairs: censorship, divorce, birth control and the special place of the Catholic Church in the new Constitution.

It may be relevant here to note that censorship was officially still in place in one form or another until the late 1980s; divorce, originally prohibited by the 1937 Constitution, was legalised in 1995 in spite of huge opposition, after an earlier failed referendum in 1986; birth control, officially illegal in the Irish Free State and subsequent Republic from 1935 until 1980 and a series of legal reforms and challenges up to 1992, while the special place of the Church in the Irish Constitution remained until 1973 and the overwhelming support (85 per cent) of the vote in favour of deleting Article 44.

So the list John Hewitt brought to that brief encounter with the Irish government minister remained elusive for almost half a century, from that churchyard ceremonial re-interment of W.B. Yeats in September 1948 to April 1998 and the Good Friday Agreement which, in a sense, left a possible, virtual federal Ireland such as Hewitt's on the table, with the collective support of the people – 71 per cent in the North and almost 95 per cent in the Republic.

John Hewitt died in 1987 before this important civic statement of cultural inclusiveness came about, and what has happened in the twenty years *since* 1998 is well beyond the scope of this chapter. But the business of legacy, guilt, political ideals and their human cost, alongside the meaning of the past, are centre stage for those with an emotional investment in the future of the country. What we *do* know is that the last fifteen or so years of Hewitt's life, after he returned from Coventry in 1972 to live in Belfast, were marked by the enduring tragedy of political violence reminiscent of that which had attended the birth of the two states on the island and the partition that had underpinned the division of the country; *reminiscent* but much worse and lasting for far longer. Hewitt's intellectual and cultural engagement with the Irish Free State and its successor, the Republic, was very much in keeping with his generation of Northern writers and, particularly, Northern artists whose work he did so much to promote at home and abroad. The divided island did not mean a divided culture, as younger scholars such as Guy Woodward[17] are showing in ever greater detail.

From quite an early age, Hewitt wrote poems (and prose) about his sense of Ireland's history and mythology, even though it was his restless probing of ideas about regionalism with which he would become much more identified. His discomfort with the Northern state is well charted ground, and his critical sense of not making contact with a readership in Northern Ireland pained him, or maybe frustrated is a better word. 'I am not speaking to my people,' he was to remark in an interview in 1980 about this fracture in communication between poet and his community, 'it is inescapable. But linked with it is the important fact of the total lack of literary interest amongst unionists of the north, the lack of any fixed literary tradition.'[18]

Hewitt's verse from *Conacre* (1943) and *No Rebel Word* (1948) all the way through to the final collections such as *Kites in Spring: A Belfast Boyhood* (1980) and *Loose Ends* (1983)[19] are inflected with a deepening consciousness of the damage done by the political exploitation of division as much as by a nostalgia for a different past, often embodied in the personae of his father, for instance in his poem, 'Going Up to Dublin' as delegate to a teachers' conference:

> When, with Partition, Protestants hived off,
> he stayed in loyally to all his kind,
> that they were teachers was to him enough,
> to sect and party singularly blind.[20]

His sketches of local life lived under the shadows of violence have a resonance for all involved in the, at times, sanitised revisiting of Irish history, particularly in this decade of commemorations, as in 'The Troubles 1922'.

> With Curfew tense,
> each evening when that quiet hour was due,
> I never ventured far from where I knew

I could reach home in safety. At the door
I'd sometimes stand, till with oncoming roar,
the wire-cage Crossley tenders swept in view.[21]

Even his youthful enthusiasm for James Connolly finds its expression in an elegy published in 1928,[22] as well as in an unpublished sonnet, identified by Frank Ormsby in his editing of the *Collected Poems of John Hewitt* with the title, 'To the Memory of James Connolly, patriot and martyr, murdered by British soldiers, May 10th 1916',[23] though, as Ormsby reminds us, Connolly was actually executed by firing squad in Kilmainham Gaol on 12 May:

When I was six years old I heard
Connolly address a Labour Crowd –
I cannot recollect a word
Yet I am very proud[.]

Alongside these simple poetic samples one can place so many much finer and more complex Hewitt poems whose concern ranges from the Great War and the Spanish Civil War to the Second World War and its bloody aftermath, both for the victorious Allies and for the cities of defeated Nazi Germany. It seems that at a very early stage of his development, John Hewitt's cultural bearings were earthed by the 1930s excitement with politics, as W.J. McCormack's *Northman* biography describes in regard to Hewitt's contact with leading figures of the Irish Republican Congress, such as Peadar O'Donnell and Frank Ryan, and writing under the pseudonym (Richard Telford) for *The Irish Democrat* and much else. Hewitt was regularly back and forth across the border to Dublin and elsewhere, as much as he was visiting in London and all the other very many different places in Europe both he and Roberta vacationed in throughout their lives together.

On 16 December 1949, just a year after that conversation with Seán MacBride in Sligo, the Hewitts were on the move again, on the 'Enterprise' train ostensibly bound for a dinner organised by the PEN Club in Dublin. 'Complex feelings of resentment, relief, guilt, and confusion shuttled across the border,' McCormack remarks, as the Hewitts temporarily left behind post-war (and blitzed) Belfast for a brief stay in post-Emergency and neutral Dublin:

> On board the 'Enterprise' they met friends, including the painter Daniel O'Neill; the journey passed quickly. They had booked into Jury's [*sic*] Hotel – 'posh' by their standards. On Saturday evening, Hewitt was surprised and pleased by Roger McHugh's knowledge of his work, less impressed by Professor H.O. White's pretences. Kenneth Reddin, a minor literary figure and a judge,[24] brought them to the Hermitage, near Rathfarnham, an eighteenth-century mansion where Patrick Pearse had conducted a school. Roberta was moved by the romantic history of the place – it had been the home of Robert Emmet's beloved [Sarah]; somebody had been hanged there. 'I became a bit of an Irish Republican in the atmosphere' [she records in her Journal].[25]

But the other reason for visiting Dublin was 'to buy goods still scarce inside the United Kingdom, several pairs of nylon stockings which Roberta smuggled inside her corset', we are told. On New Year's Eve that year (1949), the Hewitts 'again attended Mass with neighbours'[26] in the Glens of Antrim and John Hewitt would compose perhaps his best-known and most controversial poem, 'The Colony', a poem that revisits the earful Seán MacBride received the previous year. The poem's straight-talking (and, for many, offensive) persona who asks uncomfortable questions for the time: 'to be redeemed/if they themselves rise up against the spells/and fears their celibates surround them with.'[27]

Maybe it is too much of a leap of imagination (or faith) to suggest that the overshadowing of this uncomfortably independent Northern voice, which John and Roberta Hewitt and their like personified in the critical founding years of the Irish Free State of the 30s and 40s, is a story yet to be told. Told, that is, for its own sake, yes, but also for the sake of being *just* to all Irish histories and not only to those which are either more fashionable or closer to home and thereby more worthy of commemoration.

❧

CHAPTER FOUR

FROM *THE GINGER MAN* TO *KITTY STOBLING*

The 1950s represent the end of a way of life and the beginning of the world we live in today. The industrial civilisation of the British imperial project finally started to run aground in the 1950s: a culture that had spanned the globe and had produced an extraordinary legacy – of great modernising achievement on the one hand, yet on the other a battleground of colonialism. Post-war, these two powerful forces would clash in localised struggles in various parts of the remaining British Empire or countries under British influence. 'When [Harold] Macmillan became Prime Minister in 1957,' writes the social historian Dominic Sandbrook, 'no fewer that forty-five different countries were still governed by the Colonial Office, but during the next seven years Ghana, Malaya, Cyprus, Nigeria, Sierra Leone, Tanganyika, Western Samoa, Jamaica, Trinidad and Tobago, Uganda, Zanzibar and Kenya were all granted their independence.'[1]

These struggles would form the political and ultimately the social backdrop to a generation of young men and women who, in the 50s, were starting to break free from the conventional and prescribed ways of living and working: the context to much of the best in English fiction of the period such as John Braine's *Room at the Top*, David Storey's *This Sporting Life*, and Colin MacInnes's *Absolute Beginners*, as well as in the writing of poets such as Philip Larkin.

In Britain, the welfare state and the democratic opening up of educational possibilities created the foundations for a new *kind* of society that would finally emerge in the 1960s. The transformation of England, in particular, into a consumerist society, provided Ireland with the safety valve that the truly conservative nature of the Irish state and the fragility of its traditional economy obviously needed. Emigration to England, and farther afield, was both a forced and elegiac comment on the failure of de Valera's nationalism. It was also an opportunity to see the wider world and play some part in the cultural and economic changes that were taking place, although how this would have been viewed at the time is clearly a matter of perspective and of how individuals fared in their new lives 'across the water'.

The following statistic is a stark reminder of how things were: 'Of every 100 girls in Connacht aged 15–19 in 1946, 42 had left by 1951.'[2] To what kind of life and loving one wonders. Indeed, the statistics become a story in themselves: 'About 400,000 souls left in ten years for Britain, and to a lesser extent, for Canada, the United States, Australia and New Zealand.'[3] During post-war reconstruction in Britain, 634,000 Irish men and women settled in the UK; but if one stretches this cohort to include the period 1931–61, 'Irish-born' residents in Britain increased from 505,000 to 951,000 which, if one considers the numbers of those who *returned* to Ireland during the Second World War, is really quite staggering.

On a wider front, though, 1950s America and the momentum that was building up throughout that society, as well as the first mass moves towards civil rights and an end to racial segregation in the States, would politicise the English-speaking world by the end of the decade. The example of the civil rights movement in the United States would create an unstoppable cultural dynamic towards equality of races and religions with the separation of church and state.

In Ireland, the 1950s was probably the last decade in which both parts of the island, the ruling political parties and the pre-eminent role of the churches, could withstand this shifting of power in the western world. Fifties' Ireland was the beginning of the end for that unhealthy relationship, while the literature and drama of the period mark a threshold between the short-lived past of an independent Catholic Ireland and the emergence of a more modernising free state or republic that simply *had to* reconnect with Europe and, more pressingly, with its British neighbours, if it ('Ireland') was to survive. This is exactly what started to happen under the strategic shifts of economic policy initiated by T.K. Whitaker and others within the Department of Finance and in the mostly Dublin-based intellectual and political elite.[4] (A process poetically dramatized a few years later in Thomas Kinsella's long poem 'Nightwalker'.)[5]

In Northern Ireland, in a landscape still scarred by Nazi bombs, as I well remember growing up there, and its after-effects (Belfast had been blitzed in 1941 with the loss of approximately 1,000 people),[6] the momentary possibility of opening up and producing an egalitarian civic society (notwithstanding the abortive IRA campaign, Operation Harvest, during the 1950s) stuttered and stumbled into the mid-sixties before the hope of a just society was snuffed out with the eruption of the Troubles.

There are two parts to the Irish story of the 1950s — a Northern and Southern dual-narrative which sometimes interconnects but more often diverges — and it is a story that has not really been told. In 1950s Belfast, many enjoyed and prospered in the stability and quality of life provided by good schools, functioning well-run hospitals, and proliferating new roads that led into blossoming suburbs; diversifying new 'tech' factories sat alongside the traditional heavy industries of shipbuilding, aircraft manufacture, tobacco, mills and suchlike.[7] However, these industries, we now know, were becoming increasingly untenable and in a couple of decades would be extinct. A completely traditional way of industrial life, with its customs, work practices, housing and expectations was eliminated, and along with this disappearance the exposure, at almost exactly the same time, of a bigoted and repressive system of government that was blind to the poverty and inequality in its treatment of its Catholic minority and the urban poor of both religions.

The political world was redefining the power blocs of the Cold War — in Korea, in Suez, and in what became known as the Iron Curtain, behind which previously autonomous states had been colonised by the Soviet Union and would remain so for fifty years, despite brave attempts at liberation in Hungary which were ruthlessly repressed.

On the island of Ireland, the old wounding partition aside, the ingrained grievances of poverty, injustice and the dreadful inner-city housing conditions in both capitals seemed beyond the ability of either church or state to remedy. Ireland's difficulty became Britain's opportunity and, as we know, emigration flourished into a way of life. The statistics say it all.

On the cultural front, however, much was happening in Ireland and to Irish writers based abroad. Alongside the list Brian

Fallon provides in his essential portrait, *An Age of Innocence: Irish Culture 1930–1960*,[8] one can add the achievements of Elizabeth Bowen, Mary Lavin and Kate O'Brien. According to Terence Brown's study *Ireland: A Social and Cultural History 1922–2002*, the early fiction of Edna Ó'Brien, in *The Country Girls* (1960) and *The Lonely Girl* (1962), charts an emerging pattern of 'a brief idyll of youthful discovery followed by disillusionment before sending them [O'Brien's country girls] on to the more exotic attractions of London, but the young woman or man from a rural background who sought to establish a family in the city was confronted there by adjustment to the novel ways of urban family life'.[9] Brown goes on to point out that by the 1950s, 'despite the slow rate of economic growth in the country as a whole, Dublin has been transformed from the elegant, colourful, and decaying colonial centre of English rule in Ireland into a modern if rather dull administrative and commercial capital'.[10]

This change would work its way into the livelihoods of many but it would also push others towards a kind of subculture: a halfway house between the past and the emerging present, and the setting for such 'hesitancy and uncertainty' was the public house. This subculture for writers has been explored with intimate detail and knowledge in memoirs such as John Ryan's *Remembering How We Stood*,[11] the excellent *Dead as Doornails* by Anthony Cronin,[12] and in Eoin O'Brien's *The Weight of Compassion & Other Essays*.[13] The local rows, gossip and personality clashes between Dublin-based writers, such as Patrick Kavanagh and the younger Brendan Behan, was more often than not drink-related.

Drink became the arbiter of authenticity; a counter-cultural shelter, a public house for private lives, with its holy hours, after hours, Sunday closings and other licensing controls creating a lifestyle all its own, and lasting mythologies: *Such and such is a terrible man.* (Footage of a drunken Flann O'Brien being interviewed one Bloomsday bears the marks of an embittered and caustic self-parody that is itself tragic-comic.) Alcoholism, an affliction of the fifties, was as much a feature of the time as the polio epidemic of 1956 or the political collapse some years earlier of Noel Browne's Mother & Child Scheme in 1951.

Brendan Behan's success in the fifties – indeed the 1950s was very much *his* decade, with *The Quare Fellow* (1956), *Borstal Boy* (1958) and *The Hostage* (1958) – was based upon an ebullient verbal art that seemed to challenge the official sentiments of the time – in Ireland but also in Britain and the United States. As his *Borstal Boy* hit the note of 1950s' break-through, shared in novels of the period, or in a play such as *Look Back in Anger* (1956) by John Osborne, *Borstal Boy* turned the tide on English complacency and through the sheer energetic verve of his language, Behan manages to sound like a Beat poet in full flow – one minute irreverent, aggressive, the next meditative and accepting, while mocking conventional wisdom in an almost Wildean play of grievance and entitlement:

> Jesus, if they'd only let me sit there and sew away, I could be looking down at the canvas and watching my stitches and seeing them four to an inch, and passing the time myself by thinking about Ireland and forgetting even where I was, and, Jesus, wasn't that little enough to ask? What harm would I be doing them? If any of them was in Mountjoy, say, and I was there with a crowd of Dublin fellows, I wouldn't mess them about, honest to Jesus Christ I wouldn't, no matter what they were in for. And that James, that was a proper white-livered whore's melt.[14]

If the fifties were Behan's, as a one-time militant republican, jailed in England at age sixteen in the late 1930s, he came to understand England and condemn much of what was hypocritical in the Irish. His death in 1964 in his early forties makes its own telling point about the traps that were on offer in the unfolding decade of television and mass-produced popular magazines.

For, like Dylan Thomas, who had died as a result of alcoholism before Behan in 1953, and Elvis Presley, who died after him, Behan had become that most modern phenomenon: a celebrity. In the infamous live interview with Malcom Muggeridge on the BBC's *Panorama* television programme in 1956, cursing and swearing and obviously the worse for drink, and in his brawling, binge-fuelled lifestyle, Behan was bizarrely anticipating his rock-star fate. Even though it was his 'Irish' stereotype that probably fitted in with 'English' prejudice and American expectation: 'The English hoard words like misers,' wrote Kenneth Tynan in his review of Behan's *The Quare Fellow* in *The Observer*, 'the Irish spend them like sailors and in Brendan Behan's tremendous new play language is out on a spree, ribald, dauntless and spoiling for a fight. It is Ireland's sacred duty to send over, every few years, a playwright to save the English theatre from inarticulate glumness.'[15] Shaped in such 'national' terms, it is precious wonder that Behan's death as a result of diabetes and alcoholism was viewed almost as a semi-state funeral. But in a curious way, too, one of the leading roles offered to the Irish writer of the time as a 'character' was buried with him; few serious writers since Behan would follow in his footsteps.

Behan had been memorialised *before* his death, however, in J.P. Donleavy's *The Ginger Man* (1955). Behan and the Catacombs[16] feature in this richly cruel comedy of manners set in drink-besotted 1950s Dublin, as the reek and customs of the period are relentlessly exposed in Donleavy's unstoppable saga of the life of Sebastian Dangerfield and his student days at Trinity College. This is how Behan turns up at one of the gatherings of the time:

> There was suddenly a crash at the door, the centre boards giving way and a huge head came through singing.
>
> > Mary Maloney's beautiful arse
> > Is a sweet apple of sin.
> > Give me Mary's beautiful arse
> > And a full bottle of gin.
>
> A man, his hair congealed by stout and human grease, a red chest blazing from his black coat, stumpy fists rotating around his rocky skull, plunged into the room of tortured souls with a flood of song.[17]

As with *Borstal Boy* and Behan's plays, Donleavy's prose catches the absurdly mischievous, mocking, feckless playing with reality as his main characters brazen their way through the life of the capital. It is a novel seeping with a Dublin that has long since disappeared.

It is interesting, therefore, to consider how, in looking back at his own experience of living in 1950s Dublin, John McGahern interprets the scene in the posthumously published collection of his autobiographical essays, *Love of the World: Essays* (2009).[18] In speaking of his own generation of young aspiring writers, born in the provincial 1930s (the three Toms come to mind – Murphy, Kilroy, Mac Intyre) and who by the fifties were based in Dublin, McGahern is unambiguous: 'The two living writers who meant most to us were Samuel Beckett and Patrick Kavanagh.' These two 'living writers' were hugely influential, as McGahern recounts:

They belonged to no establishment, and some of their best work was appearing in the little magazines that could be found at the Eblana Bookshop on Grafton Street. Beckett was in Paris. The large, hatted figure of Kavanagh was an inescapable sight around Grafton Street, his hands often clasped behind his back, muttering hoarsely to himself as he passed. Both, through their work, were living, exciting presences in the city.[19]

Patrick Kavanagh would become a significant figure in McGahern's own fiction, as we shall see, while Beckett's influence on another writer who emerged out of the 1950s, Brian Friel, is important to note here. Brian Friel's early drama, such as *Philadelphia, Here I Come!* (1964), has Beckettian undertones in the play's view of language and memory – such as the father's inability to recall details that matter to the departing (emigrating) son, the 25-year-old Gar. Friel's play also embraces the increasing allure of American popular culture: 'I'll come home when I make my first million,' Gar protests, 'driving a Cadillac and smoking cigars and taking movie films',[20] as well as conveying the sense of 'having to' leave Ireland because of its claustrophobic provincialism.[21] As Gar puts it, picking up terms he has heard earlier from his drunken old schoolmaster:

All this bloody yap about father and son and all this sentimental rubbish about 'homeland' and 'birthplace' – yap! Bloody yap! Impermanence – anonymity – that's what I'm looking for; a vast restless place that doesn't give a damn about the past. To hell with Ballybeg, that's what I say![22]

In his short story, 'High Ground', set in the 1950s but published in 1982 and collected in *High Ground* (1985), John McGahern puts in the mouths of his timber workers a complex web of self-recognition and ironic delusion as they sup their pints with another alcoholic old schoolmaster after hours in Ryan's Pub. The young Moran (a literary brother to Gar in *Philadelphia*) pauses outside by the church, having gone to the well for spring water, the pressure of having been offered his old teacher's job pressing upon his mind and he overhears the pub conversation:

> 'Ye were toppers, now. Ye were all toppers,' the Master said diplomatically.

> 'One thing sure is that you made a great job of us, Master. You were a powerful teacher. I remember to this day everything you told us about the Orinoco River.'

> 'It was no trouble. Ye had the brains. There are people in this part of the country digging ditches who could have been engineers or doctors or judges or philosophers had they been given the opportunity. But the opportunity was lacking ...' The Master spoke again with great authority.[23]

Patrick Kavanagh could well have been one of those voices. Indeed, in some of his poems he seems to be deliberately improvising the innocent circumspection similar to these characters' knowledge, intimacy and understanding.

After years of hard dedication to his craft, that would produce one of the mid-century Irish 'classics' in *The Great Hunger* (1942), and having fought against what he saw as the establishment in Dublin (and elsewhere), Kavanagh's health, like Behan's before him, gave out. But out of *his* illness – lung cancer and the complications of an unsteady lifestyle based around the pub – Kavanagh's rebirth took place in the mid-1950s, as he was to remake his writing life by the Grand Canal:

So it was that on the banks of the Grand Canal between Baggot and Leeson Street bridges in the warm summer of 1955, I lay and watched the green waters of the canal. [...] I was born in or about nineteen fifty-five, the place of my birth being the banks of the Grand Canal.[24]

Come Dance with Kitty Stobling,[25] which was finally published in 1960 after Kavanagh's arduous search for a publisher, is addressed to his muse and contains a great lyrical lightness of touch, surrounded by some scars of struggle, as health and moral freedom are restored. It is a great book, as important in its way as, say, W.B. Yeats's magnificent volume of 1928, *The Tower*. *Come Dance with Kitty Stobling* is a hymn to rebirth but it is also a remarkable poetic testament to the resilience of the imagination and the ability of Kavanagh to transcend the demeaning, niggardly and cramped atmosphere that had contaminated so much of the Irish literary scene by the 1950s.

As the Northern Irish, London-based poet Louis MacNiece remarked of the Dublin of a decade and a half beforehand, in 1939 just as the Second World War is declared:

I was alone with the catastrophe, spent Saturday drinking in a bar with the Dublin literati; they hardly mentioned the war but debated the correct versions of Dublin street songs. Sunday morning the hotel man woke me (I was sleeping late and sodden), said, 'England has declared war'.[26]

Kavanagh's *Kitty Stobling* takes on what remains of this 'literary world' post-war in 'The Paddiad; or, The Devil as a Patron of Irish Letters', while caustically pointing his finger at those who promote its fading glories outside the country. This is the prefacing note to the poem:

This satire is based on the sad notion with which my youth was infected that Ireland was a spiritual entity. I had a good deal to do with putting an end to this foolishness, for as soon as I found out I reported the news widely. It is now only propagated by the BBC in England and in the Bronx in New York and the departments of Irish literature at Princeton, Yale, Harvard and New York universities.

I have included this satire but wish to warn the reader that it is based on the above-mentioned false and ridiculous premises.

A timely warning for those today uncritically advancing the notion that Ireland is a unique 'cultural nirvana'. But the poems kick free of this kind of polemic and become 'spiritualized' – airy contemplations on the meaning of being; a cumbersome phrase for what is, in Kavanagh's idiomatic English, so deceptively easy on the ear.

The sonnets, opening with 'Canal Bank Walk' and 'Lines Written on a Seat on the Grand Canal, Dublin' continue throughout the collection with 'October', 'Dear Folks', 'Yellow Vestment', 'Come Dance with Kitty Stobling', 'Miss Universe', 'Epic', 'Winter', 'Question to Life', 'Peace', 'Nineteen Fifty-Four' and 'The Hospital'. They form the poetic core of the collection. And in this re-centred world of his imagination, Kavanagh created what, in John McGahern's words, was a lasting vision, one of the great legacies of the period.

'[Kavanagh had] in *The Great Hunger*,' McGahern remarks,[27] 'brought a world of his own vividly to life. The dumb world of de Valera's dream had been given a true voice.' McGahern continues: Kavanagh 'had an individual vision, a vigorous gift for catching the rhythms of ordinary speech, and he was able to bring the images that move us into the light without patronage and on an equal footing with any great work'.

Patrick Kavanagh's is a truly pitch-perfect, Irish-inflected voice, talking away to itself in these sonnets and is no longer troubled by the literary business of reputation and/or recognition. It is a wonderful achievement which Kavanagh would bequeath to a generation of poets coming behind, who would, unlike him, achieve international acknowledgement. Alongside the early books of Thomas Kinsella and John Montague, and the breakthrough of Austin Clarke's *Ancient Lights* (1955), *Come Dance with Kitty Stobling* set a high watermark for Irish poetry, particularly when placed alongside the achievements of, say, Philip Larkin's *The Less Deceived* (1955) or Robert Lowell's masterful, shape-changing volume, *Life Studies* (1959). In poems such as 'The Hospital' or 'Lines Written on a Seat on the Grand Canal, Dublin', Kavanagh's imagination declares a revelation earned and honoured through hard-won experience:

> And look! a barge comes bringing from Athy
> And other far-flung towns mythologies.
> O commemorate me with no hero-courageous
> Tomb – just a canal-bank seat for the passer-by.[28]

Though published in the first year of the 1960s, *Come Dance with Kitty Stobling* ponders the past decade from its mid-point, and in 'Nineteen Fifty-Four' secures a most potent image of the time. We should recall that Kavanagh had been through a lot personally – he had lost a court case for libel against the *Leinster Leader* newspaper, experienced increasing ill-health, and cancer would be later diagnosed. He was fifty at the time, a relatively young man to our way of thinking; yet, in a poignant sense, 'Nineteen Fifty-Four' is a reflection, as is much else in *Come*

Dance with Kitty Stobling, on Kavanagh's surviving his own life and times. The last line, both as realisation and freedom, carries a powerful resonance to this very day;

> But tonight I cannot sleep;
> Two hours ago I heard the late homing dancers.
> O Nineteen Fifty Four you leave and will not listen,
> And do not care whether I curse or weep.[29]

Whether to 'curse or weep' as time passes is a perennial question, but perhaps Brian Fallon has defined best the cultural legacy of the 1950s:

> Yet many still remember the Fifties as a grim, grey, rather bitter decade, which no doubting some respects they were. Internationally the Cold War had reached a stage of permafrost, and the mushroom-shadow of the Atomic Bomb hung over Europe, though there was still real faith in the capacity of the United Nations [Ireland was admitted in 1955] to maintain an international balance of power. Money was short, so too were jobs, and writers and artists in particular were badly paid; it was a period when many of them had to take casual employment of all kinds to tide them over until better times, and a number emigrated temporarily to London ... Yet underneath it all there was in fact a considerable life force.[30]

The 1950s are a kind of alter-image of today[31] when what we now know was happening was not exposed publicly or challenged politically – the sexual abuse of children in the care of the Catholic Church; the appalling conditions that young women were condemned to work under in the Magdalene laundries; the narrow-minded complacency of the ruling elite.

Lessons are rarely learnt from history, but the 1950s certainly show how best to counter the understandable anger and rage about political and moral failure of both church and state in the Ireland of that time.

In 1950s Ireland we can see our younger selves reflected as an age of innocence but also one full of dark secrets and wrongs. This proves the incontestable point that we neither need to go, nor should even consider going, backwards to realise that a soft-centred, remodelled nationalism – the very thing that Patrick Kavanagh railed against – is not what is needed today to rectify Ireland's problems, simply because it does not work, any more than a refashioned imperial nostalgia works for Britain. If the 1950s prove anything in *Ireland*, it is by way of a rebuke and an inspiration; about the political need for a level-headed Mark II of the Whitaker generation who will coolly and calmly focus upon the historical fault-lines and fissures in Irish society in an effort to work through and plan how best to fix these while, at the same time, realistically appraising Ireland's future standing in the eyes of its own citizens, as well as in the rest of the world.

CHAPTER FIVE

THE PASSIONATE TRANSITORY: JOHN MCGAHERN

On the occasions when I met John McGahern in Galway or Dublin, or once farther afield in Poland, the conversation often gravitated towards poetry. He had both an imaginative understanding of poetry and the professional interest of a one-time teacher and university lecturer, but also as an observer of the literary world in Ireland, Britain and in the United States, where poets featured either as individuals he had come across or whose work he knew by heart. McGahern's knowledge of poetry is shown throughout his own writing, both in the fiction but also in the literary journalism he published over many years. He was an intensely lyrical writer himself and the sense of language in which his fiction revels is very close to a poet's understanding. In the short piece called 'The Image' he remarks, 'The Muse, under whose whim we reign in return for a lifetime of availability, may grant us the absurd crown of Style, the revelation in language of the unique world we possess as we struggle for what may be no more than a yard of lead piping we saw in terror or in laughter once.'[1]

That sense of things conveying *emotional* meaning filtered through the imaginative control of his prose is a discipline close to the highest forms of poetry-making. It is little wonder that of the poets McGahern returned to most – Philip Larkin, Patrick Kavanagh and, less often, W.S. Graham – each is known for his lyrical control of difficult emotional states, existential mindscapes and desires, and the 'struggle' to re-enact transcendent silences.

It is possible to read McGahern's fiction as an epic search for a prose equivalent of poetry; to render in descriptive English the speech rhythms of a way of saying and seeing things, infused with the intellectual and literary allusions of his own educational upbringing in Ireland, alongside the cultural inflections of the life he discovered as a young writer in the Dublin of the 1950s and beyond, growing into the artist he became.

It would take quite a bit of ground indeed to cover it all – examining the role of the national syllabus in which John McGahern was taught and which he in turn taught, tuned to an English literary tradition of 'the greats', with its strong emphasis on learning passages by rote; 'very quotable', as it has been described to me.[2] Upon this foundation, McGahern would develop his own tastes in reading widely in French and other European writing, as well as in British and North American literature. Instead, I'll focus on the intriguing *poetic* nature of McGahern's writing, look at what he wrote about poets and poetry and also show how, in one of his best-known stories, 'Bank Holiday',[3] poetry becomes the *essential* part, the fulcrum of the fiction itself, before finishing with a brief reference to the ending of his novel, *The Leavetaking*.

John McGahern's work is so full of lyricism, it is difficult to select only one or two examples to illustrate the value he placed upon getting the words right. So often it is the visual quality of his language that carries the moral freight of his meaning. Think of this setting, for example, in the poignant, pitch-perfect 'Faith, Hope and Charity':

> All the doors of the house were open when he got to Cunningham's but there was nobody in. He knew that they must be nearhand, probably at the hay. There is such stillness, stillness of death, he thought, about an empty house with all its doors open on a hot day. A black and white sheepdog left off snapping at flies to rush towards him as he came through the gate into the meadow. It was on the side of the hill above the lake. In the shade, a tin cup floated among some hayseed in a gallon of spring water. Across the lake, just out from a green jet of reeds, a man sat still in a rowboat fishing for perch. They were all in the hayfields, the mother and father and four or five children. The field had been raked clean and they were heading off cocks. All work stopped as the hatted man came over the meadow. The father rose from teasing out hay to a boy winding it into a rope. They showed obvious discomfort as they waited, probably thinking the teacher had come to complain about some of the children, until they saw the pale green envelope.
>
> 'I'm sorry,' the hatted man said as he watched the father read, 'If there's anything I can do you have only to tell me.'[4]

The details accumulate inside the wider frame of the empty house 'until they saw the pale green envelope' and the spoken words which break the hypnotic silence: 'I'm sorry.' Apart from the narrative value of the passage – the bringing of bad news within the workaday routine of haymaking – the sense of timelessness and of expectation are poetically charged by precise and specific images: the sheepdog left off snapping at flies and that tin cup in a gallon of spring water. Life goes on in its own circular way, no matter what grief or tragedy comes along. The stated 'such stillness, stillness of death ... about an empty house with all its doors open on a hot day' has the ring of a poetic line, fulfilled by those details and the varieties of light and shade, inaction, expectation. It really is wonderfully achieved lyricism.

Or take the following passage from 'Doorways', a simple enough paragraph of description to which the appended dialogue brings a surprising shift in perspective:

> As we walked I pointed to the stream of cars going slowly down to the sea. The roofless church was two miles from the hotel. At first, close to the hotel, we had come among some half-circles of tents in the hollows, then odd single tents, and soon there was nothing but the rough sea grass and sand and rabbit warrens. Some small birds flew out of the ivy rooted in the old walls of the church, and we sat across the faceless stones, close to a big clump of sea thistle. Far away the beach was crowded with small dark figures within the coastguard flags.
>
> 'In America', she said, looking at the lighthouse, 'they have a bell to warn ships. On a wet misty evening it's eerie to hear it toll, like lost is the wanderer.'
>
> 'It must be,' I repeated. I felt I should say something more about it but there was nothing I could say.[5]

The images of ruin and the slightly gothic setting of the scene are spiked with tension that surfaces with that curious literary-like reference, 'like lost is the wanderer'.

But if McGahern's fictional characters are self-conscious at times, they are also quite literary-minded. In 'Strandhill, the Sea', the guests staying in Parkes' Guest House in County Sligo take refuge from the inclement weather in language games, naming things, swapping quotations with one another:

> 'Names are a funny thing,' Ryan said without thought.
> 'Names are a funny thing, as you put it,' Ingolsby repeated sarcastically.[6]

The story deals with literary value in an ironic and playful manner. The narrator is chastised for having 'comics' – which he has lifted from the local shop without paying for them: 'Why have you to be always stuck in that trash? Why can't you read something good like Shakespeare that'll be of some use to you later?'[7] (Shakespeare and Bernard Shaw pop up again in 'Hearts of Oak and Bellies of Brass',[8] as testers of character.) In the guesthouse the discussion of Shakespeare's 'validity for the modern world' leads in turn to the following exchange among some of the guests:

> The people in the room had broken up into their separate groups, and when Miss Evans raised her arms in a yawn out of the chair Haydon leaned forward to say, 'There must have been right old sport last night.'

> 'I beg your pardon, Mr Haydon,' she laughed, pleased.

> 'The way all women are, all on their dignity till the business gets down to brass tacks and then an almighty turn of events. And who'd object to an old roll between the sandhills after the dance

anyhow?' He raised his voice, as if to irritate Ingolsby, who was pressing a reluctant Ryan on Wordsworth.[9]

Ingolsby, the retired lecturer in English, meets 'hostility' to the 'themes of [his] ponderous conversations',[10] and as the story reaches its conclusion, McGahern seems to pitch the teacher's self-importance against the narrator's imagining inside the house by the sea, a subtle rendering in which poetry and its authority are relocated in the much more modest yet pleasurable form of reading a comic:

> It was some consolation to Ryan that he'd [*Ingolsby*] abandoned the poets, but his eyes still apologized to the room. He'd make his position even clearer yet, in his own time.

> The turning of the pages, without reading, pleasure of delaying pleasure to come. Heroes filled those pages week after week. Rockfist Rogan and Alf Tupper and Wilson the Iron Man. The room, the conversations, the cries of the seagulls, the sea faded: it was the world of the imagination, among the performing gods, what I ashamedly desired to become.[11]

'Strandhill, the Sea' is about the poetry of the prosaic and ends with a poetic riff to the mundane transformed in the eye of the beholding narrator. In 'My Love, My Umbrella', one of McGahern's most 'Frenchified' tales, reminiscent of Jean Paul Sartre's shorter fiction, the Dublin-based lovers' first encounter with each other is mediated through the presence of 'a poet' as they sit in Mooney's Bar in Lower Abbey Street, eating beef sandwiches with their glasses of stout:

Soon, in the drowsiness of the stout, we did little but watch the others drinking. I pointed out a poet to her. I recognised him from his pictures in the paper. His shirt was open-necked inside a gabardine coat and he wore a hat with a small feather in its band. She asked me if I liked poetry.

'When I was younger,' I said. 'Do you?'

'Not very much.'

She asked me if I could hear what the poet was saying to the four men at his table who continually plied him with whiskey. I hadn't heard. Now we both listened. He was saying he loved the blossoms of Kerr Pinks more than roses, a man could only love what he knew well, and it was the quality of the love that mattered and not the accident. The whole table said they'd drink to that, but he glared at them as if slighted, and as if to avoid the glare they called for a round of doubles. While the drinks were coming from the bar the poet turned aside and took a canister from his pocket. The inside of the lid was coated with a white powder which he quickly licked clean. She thought it was baking soda. Her father in the country took baking soda for his stomach. We had more stout and we noticed, while each new round was coming, the poet turned away from the table to lick clean the fresh coat of soda on the inside of the canister lid.[12]

Poets and poetry, language and literary allusion abound in McGahern's shorter fiction. His characters and narrators often refer to their own education (as in the ending of 'High Ground')[13] and in drawing upon that experience they sometimes allude to various influences such as Church language, which appears in conversation in 'The Wine Breath'.[14] In the same story discussion takes place about the understanding of 'common names' and how this links in with the poetry inherent in the naming of things – flowers, townlands and religious ceremonies. In this extract the exchange opens with reference to the Scottish poet Hugh MacDiarmid's poem 'The Little White Rose':

> 'And, no doubt, the little rose of Scotland, sharp and sweet and breaks the heart,' he heard his friend quote maliciously. 'And it's not the point. The reason the names of flowers must be in Latin is that when flower lovers meet they know what they are talking about, no matter whether they're French or Greeks or Arabs. They have a universal language.'[15]

And when his characters are not thinking aloud about such language matters, reference can be made to how religion and poetry combines in their minds, such as poor old McMurrough, who in 'The Recruiting Officer' 'now lay in the Sligo madhouse reciting poetry and church doctrine'.[16] McGahern also draws attention to the cultural space of 'books' as the physical embodiments of a kind of imaginative freedom, from the autobiographical opening of his essay 'The Devil Finds Work for Idle Hands'[17] and his praise of the Moroney's Library of his young boyhood, to his experiences of reading Kavanagh and Beckett in 1950s Dublin.

Literature, and its quintessential beat, poetry, are *material* things which matter to McGahern, and the essays collected in *Love of the World* reveal as much. Here, McGahern's indebtedness is clearly expressed in an extraordinary range of poets, many of whom he refers to with pleasure and real enthusiasm. W.H. Auden, William Blake, Louise Bogan, George Mackay Brown,

Hart Crane, T.S. Eliot, David Gascoyne, Allen Ginsberg, W.S. Graham, Seamus Heaney, Patrick Kavanagh, Thomas Kinsella, Philip Larkin, D.H. Lawrence, Louis MacNeice, Eugene Montale, Edwin Muir, Richard Murphy, Sylvia Plath, Alexander Pope, Ezra Pound, Rainer Maria Rilke, Stevie Smith, William Carlos Williams, William Wordsworth, David Wright, Yeats and the poet's father, John Butler Yeats, whose correspondence with his son McGahern abridged.[18]

What McGahern drew from these varied poetic sources – American poets, less well known British poets such as Gascoyne, Wright and Graham, fellow Irish writers – and his use of quotation in his fiction from Burns, Matthew Arnold, and Shakespeare, among others, is the subject of a study all to itself. If I can isolate a few quotations, however, it might show how the figure of the poet and the power of poetry were integral to the very fabric of McGahern's fiction-making and also, possibly, to the Ireland out of which he came.

As I've already mentioned, of the two living writers who meant most to the young McGahern in 1950s Dublin, Patrick Kavanagh and Samuel Beckett, Kavanagh was pre-eminent, and recollecting the time McGahern writes: 'I wish I could open a magazine now with the same excitement in which I once opened *Nimbus*: "Ignore Power's schismatic sect/Lovers alone lovers protect."'[19] The two lines McGahern quotes here are from the ending of Kavanagh's poem 'Prelude' included in *Come Dance with Kitty Stobling and Other Poems*,[20] a book of poems that will figure large in McGahern's own writing. In a 1987 review of Peter Kavanagh's portrait of his poet brother, McGahern considers how Patrick had such a powerful 'individual vision, a vigorous gift for catching the rhythms of ordinary speech, and ... was able to bring the images that move us into the light without patronage and on an equal footing with any great work.'[21] In the same review, McGahern identifies Kavanagh's *Kitty Stobling* as a 'new world' recovered:

> These later poems are steeped in space and time while still happening in one clear, specific place. What they have in common with the early poems is the genius that restores the dramatic to the ordinary and the banal. I remember well the excitement of reading poems like 'Prelude' or 'Auditors In', or 'Kerr's Ass' or 'The Chest Hospital' for the first time in manuscript.[22]

Incidentally, McGahern tells us in 'The Bird Swift',[23] a memoir of the painter Patrick Swift, that the manuscript he read was a typescript of *Kitty Stobling* made for Kavanagh by another member of the Swift family. It was through Patrick Swift that McGahern met in London the ex-South African poet David Wright, who with Swift was editing the magazine *X*, which had accepted for publication McGahern's first piece of prose.[24]

In the closing (and uncharacteristically rhetorical) flourish to the review of Peter Kavanagh's book, McGahern paints a picture of Patrick Kavanagh that is both homage and echo of the slightly earlier representation of the poet in 'Bank Holiday',[25] which is such a key focus to what happens emotionally in the story:

> His extraordinary physical presence, whether seated in a chair or walking up a street with his hands clasped behind his back, always managed to convey more the sense of a warring crowd than of a solitary person. He was also a true poet and I believe his violent energy, like his belief that people in the street steered by his star, raised the important poems to

permanence. They have now moved from Mucker by way of the Grand Canal and the Chest Hospital to their own place on Parnassus.[26]

'Bank Holiday' is a richly seductive portrait of Dublin as seen through the eyes of a 50-year-old civil servant, who has in quick succession lost both his parents and seen his marriage dissolve. His bachelor life is conveyed in quick flashes of wit, while a sense of Larkinesque pique attends his lonely existence. In Webb's Bookshop, the poetically named Patrick McDonough[27] is discomfited by the brown-overalled manager as he peruses some books before leaving, hot and bothered, only to discover back in his flat that an old friend, James White, has suggested to Mary Kelleher, a young visiting American academic (her research is mediaeval poetry), that she should look up McDonough when she is in Dublin. They meet and start to fall in love in Bernardo's Restaurant in Lincoln Place. The story circles in and out of a poetic vortex of walking and talking which takes them through the Bank Holiday heat towards the East Wall and strand:

> 'Oh, it's cold.' She shivered as she came out of the water, and reached for her sandals.

> 'Even in heatwaves the sea is cold in Ireland. That's Howth ahead – where Maud Gonne waited at the station as Pallas Athena.'[28] He reached for his role as tourist guide.

> 'I know that line,' she said and quoted the verse. 'Has all that gone from Dublin?'

> 'In what way?'

'Are there ... poets ... still?'

'Are there poets?' he laughed out loud. 'They say the standing army of poets never falls below ten thousand in this unfortunate country.'

'Why unfortunate?' she said quickly.

'They create no wealth. They are greedy and demanding. They hold themselves in very high opinion'.[29]

The 'all that' to which Mary refers is poetry and its presence in the public sphere of the city, and as she is about to discover, it is all very much visible:

It was into this quiet flow of the evening that the poet came, a large man, agitated, without jacket, the shirt open, his thumbs hooked in braces that held up a pair of sagging trousers, a brown hat pushed far back on his head. Coughing harshly and pushing the chair around, he sat at the next table.

'Don't look around,' McDonough leaned forward to say.

'Why?'

'He'll join us if we catch his eye.'

'Who is he?'

'A poet.'

'He doesn't look like one.'

'That should be in his favour. All the younger clerks that work in my place nowadays look like poets. He is the best we have. He's the star of the place across the road. He's practically resident there. He must have been thrown out.'

The potboy in his short white coat came over to the poet's table and waited impassively for the order.

'A Powers,' the order came in a hoarse, rhythmical voice. 'A large Powers and a pint of Bass.'[30]

The connection here between Patrick McDonough and Mary Kelleher, like the relationship dramatised elsewhere in 'Peaches',[31] for example, is revealed through the life of poetry and the perceived public place of 'the poet' in modern society. The individuals are seen, and in turn see each other, in terms of how the imaginative life is reflected (sometimes comically, sometimes perversely) in Irish society's altering self-consciousness during a decade of increasingly fraught social and economic change.

In 'Bank Holiday', the lovers' blossoming romance begins with a poem – W.B. Yeats's 'Beautiful Lofty Things' – and is conveyed through an encounter with Patrick Kavanagh, the unnamed poet ('the best we have'),[32] before concluding with the unnamed book of his which, by the look of it, is Kavanagh's *Come Dance with Kitty Stobling*. You can read this fictional encounter in 'Bank Holiday' with the knowledge that, according to Antoinette Quinn's essential biography of Patrick Kavanagh,[33] the event in the story had its roots in an actual experience of McGahern's. In the fictional reimagining, McDonough (a kind of latter-day Gabriel Conroy) is, for a second time, rattled by the poet's comment:

'You're a cute hoar, McDonough. You're a mediocrity. It's no wonder you get on so well in the world', the poet burst out in a wild fury … and stalked out, muttering and coughing.

'That's just incredible', she said.[34]

Incredible too that when McDonough and Mary return to McDonough's flat, Mary asks, 'Do you have any of the poet's work?' to which her soon to be lover retorts:

'You can have a present of this, if you like.' He reached and took a brown volume from the shelf.

'I see it's even signed,' she said, as she leafed through the volume. 'For Patrick McDonough, With love', and she began to laugh.[35]

As the narrative deepens into the couple's romantic and physical attraction, that poetry book travels with Mary on her journey to in-laws in Dundalk (where else? – Kavanagh country!) and when she returns she remarks: '"I read the poems at last". She put the book with the brown cover on the table. "I read them again on the train coming back. I loved them."'[36] Why not just put 'the book back'? The fact that we have that 'brown cover' mentioned twice suggests a definite bond with an actual book, *Come Dance with Kitty Stobling*, which did indeed have a brown cover. And in the Chekhovian passage that follows, McGahern and his character McDonough reveal their hand, for the 'very pure love sonnets' which McDonough refers to are undoubtedly the self-same sonnets in *Kitty Stobling* by which the real-life Patrick Kavanagh would be recognised for generations of readers to come:[37]

'I've long suspected that those very pure love sonnets are all addressed to himself ... That was how the "ignorant bloody apes and mediocrities" could all be short-circuited.'

'Some are very funny.'

'I'm so glad you liked them. I've lived with some of them for years.'

Later, over dinner, McDonough asks Mary to marry him. So the phantom book of poems becomes quite literally a love token shared between both characters as the unlikely and contradictory poet-figure of Kavanagh turns into an ungainly muse-like cupid. This is not quite as fanciful as it might appear, since McGahern has got form in this regard.

McGahern's novel *The Leavetaking* ends where 'Bank Holiday' begins – with Howth and the rapturous 'My love waits for me in a room at Howth'.[38] As the narrator walks past Howth Station, the 'full tide surges against the wall and boats, withdraws, and surges back'.[39] The sensual music of the sea brings to the young teacher's mind Matthew Arnold's poem 'Dover Beach'[40] as he anticipates leaving with his girl 'on the boat to London'.

At so many points of contact in his fiction and in his other writing, McGahern demonstrates just how indispensable poetry is to his characters' formation and the possibilities they share. Poetry acts as an emotional barometer. It is a form of self-knowledge and provides an essential guide to McGahern's country of the mind, while in the guise of 'The Poet' and his revelations, we register how healthy or unhealthy a society is. Poetry, for McGahern, was both a form of art and its own self-constituted *imagined* world, with its peculiar ways of being. What's more, poetry as revelation could be found in McGahern's fiction writer's sense of what Kavanagh called in one of those sonnets, 'The Hospital', 'the common and banal' and in many ways these lines are a perfect résumé of John McGahern's achievement and ambition as a writer:

> Naming these things is the love-act and its pledge;
> For we must record love's mystery without claptrap,
> Snatch out of time the passionate transitory.[41]

CHAPTER SIX

Fatal Attractions: John Berryman in Dublin

Literature in my early days was still something you lived by; you absorbed it, you took it into your system. Not as a connoisseur, aesthete, lover of literature. No, it was something on which you formed your life, which you ingested, so that it became part of your substance, your path to liberation and full freedom. All that began to disappear, was already disappearing, when I was young.[1]

*I*n his memoir about John Berryman's stay in Dublin from 1966 to 1967, John Montague describes the man he had met in the Majestic Hotel, Baggot Street as 'enthusiastic, hilarious, drunken, as splendid and generous a man as one might meet, who fitted into the roar of Dublin pub life with ease'.[2] Some twelve years earlier, Montague had met a completely different Berryman in Iowa: 'nervous, taut, arrogant, uneasy; very nearly a caricature of the over-trained, fiercely cerebral, academic poet of the fifties; a man hair-triggered for insult, and quite capable of getting angry with a student' – which is precisely what happened 'one autumn evening in that second week of term;

70

Berryman hit or at least scuffled with someone and was landed in the town jail'.[3] He was subsequently dismissed from his post.

The previous year, 1953, Berryman had witnessed the final days of Dylan Thomas's life, Thomas having collapsed into a coma in November in the Chelsea Hotel in New York where both poets were staying. They had previously met in England back in March 1937, when the 23-year-old Berryman was a graduate student at Cambridge and Thomas had come to St John's College to give a reading. Thomas went on a binge for the week he stayed there and Berryman followed suit, only to enter, in the words of his biographer, John Haffenden, 'a period of despondency lasting at least another week, worrying [about] his sense of incompetence and unfilled ambition'.[4]

The next month Berryman made his first trip to Ireland, only to discover that the object of his journey, W.B. Yeats, was in London. Undeterred, Berryman wrote to Yeats and a meeting was arranged for Friday, 16 April 1937 at the Athenaeum Club in London. As Berryman recounts in his *Paris Review* interview (1971), Thomas shows up again:

> Thomas had very nearly succeeded in getting me drunk earlier in the day. He was full of scorn for Yeats, as he was for Eliot, Pound, Auden. He thought my admiration for Yeats was the funniest thing in that part of London. It wasn't until about three o'clock that I realised that he and I were drinking more than usual. I didn't drink much at that time; Thomas drank much more than I did. I had the sense to leave [and] just made it for the appointment.[5]

From the wide-eyed, graduate student poet of the 1930s to the thrice-married, world-weary poet and teacher of the 1960s, Berryman's relatively short life (he died at the age of fifty-seven) reveals a fatal attraction to self-destruction perversely echoed throughout his generation of American writers and painters, whose constant companions seemed to be alcohol and depression. As Robert Lowell has it in one of his valedictory poems, 'For John Berryman':

> Yet really we had the same life,
> the generic one
> our generation offered[.][6]

In the Afterword to her memoir, *Poets in their Youth*, Eileen Simpson lists the fallen: Dylan Thomas, Theodore Roethke, Randall Jarrell, R.P. Blackmur, Delmore Schwartz, and by extension, Louis MacNeice (a one-time drinking buddy of both Berryman and Thomas) and Lowell, who outlived Berryman.[7] All had died at (relatively speaking) an early age. The transformation, which Montague noted in his memoir, is nevertheless shocking, and all the more so when one bears in mind Montague's own gloss on Berryman's writing life:

> This is something I want to make clear: Berryman is the only writer I have ever seen for whom drink seemed to be a positive stimulus. He drank enormously and smoked heavily, but it seemed to be part of a pattern of work, a crashing of the brain barriers as he raced towards the completion of the *Dream Songs* ... He had come into his own and radiated the psychic electricity of genius.[8]

In Montague's view, Berryman thrived in that 'glorious year', living in a 'trim suburban villa' in Ballsbridge, Dublin, a regular of Ryan's Bar. Indeed, Montague recalls taking Berryman to meet Garech Browne and at a party in the Dublin hills:

> John seemed to be drinking at random. There was a tray on the lawn, for instance, and instead of keeping to one drink [Berryman] just poured whatever was nearest to him into his glass, whiskey, gin, vodka, white wine, an impossible mixture.[9]

Anyone who has seen that kind of manic drinking knows how lethal it becomes for the alcoholic. Again, Montague's memoir takes up the story not long before Berryman's suicide. At a reading he gives at the University of Minnesota, Montague meets Berryman again. On this occasion, the American is a relic of his former self:

> He shuffled out of an Alcoholics Anonymous lecture, hands twitching, face pale and uneasy as he greeted me ... The contrast between our previous meetings in Dublin when he would roar out his latest dream songs, good, bad, or indifferent, lovely or awful or 'delicious' (his own phrase for praise), was too abrupt.[10]

Berryman seemed 'clearly ill at ease in such a restrained life' and, according to Montague, the reason was clear. '[N]ot only his habits but his habits of work were linked with drink; the ramshackle structure of the *Dream Songs* is based as much upon the ups and downs of the chronic drunk as anything else.'[11] This transformation towards the close of his life, and the all too short respite of his final year with the birth of his second daughter – 'eleven months of abstinence, half a year of prolific rebirth, then suicide', as Lowell defined it[12] – is mirrored in the earlier shift of self-image.

From that 'academic poet of the fifties', described by Saul Bellow as 'The Princeton John' – 'tallish, slender, nervous', who had 'many signs that he was inhibiting erratic impulses' – into the long bearded, guru-like Beat figure of the late 1960s, 'High shouldered in his thin coat and big homburg, bearded, [who] coughed up phlegm [and] looked decayed', Berryman ends up a haunted version of himself.[13] The changes might have been liberating for the hidebound Berryman even while producing the claustrophobic hothouse atmosphere of many of the *Dream Songs*. At another level they were to prove distorting and costly. Could it really be this 'easy' to make up poems for Henry to think and say?

The constant need for the reaffirmation of his friends' approval seems to suggest otherwise. The scholarly side of Berryman's training probably cast some inner doubt, but by that stage the bardic persona had won and there was no way out. The mask had stuck. Berryman, the elegist of his generation of fellow poet–teachers who burned out on ambition, alcohol, drugs and depression, is a talismanic figure, representative of a literary culture that in the decade following his death also passed away. As the headily politicised 1970s and 1980s scorned the apparent egotism and introversion of the 'victim-hero' poets, by the 1990s poetry was viewed much more as a career than as a complex fate. So perhaps the tangled lives of Berryman's generation have in fact more in common with today's 'pop' culture than would have seemed possible ten or fifteen years ago. The culture that Berryman and his generation embraced, almost in spite of its antipathetic nature, is told with great verve by one of Berryman's good friends, Saul Bellow, in *Herzog* (1964) and in *Humboldt's Gift* (1975) where Fleisher is emblematic of the angst and ambition of that fateful generation. Here narrator Charlie Citrine meditates on the significance of Humboldt's death:

> For after all Humboldt did what poets in crass America are supposed to do. He chased ruin and death even harder than he

chased women. He blew his talent and his health and reached home, the grave, in a dusty slide. He plowed himself under. Okay. So did Edgar Allan Poe, picked out of the Baltimore gutter. And Hart Crane over the side of a ship. And Jarrell falling in front of a car. And poor John Berryman jumping from a bridge. For some reason this awfulness is peculiarly appreciated by business and technological America. The country is proud of its dead poets. It takes terrific satisfaction in the poets' testimony that the USA is too tough, too big, too much, too rugged, that American reality is overpowering. And to be a poet is a school thing, a skirt thing, a church thing.[14]

Echoing Montague's view, Bellow recalls in 1973 the real-life Berryman in the following stark terms: 'Inspiration contained a death threat. He would, as he wrote the things he had waited and prayed for, fall apart. Drink was a stabilizer. It somewhat reduced the fatal intensity.'[15] Looking at Ireland, it has to be said that such 'fatal intensity' afflicted Kavanagh, Behan, Flann O'Brien, Louis MacNeice and, a little later, the hugely talented Seán Ó Riada, who were among those who died relatively young with drink the great de-stabiliser.

Berryman's writing life prefigures many of the features of contemporary 'lifestyle' popular culture. From the Chelsea Hotel where Berryman held vigil over Dylan Thomas's last days (and Thomas was, of course, to become immortalised as one of the great folk heroes of the 1960s) to his own death almost twenty years later in January 1971, Berryman's life story is so familiar today.[16] Even the manner of his death has the ring of rock myth about it. He 'walked unto the west end of the Washington Avenue Bridge high over the Mississippi River' and 'at about nine o'clock' in the morning, according to one eyewitness, 'jumped up on the railing, sat down and quickly leaned forward [and] never looked back'; the *Minneapolis Star*, Haffenden recounts, 'reported a witness who observed that he apparently "waved goodbye"'.[17]

The rock hero beset by the search for calibrated pre-eminence and celebrity, shifting from gig to gig (albeit with universities as the venues), the late night speak-fest, ceaseless drinking, ultimate addiction, the non-stop touring and the temporary respite – all have the hallmarks of a 'star' on the move and (alas) on the wane. What Berryman felt he was losing back home in the pressure cooker literary world of America, he tried to restore in the intimate, yet oddly respectful, space of his brief life in Dublin. Some of the best of the *Dream Songs* is the result.

'Ireland' provided a source of fascination and inspiration for Berryman in the shape of the 'majestic shade' of Yeats, and latterly there was the fatal allure of the infamous 'drink' culture. With booze so much a part of the literary culture, who would notice another literary genius in the corner? He could fit in, at last. His looks were even part of the fashion of the time; he could have been mistaken for one of The Dubliners. Indeed, it is curious to see Berryman's generation in parallel with the Irish generation of the 1940s and 1950s as they too struggled with addiction and depression. And it is telling to note how and why fellow American poet-teacher, the much-troubled Theodore Roethke ('a daring & true & beautiful poet' in Berryman's words)[18] had been there before Berryman, when he visited (and had been hospitalised) in Ireland in 1960. Therein lies another story of tragic loss and obsession.

CHAPTER SEVEN

HISTORY LESSONS: DEREK MAHON & SEAMUS DEANE

This is how Ezra Pound opens Chapter Three of his fascinating little book, *ABC of Reading*:

> Literature does not exist in a vacuum. Writers as such have a definite social function exactly proportioned to their ability AS WRITERS. This is their main use. All other uses are relative, and temporary, and can be estimated only in relation to the views of a particular estimator.
>
> Partisans of particular ideas may value writers who agree with them more than writers who do not, they may, and often do, value bad writers of their own party or religion more than good writers of another party or church.
>
> But there is one basis susceptible of estimation and independent of all questions of viewpoint.

Good writers are those who keep the language efficient. That is
to say, keep it accurate, keep it clear.[1]

Derek Mahon fulfils Pound's key critical exhortation that
good writers 'are those who keep the language efficient. That
is to say, keep it accurate, keep it clear.' As it happens, Pound
makes an appearance in Mahon's poetry, so the connection
between both poets is not entirely gratuitous. Along with other
leading figures of the English language Modernist movement
of a hundred years ago, among them Ford Madox Ford and
Wyndham Lewis, Pound features in Mahon's 1984 poem 'A
Kensington Notebook'. Indeed, Pound's poem 'Hugh Selwyn
Mauberley' (1920) provides 'A Kensington Notebook' with
its structure, bilingual rhymes and theme of alienation. 'A
Kensington Notebook', like Pound's 'Hugh Selwyn Mauberley',
is a meditation on the place of art and the poet in western
society at the critical point of cultural crisis and re-imagining
that followed the end of both world wars:

> Ford dies abroad
> A marginal figure still;
> And Lewis, self-condemned,
> Eyeless in Notting Hill.
>
> Pound, released, reads
> To his grandchildren; 'helps'
> With the garden; doses off in a high
> Silence of the Alps —[2]

Pound is also present – as a preceding context, if not directly
– in Mahon's highly tuned literary sensibility and in the
Irish poet's embrace of literatures and cultures other than

the Anglophone. For instance, Japanese and French literatures provide important countervailing influences throughout Mahon's writing. In 'Beyond Howth Head', the first of his extended poems, comparable to a verse letter, Mahon presents the following scene:

> Chomēi at Tōyama, his blanket
> hemp, his character a rank
> not-to-be-trusted river mist,
> events in Kyōto all grist
> to the mill of a harsh irony,
> since we are seen by what we see;[3]

While in 'The Snow Party', Mahon, in the clearest English, identifies himself with the seventeenth-century haiku poet, Matsuo Bashō. In *Harbour Lights*, Bashō quite literally appears in Kinsale, County Cork, where Mahon lives. As Naomi Miki has amply demonstrated, Mahon's involvement with Japanese literature and culture is a complex and multi-levelled process, not unlike Pound's.[4] His panoramic view of the world, his scanning of literatures and cultures beyond the Anglophone, along with an unrelenting vigilance that he sees as the artist's obligation in the face of a flawed and inadequate contemporary culture, is very close to Mahon's viewpoint. I have in mind here Mahon's powerful visionary range: the critical mediation between self and the world that characterises his poetry and the level of artistic control, verbal dexterity and formal inventiveness which has made Mahon such an influential poet. An influence, I should say, not without its own irony.

Mahon was born in north Belfast, in 1941, where he attended the Royal Belfast Academical Institution (better known as 'Inst') in the 1950s before studying at Trinity College Dublin in the early 1960s. After a brief time studying at the Sorbonne in Paris, Mahon travelled extensively. During the past thirty years or so, he has held various journalistic jobs – theatre critic for *The Listener*, poetry editor at the *New Statesman*, features editor at *Vogue*, and reviewer and columnist with the *Irish Times* – as well as academic positions in Irish and American universities, including the University of Ulster, Trinity College, Dublin and New York University. Throughout these years he has produced a substantial body of work, including the following volumes of poetry: *Night Crossing* (1968), *Lives* (1972), *The Snow Party* (1975), *The Hunt by Night* (1982), *Selected Poems* (1991), a new *Selected Poems* (1993), *The Hudson Letter* (1995), *The Yellow Book* (1997), *Collected Poems* (1999), *Harbour Lights* (2005), *Life on Earth* (2008), *An Autumn Wind* (2010), *New Collected Poems* (2011) and *New Selected Poems* (2016). In the intervening years, Mahon has been prolific with *Selected Prose* (2012); a collection of translations, *Echo's Grove* (2013); and two fascinating prose collections of literary and autobiographical essays, *Red Sails* (2014) and *Olympia and the Internet* (2017).

Along with writing adaptations of plays[5] by Molière, Euripides and Edmond Rostand's *Cyrano de Bergerac*, he has written screenplays of well-known Irish novels – Jennifer Johnston's *Shadows on our Skin* and *How Many Miles to Babylon?* and Elizabeth Bowen's *The Death of the Heart*. Mahon has also edited two anthologies of Irish poetry, as well as edited the poetry of the neglected Irish poet Patrick MacDonogh (1902–61), and the universally acclaimed Welsh poet Dylan Thomas.

Mahon's poetry has been recognised with several distinguished awards, including the Denis Devlin Poetry Award, the *Irish Times*/Aer Lingus Poetry Prize, and the C.K. Scott Moncrieff Translation Prize. He has also been awarded two of the most significant literary honours available in America, the Lannan and Guggenheim fellowships: a rare achievement for an Irish poet. In 2007 he was awarded the prestigious David Cohen Prize for Literature.

Mahon is regarded not only as one of Ireland's finest poets; his critical reputation is acknowledged by many leading critics and scholars as the most significant poet writing in English today.[6] His influence upon a younger generation of poets writing in Ireland, and elsewhere, is also noticeable. Yet there is a profound irony in all this because over the recent past Mahon has receded further from the public platform on both sides of the Atlantic. He rarely gives poetry readings, and at his own request his books of poetry were not sent for review to newspapers for a period of time, so disaffected had Mahon become with the literary 'scene'. He spurns the blandishments of media attention, refusing interviews, book launches and maintaining an almost Beckettian silence in relation to his work, which he believes should speak for itself.

Selected as one of the poets for the millennial programme *Reading the Future*, broadcast on RTÉ, the Irish national radio station, Mahon, unlike all but two (Brian Friel and Thomas Kinsella) of the twelve selected writers, did not appear in person. In the subsequent publication of *Reading the Future*, a book based upon the series of interviews, his shadowy presence was neatly caught by a photograph in profile, reminiscent of Alfred Hitchcock, the great director of filmic suspense.[7]

Mahon's own poetry pays homage to artists and fellow writers such as Samuel Beckett, Bertolt Brecht and Albert Camus. For these writers share both Mahon's 'emigrant sensibility' (the phrase comes from Brown's invaluable introduction to *Journalism*) and opposition to what he sees as the fatal allure of the inauthentic, the fake, the sham; the inconsequence of much that constitutes contemporary life and culture. 'It's one more sedative evening in Co. Cork,' he writes in 'Harbour Lights':

> The house is quiet and the world is dark
> while the Bush gang are doing it to Iraq.
> The flesh is weary and I've read the books;
> Nothing but lies and nonsense on the box[.][8]

Lies and nonsense on the television screen in Cork, but not in dear old France, one of the last remaining shelters for the real thing, as Mahon remarks in 'Resistance Days', addressed to his friend the photographer John Minihan. The reference in the last of the following lines is to the highly respected and desired French female actors, the 'real stars', Isabelle Adjani and Juliette Binoche:

> Still sceptical, statistically off-line France
> resists the specious arguments most advance,
> the digital movies and unnatural nosh,
> to stick with real tomatoes, real *brioche*
> and real stars like Adjani and Binoche.[9]

Mahon is at times a poet of misanthropy and existential regret. The radical nostalgia that underpins much of his more 'conversational' poetry, from *The Yaddo Letter* (1992) on, is double-edged: ironic lamentations that what is currently on offer (what makes the present inadequate and misconceived) should be dramatically exposed in *writing*. As a poetic chronicler of the world today, Mahon's displeasure and dissatisfaction is satirical, infuriated and resigned. This is the Pound position, 'a tawdry cheapness' which 'shall outlast our days', as he described it in the third section of 'Hugh Selwyn Mauberley'.[10] Like

Pound, Mahon achieves his measurement of how things have grown worse both in artistic and cultural terms, and regarding other traditions – literary ('high' and 'low'), visual art and cinema. In so doing, he echoes the ambition of Pound but also that of a poet much closer to home, his fellow Northern Irish poet Louis MacNeice, whose *Autumn Journal* (1939) can be read as a template for Mahon's more recent work. Mahon also looks back in the birthday poem 'St. Patrick's Day' to Jonathan Swift, the great Irish satirist, as an inspirational antecedent; significantly, the poem closes Mahon's *Collected Poems* and sets the terms for much of *Harbour Lights*.

Known worldwide as the name of Ireland's patron saint and of the national holiday, St Patrick's is also the name of the hospital in Dublin which Swift established for 'fools and mad'; it is mostly used now as a medical unit for recovering alcoholics and for post-trauma convalescence, a fact alluded to by Mahon in an earlier poem, 'Dawn at St. Patrick's'.[11] The long library mentioned in the opening line of 'St. Patrick's Day' probably refers to the Long Room, the impressive library that houses the *Book of Kells* in Trinity College where Swift (and Mahon) had studied. The poem is clearly not *only* about commemorating Swift, though he rises, Leviathan-like, as an inquisitorial figure out of the poem's depths.

Taking its bearings from Swift, 'St. Patrick's Day' is an audit of the present. The switching attention of the poem, from the distant past to the here and now, from Dublin to New York via the tourist routes, takes in the corporate world we all inhabit, where Swift's legacy is momentarily, bizarrely, instated, before Mahon concedes his folly. The individual imagination, he suggests, cannot resist the all-powerful forces of 'consensual media, permanent celebration,/share options, electronic animation,/wave motion of site-specific daffodils,/and video lenses in the new hotels'. The poem is an act of renunciation ('I now resign these structures and devices,/these fancy flourishes and funny voices') and becomes an acknowledgement of 'the perpetual flow' of life; the recognition and respite found in ordinary domestic subjects, not 'middle age and misanthropy' but:

> prismatic natural light, slow-moving cloud,
> the waves far-thundering in a life of their own,
> a young woman hitching a lift on a country road.[12]

These are the things that matter. 'St. Patrick's Day' is an important 'representative' poem by Mahon in the sense that it points to an enduring tension in his work between the panoramic, troubled vision of transcendence and the unexpected bounty of the everyday.

Time and again, Mahon has homed in on the contrary pulls of the imagination, away from the 'dying light of faith' when 'God gutters down to metaphor'[13] to 'the anxiety of a last word/When the drums start',[14] the intersection between dream and reality. In 'The Mayo Tao', he breaks cover and speaks his mind:

> I am an expert on frost crystals
> and the silence of crickets, a confidant
> of the stinking shore, the stars in the mud –
> there is an immanence in these things
> which drives me, despite my scepticism,
> almost to the point of speech,
> like sunlight cleaving the lake mist at morning
> or when tepid water
> runs cold at last from the tap.[15]

One can almost hear the advice of Bashō in the background to this resolution: 'Your poetry issues of its own accord when you and the object have become one – when you have plunged deep enough into the object to see something like a hidden glimmering there.'[16]

In this heightened awareness of 'an immanence' in things (Bashō's 'hidden glimmering') 'a shirt-hanger/Knocked in an open wardrobe' is 'a strange event/To be pondered on for hours'[17] and 'a rare stillness/Lies upon roof and garden – Each object eldritch-bright'.[18] Such attention to the momentariness of life turns things upside down: 'a single bird' can 'Drown with a whistle' the residual roar of 'Rock Music';[19] 'Tacitus believed mariners could *hear*/The sun sinking into the western sea',[20] while 'in the window-frame a persistent fly/buzzes with furious life which will never die'.[21] In other words, poetry clarifies life and remakes it; a version of what is seen or heard or thought or felt is rendered real in another kind of medium; artistically, through the efficient use of language. In one of his rare interviews, Mahon corroborates this view:

> For me, poetry is about shape and sound. It's about taking the formless and making it interesting … creating form out of formlessness. Poems may appear to be about history or politics or autobiography, but it is essentially an artistic activity.[22]

Eileen Battersby's accompanying gloss reads: 'Mahon's own view is that the best kind of artistic tension exists between public and private concerns.' And this simple statement neatly summarises Mahon's art. It was also around the time of this interview (1990) that Mahon was moving increasingly towards a more open conversational poem that has since characterised his writing. The three collections, *The Hudson Letter*, *The*

Yellow Book and *Harbour Lights*, are crammed full of the world as we know it today – a global, urban, corporate cyberspace dominated by soundbites and video grabs, controlled by an impatient and swamped media. This is how Mahon views our brave new world:

> News-time
> in the global village – Ethiopian drought,
> famine, whole nations, races, evicted even yet,
> rape victim and blind beggar at the gate –
> the images forming which will be screened tonight
> on CNN ...[23]

Against this public onslaught, the individual poetic imagination finds strength and release in whichever way it can. For Mahon, the popular culture of the mid-twentieth century is often summoned. In his recent work, in particular, writers such as the Irish poet Austin Clarke are recalled from relative neglect.[24] In an earlier version of 'The Sea in Winter', originally published in 1979, Mahon, situated in 'a draughty bungalow in Portstewart', addresses his fellow Irish poet Desmond O'Grady with a reference to 'This is where Jimmy Kennedy wrote "Red Sails in the Sunset".'[25] Northern-Ireland-born, fellow Trinity College graduate, and one of the great lyricists of the last century, Jimmy Kennedy turns up again twenty-five years later, supplying Mahon with the title for *Harbour Lights*.[26] Kennedy also provides one of the finest poems in the collection 'Calypso', with its critical turning point between the classical world of Homer's Ulysses and the landscape of an imagined home:

> Red sails in the sunset where the dripping prows
> Rapped out a drum-rhythm on uncertain seas

> Of skimming birds, a lonely pine or shrine –
> But the seer's secrets diminished on dry land,
> Darker than they could know or understand.[27]

So the archetypal vision of Homer's Ulysses searching for Ithaca, his home, finds an unpredictable congruence in the sentimental lyrics of Jimmy Kennedy's 'Red Sails in the Sunset'.

Mahon's ability to make these correspondences without self-regarding knowingness or shrill post-modern trickery points back towards Pound's assertion that good writers 'are those who keep the language efficient … accurate … clear'. The exchange, which takes place in Mahon's work between literature, art and popular culture, between Homer and Jimmy Kennedy, invigorates his poetry and maintains efficient lines of communication. At the same time, Mahon's critical understanding of our present moment is open, sometimes abrasive and mostly questioning. It is probably this latter attribute, the quizzical, outsider-like view, the occasional patrician note of disdain, undercut by a playful mocking tone – along with the achieved status of some of his earlier poems ('Ecclesiastes', 'A Disused Shed in Co. Wexford', 'The Globe in Carolina', amongst others), that makes Mahon such an important and influential poet with a younger generation of poetry readers and poets seeking a genuinely *poetic* response to their world.

Derek Mahon's contemporary Seamus Deane offers a fascinating comparison in that born a year before Mahon in the maiden city of Derry, and like Mahon and Heaney, a scholarship boy, Deane's imaginative life seems to have struggled to free itself from the historical roots of his upbringing. The border city, which was a harbour much engaged with a substantial military camp and naval fleet during the Second World War, had been very badly treated since the foundation of the new

Northern state in 1922. Throughout the early decades of Northern Ireland unemployment was notoriously high – one of the highest in Europe – housing conditions were appalling and the normal practices of democratic representation were riven by the sectarian gerrymandering of the Unionist government.

Overlooking the Foyle River and estuary and backing into the most westerly and dramatic of the northern counties, Donegal, which as a result of the partition of the island was across the Irish border, Derry's famous walled inner world of battlements and rising streets has been caught between two worlds. For the sense of a landscape of great coastal beauty on one's doorstep could not compensate for the heavily policed atmosphere of the post–Second World War era, when ineffective IRA attempts to challenge the government militarily led to the increasing use of a sectarian force of auxiliary police called the 'B' Specials in controlling the largely Catholic and nationalist areas of Derry, such as what became known first as the Bogside and later the Creggan.

Deane grew out of this world and, like his life-long friend and fellow poet Seamus Heaney, attended the city's well-known Catholic grammar school, St Columb's – Deane as a day boy, Heaney as a boarder (1951–7). The story of their relationship is neatly captured in Deane's article, 'The Famous Seamus',[28] an honest and occasionally acerbic portrait of both school pals and their later development as poets and critics, firstly at Queen's University in Belfast (1957–61), which they attended together and then went their separate ways immediately thereafter – Seamus Deane came up to Pembroke College in 1963 and was approved for a doctorate in May 1968, graduating in Easter of that year. The title of his PhD was 'The Reception and Reputation of Some Thinkers of the French Enlightenment in England between 1789 and 1824'.

After a few years teaching in Berkeley, California, Deane returned to Dublin, first as a lecturer in University College Dublin, before being appointed Professor of Modern English and American Literature, a position he held until 1993 and his appointment as Professor of English and Donald and Marilyn Keough Professor of Irish Studies at the University of Notre Dame, Indiana, from which he retired some years ago. To have some sense of Deane's presence as a teacher during his early years in Dublin, I asked the Dublin-born poet Gerard Fanning for his recollection of Deane in UCD during the late sixties:[29]

It was September 1969, and I, 17, naïve and gauche to boot, started in University College Dublin, Earlsfort Terrace as a First Arts student. My subjects were Philosophy, Political Economy and English. At the time, that area of Dublin – Earlsfort Tce., Leeson Street and St. Stephen's Green – was wonderfully irreverent and lively. There were student boarding houses, squalid bed-sits, draughty flats, Alexandra College in its posh secluded grounds, St Vincent's Hospital and a bunch of public houses that seemed to be packed all day. And on a string of soon to be demolished 19th Century tenements leading up to the University, someone had scrawled 'Desolation Row'. The formidable Prof. Denis Donoghue presided over the English Department. A serious man, we knew he was in constant correspondence with the movers and shakers of American Literature (now there is 'a collected letters' worth publishing) and had only a passing interest in the local scene.

At each academic year start, he perceived as his primary duty to shatter the complacency of new undergraduates, so the Michaelmas Term would consist of prosody and more prosody. But we also knew that a brilliant, young Northern lecturer,

Seamus Deane, had joined the Department the previous year. Professor Donoghue's mood seemed to have lightened. At last, here was someone with whom he could really converse. Seamus Deane was marvellous and exhilarating in the lecture theatre. We were to study Jane Austen (*Emma*) and Albert Camus (*The Plague*) amongst others. There was perfection here and it was up to us to identify, contextualise and then hold dear for the rest of our lives. The lectures were mesmerising. He seemed to start with the bones of a thesis, but as he walked up and down by the lectern, new ideas, associations and tentative conclusions would spark and collide. He effortlessly made the sociological, ethical, ontological and economic strands of his evolving argument cohere into a formidable thesis, only to deconstruct his argument, begin again, and offer counter interpretations. And all conducted as if he took us seriously, a conversation between equals. We were to believe that he trusted us to keep up, and trusted us with the same thought processes.

Being First Arts, and the winnowing not yet complete, lectures were held in the largest theatre available, but two more theatres were always on stand-by to relay the lectures with loudspeakers. There might have been some slippage in attendance at some of Desmond Connell's metaphysical ramblings in the Philosophy Dept. but not with Seamus Deane. We knew he was part of that miraculous grouping from Northern Ireland (Heaney, Mahon etc.) and his first poetry collections would appear in the 70s and 80s.

In my second year I dropped English to pursue a degree in Philosophy & Economics. The Arts Faculty moved out to Belfield, St Vincent's Hospital moved to Elm Park, Alexandra College moved to Milltown. That once vibrant area of Dublin relaxed into its present anonymity – ghosts of junior doctors, nurses in uniform and posh school girls, forever young, flitting into bar back rooms and snugs, long gone. But Seamus Deane made that time bright for many of us, raising literature to an exploded view, seeing Shakespeare as our contemporary and positing the University as a real place for the imagination.

Mr Deane was indeed like a tight coil, eating cigs. Very nervy. There was a kind of impatience, like 'let's get all this guff about the basics of narrative out of the way and get on with the philosophical imperative'. I'm not saying he was in thrall to the way Existentialism was very big at the time, particularly the way it bled into Lit. Crit., but we students were, and he seemed sympathetic. It suited me too, a very young 17-year-old, to connect with my other subjects. His own poetry wasn't in book form at the time, though we knew he was writing. I think I'm right in saying he was invited to read at the English Lit. Society and was very edgy and nervous. I think we liked him for that too. The few poems I saw at the time seemed a match with his Northern contemporaries, but then there was so much happening, our own *St Stephen's* (edited at the time by Brian Earls. Ruth from Books Upstairs involved), *HU*, *Dublin Mag.*, *Hibernia* and *New Irish Writing*. I'm not surprised he gave it up though. Also, I never attended a lecture on poetry. I do remember a mention of his admiration for the Up-State New York poets of the 'deep image'. Would that be Robert Duncan?[30]

Deane's first collection, *Gradual Wars*, was published in 1972 when he was a lecturer in UCD, though a pamphlet of his poems, *While Jewels Rot*, had appeared somewhat earlier, in 1966, in the famous Festival Publications series at Queen's, but

Deane rejected the poems and at £699 or more per copy on AbeBooks it might be just as well!

At thirty-two years of age, in contrast to his contemporaries Seamus Heaney, Derek Mahon and Michael Longley, Deane's was a slightly later entry into the public world of publishing a *book* of poems. For instance, Heaney had already published *three* volumes – *Death of a Naturalist* (1966), *Door into the Dark* (1969) and *Wintering Out* (1972) – and Mahon's *Night-Crossing* (1968) and *Lives* (1972) had appeared to critical acclaim. *Gradual Wars* received the prestigious Æ Memorial Award for Literature in Ireland and was followed by *Rumours*, published by Dolmen Press in 1977; six years later *History Lessons* appeared with The Gallery Press in 1983 and five years after that, a volume of *Selected Poems*, including a section of new poems and translations, was published in 1988. After that – on the poetry front, silence.

Deane's scholarly, critical and editorial work, however, took off, producing seminal studies of Irish writing and its European contexts in book after book. The 1980s saw publication of the highly influential collection *Celtic Revivals: Essays in Modern Irish Literature 1880–1980*, *A Short History of Irish Literature* and *The French Enlightenment and Revolution in England*. He had also been an inspirational presence in establishing *The Crane Bag* journal (1977–85) edited by philosophers Mark Patrick Hederman and Richard Kearney.

In the 1990s, Deane was the driving force behind the publication of the *Field Day Anthology of Irish Writing 550–1988*, a controversial anthology originally in three volumes, which had come out of the theatre and publishing collective he joined with founders Brian Friel and Stephen Rea, along with Thomas Kilroy, musician and film-maker David Hammond and poets Seamus Heaney and Tom Paulin. In 1997, his 1995

Clarendon Oxford Lectures were published as *Strange Country: Modernity and Nationhood in Irish Writing Since 1790*, echoing the opening lines of his poem 'Strange Country' from *Rumours*, twenty years earlier:[31]

> It is too simple
> To say I miss you.
> If there were a language
> That could not say 'leave'
> And had no word for 'stay'
> That would be the tongue
> For this strange country[.]

In the new century, Deane as general editor oversaw the publication of the Penguin Classic *James Joyce* series, a major undertaking, alongside co-editing the *Field Day Review*, an annual Irish Studies journal, as well as mentoring a book series on Irish Studies co-published by the University of Notre Dame Press and Cork University Press. It was, however, his autobiographical novel, *Reading in the Dark* (1996), winner of the Irish Times International Fiction Prize, the Irish Literature Prize, The Guardian Prize, Booker-short listed and translated into numerous languages, which brought Deane's name to a much wider audience, producing the kind of critical and popular recognition that his fellow student at St Columb's and Queen's University had experienced since publication of his first collections back in the heady days of the 1960s. But far too much can be read and *has* been read into these relationships of well over half a century ago. On an individual level, it's clear that Deane's remarkable achievement *across* literary disciplines suggests a completely different kind of imaginative and intellectual bearing than that of a contemporary such as Derek

Mahon with whom Deane, along with others, edited the short-lived magazine *Atlantis* in the early 1970s, or Seamus Heaney, with whom he is much more often identified.

In what follows I'm interested in looking at a very small sample of the poems – a little over one hundred or so – and what they tell us about the history of Deane's life and times to date, but also about History itself, the monolith he has struggled with (at least so it seems to this reader) since he kicked a football in the descending dusk of a Derry back field in the late 1940s and early 1950s. Clearly, I have to radically select from his four collections a number of 'stand out' poems to illustrate my theme. But if ever there was a subject awaiting the attention of a younger generation of scholars, Deane as poet, critic and scholar is an abundant source of intellectual challenge, as can be seen in the extensive archive held at the Emory University Stuart A. Rose Manuscript, Archives, and Rare Book Library in Atlanta, Georgia. That is for another day, although it is good to report that Rosie Lavan is energetically engaged on a project, 'Representing Derry, 1968–2013', which 'examines representations of Derry in a range of forms and genres – poetry, fiction, drama, memoir, criticism, photography and documentary film'.[32] Lavan goes on to state that:

> [T]hrough their resistance to straightforward generic classification, many of the works under discussion, including Seamus Deane's autobiographical novel *Reading in the Dark*, put pressure on the process of literary interpretation itself. Mindful particularly of his engagements with form, I consider Deane's novel in relation to his poetry, and in the context of his convictions about literature and history expressed in his criticism from the 1970s to date. In addition, I am particularly interested in re-approaching his

criticism of the 1970s and '80s now – mindful of its original provocations, and of the very particular climate in which it was produced – and considering the place it claims both in our increasingly historicised understanding of that period, and in contemporary cultural debates.[33]

So maybe we are beginning to see a wider reassessment of the creative and scholarly writing from contemporary Ireland, and a much-needed widening of the critical franchise. But the first point of reference I'd like to make is how Deane has described himself in an interview: 'I have no substantial connection with the Northern poets' group or groups. I learned of it via Seamus Heaney when he came to visit me in Cambridge armed with a prize and a bottle of whiskey.'[34]

The characteristic homing instinct of his early poems, the journeying back, is a powerful motif in Deane's poetry; not only in terms of the city, imagined as an embattled and at times mystical place – like a Gothic castle – but also the inner décor of the family home and the surrounding streetscapes take on an estranged and ominous reality. The 'sirens settle/to a blue yap', clocks and telephones, wallpaper and doors, backyards and street corners hold a kind of philosophical meaning of threat and desire mixed up with fearfulness and anxiety:[35]

> Look! The razors
> Of perception are now
> So honed they cut
> The lying throat of song.

Why 'song' has a 'lying throat' is a bigger question that I have space for here, but it summons up the figures of Theodore Adorno and Walter Benjamin,[36] both of whom feature pervasively in Deane's critical thinking. If the narrator of the poems in *Gradual Wars* is 'snared in my past',[37] there is an ongoing sense of danger in even the most familiar atmosphere:[38]

> I fear more
> The ghost that comes by the wall,
> The patterned face upon the curtain
> The sight that can unhinge
> The stable doors of the sty
> And maraud for revenge.

Deane's Derry is a knowable place from the beginning. *Gradual Wars*, dedicated to his father and mother, opens with a sequence based around a family home (no. 38) and elegises those murdered on Bloody Sunday ('After Derry, 30 January 1972').[39] The collection is full of names – Sean Cassidy, Peter Doherty. Dermot Felon, and the names of the immediate family – Ciaran, Maeve, Richard, Joe, Emer, Conor, Marian. But sitting alongside this intense intimacy, other landscapes emerge in 'the wide American night',[40] such as San Francisco, and with them an unfolding sense too of the poet's transference to another kind of language, as in the Wallace Stevens-sounding 'On the Mimicry of Unnatural Objects' and 'Landscape into Art'. But the overriding mood of the volume is of a distinct and present danger embedded in the home place.[41]

Rumours, his second collection, seems comparatively more secure in its revisiting of the past. Dedicated in memoriam to Frank Deane, the poet's father, there is an achieved balance between the stern retrospection of Deane's Northern life in his poem 'Going Northward' and Belfast in 'The Brethren', but also a releasing fondness conveyed in 'Shelter':[42]

Two years after one war,
And some time before another,
In nineteen forty-seven,
Came a heavy fall of snow
That drifted over the slab of the air-raid roof.

And concludes with a portrait of his ('unsheltered') mother, 'Doing the sums/For food and clothes, the future/In endless hock'. There might be an element of wish-fulfilment in the older poet looking back to 1947 and his 7-year-old self's consciousness of being 'weather-proof', but the poem's mention of 'Two years after one war/And some time before another' brings into frame the mindfulness of Deane's poems with the play of language in the processes of history-making.

In the chapter 'Grandfather: October 1952' from the haunting and haunted novel, *Reading in the Dark*, there is a wonderful portrait of 'great uncle Constantine, on my mother's side … the sole family heretic' who 'hung a placard on the wall of his living room, with the slogan CRUSH THE INFAMOUS ONE painted in red on a black background; he said that was his and Voltaire's Declaration of Faith. Then he went blind, became ill and caved in by being restored to the bosom of the Church before he died.'[43]

Sitting with his grandfather, the young boy is asked what he is doing and the conversation follows:[44]

'Just some French exercises.'

'French! What do you want to be bothered with French for? Sure who speaks French round here? Waste of time. Fit you better to be studying Irish, your own language.'

'An' who speaks Irish round here?'

'Frankie Mennan, Johnny Harkin. That's two. And plenty more. And look at what French did to Constantine. Lost him his sight, then, they say, his soul.'

'Constantine? Sure he died a Catholic.'

'He did not. He didn't. He died a heretic. Refused to see the priest and died holding that French book across his chest that they tried to get off him.'

'I heard diff ...'

'Of course you did. They cooked up the story so's not to give a bad example. But old Con, he's down there roasting with all the other atheists. God rest him.'

At that he laughed suddenly, and so did I.

'Aye, God rest him in his wee suit of fire, reading his fancy French book.'

Language really is a matter of life and death and possibly, if there's autobiographical truth in the incident, maybe no surprise that Deane's interest in some thinkers of the French enlightenment should form part of his own intellectual development. But also precious wonder that Deane should publish a volume called *History Lessons* which mediates between how the big frame of History, with a capital 'H', imposes order and authority upon the workings of ordinary family life 'underneath'.

Opening with a poem on the Russian poet Osip Mandelstam as a figure of the poet *in extremis*, the volume is backlit by other 'great' literary presences, including a dramatic vignette on Edmund Burke ('Christmas at Beaconsfield') – on whom Deane would publish several key essays[45] – John Mitchel, the nineteenth-century Irish republican activist and, in the title poem, a meditation on a journey taken to Moscow.

As with the earlier volumes, *History Lessons* relives different kinds and sources of history: the local, familial, unvoiced world of Deane's upbringing and the authorising, validating structure of state and imperial power. 'All my work,' he states in an interview, 'is about uncovering, especially uncovering of voices that speak without governance, or that speak without being heard'[46] – something he has discussed at length in his readings of the playwright Brian Friel.[47] The contrasts within *History Lessons* couldn't be starker than in the following two poems, which, like a metronome, provoke in 'Breaking Wood', the poem to his father, the reader's sympathy at the very same time as questioning how the individual is at the mercy of the grander designs of History in the title poem, 'History Lessons':[48]

Elections, hunger-strikes and shots

Greeted our return. Houses broke open
In the season's heat and the bulb
Burned in the ground. Men on ladders
Climbed into roselight, a roof was a swarm of fireflies
At dusk. The city is no more. The lesson's learned.
I will remember it always as a burning
In the heart of winter and a boy running.

There is much else in the poetry of Seamus Deane than I have rendered here. I'm thinking of the domestic poems of love and loss, the songs of praise and pleasure in the landscape, although even 'Hummingbirds' can't quite avoid some part of a history lesson and the ornate, somewhat arcane English of many other poems, such as 'Street Singers' and 'Guerrillas', deserve more than a note in passing.

What is required is a new edition of all Deane's poems in one collected volume and then we can read it in its diversity and unique range of reference, although I don't recommend holding our breaths waiting for that to happen. In the almost thirty years that followed publication of *Selected Poems* in 1988, Deane seems to have revoked his poetic deeds. Asked if there was any cache of post-1988 poems I should know about, the two-word reply said it all, 'No danger'![49]

In a fascinating interview with John Brown, from which I have been quoting, Deane speaks of poetry very much against the grain of current fashion: 'If poetry has any enhancing powers for the poet,' Deane wonders aloud, 'they surely must include the belief that you must make the effort to break from what formed you, even though this itself is part of an almost predetermined formation.'[50] He then goes on to challenge one of the most popular and entrenched views of the values of *Irish* poetry:[51]

> In Ireland there is such an ideological investment in the idea of the artist, the privatisation of writing, the absurd pretensions to a cheap universalisation of feeling and of authority with that, that it is difficult to keep a sense of proportion. Writing that treasures narcissism, writing that is mere propaganda – between these polarities there is very little that is worth remembering. And it is difficult to enter into the wider world without denying the inner world. It is not just an escape from nationality, of the British or the Irish variety; it is an escape into the belief that one is 'free', that one is the maker of the world he

sings. I think this is a glamorous and vacuous notion. At least in its pseudo-liberal therapeutic form, it is mere garbage, although widely canvassed and admired.

In the final poem collected in his *Selected Poems*, 'Reading *Paradise Lost* in Protestant Ulster 1984', a bulky poem of Spenserian stanzas such as Yeats had employed in, among other volumes, *The Tower* of 1928, the twin peaks of Deane's writing life come together – his scholarship and the wayward trip of his imaginative energies. I am not sure when the poem was actually drafted but it may well refer to his time living in Belfast as a student at Queen's University which he recalls in his *New Yorker* portrait of Seamus Heaney. In the following extract, Deane recounts his lecturer in literature at Queen's, the South African poet and critic Laurence Lerner, who had 'reordered the local tyranny in our minds, by showing us how deeply introjected the sour hegemony of our sectarianism had become'. It is Belfast in the late 1950s:[52]

I think that [Lerner's] lessons were silently meant to teach us how to read literary texts in a living way – reminding us that our lives, too, were embroiled with these books. I remember the oddness of seeing Protestant working-class Belfast for the first time: I would cross its most notorious street, Sandy Row, and hear the Saturday-night evangelicals screaming and raving through loudspeakers about Popery and repentance, and pass by the clamorous shops, and smell the sweet aromas from the Erinmore tobacco factory, above the railway bridge, and then return to my rented room in a nearby Catholic neighbourhood, to read Milton and Dickens – whose seventeenth- and nineteenth-century worlds were suddenly coexistent with my own. I knew the bitterness of Protestantism, and its philistine pride, but for the first time I began to sense its magnificence. Lerner brought the streets of Belfast and the poems and novels we read into contact with one another. It was a salutary lesson.

'Reading *Paradise Lost* in Protestant Ulster, 1984' presents us with a very powerful sense of Seamus Deane's own coming to terms with the past at the very point his poetry was questioning whether or not history really has any 'lessons' we can learn from or if we can ever really 'let go'. It is that struggle which makes his poems unique and important expressions, deserving of our critical attention along with so much else of his challenging work of over half a century:[53]

> Our 'sovran Planter' beats
> Upon his breast, dyadic evil rules;
> A syncope that stammers in our guns,
> That forms and then reforms itself in schools
> And in our daughters' couplings and our sons,
> We feel the fire's heat, Belial's doze;
> A maiden city's burning on the plain;
> Rebels surround us, Lord. Ah, whence arose
> This dark damnation, this hot unrainbowed rain?

CHAPTER EIGHT

THE GREEN LIGHT: STEWART PARKER

At the end of *Northern Star*, Stewart Parker's play set in the 'continuous past' – where, in his own words, 'pastiche' is 'a strategy' and the eighteenth century of the play forms part of the 'common enterprise' which, with *Heavenly Bodies* and *Pentecost*, takes us up to the infamous Loyalist Workers' Strike of 1974 – Henry Joy McCracken addresses his audience:

> Why would one place break your heart, more than another? A place the like of that? Brain-damaged and dangerous, continuously violating itself, a place of perpetual breakdown, incompatible voices, screeching obscenely away through the smoky dark wet ... And yet what would this poor old fool not give to be able to walk freely again from Stranmillis down to Ann Street ... cut through Pottinger's Entry and across the road for a drink in Peggy's ... to dander on down Waring Street and examine the shipping along the river, and back on up to our old house ... we can't love it for what it is, only for what it might have been, if we'd got it right, if we'd made it whole. If.

It's a ghost town now and always will be, angry and implacable ghosts. Me condemned to be one of their number.[1]

It is a chilling moment, that marries the tragic note with the farcical, the sentimental with the shock of reality: McCracken's execution by hanging. When first staged in Belfast in November 1984 at the Lyric Players' Theatre, the scene, played in the very depths of the Troubles, sent a shudder of challenging recognition through the audience. For 'the citizens of Belfast' were listening, and, in my understanding of Stewart Parker, the epicentre of not only *Northern Star* but of his writing life is symbolised in that reverie: 'what would this poor old fool not give to be able to walk freely again from Stranmillis down to Ann Street … cut through Pottinger's Entry and across the road for a drink in Peggy's … to dander on down Waring Street and examine the shipping along the river, and back up to our old house'.

Stewart Parker's plays are about the complex, conflicting and emblematic relationship between 'our old house', the physical and civic embodiment of personal history and family tradition, and the city of Belfast, a relationship that I would like to descriptively explore in Stewart Parker's own words. The house as a metaphor embraces, most tellingly, Lily Mathews's 'parlour house' in *Pentecost*, 'a house eloquent with the history of this city', as Marian describes it.[2] A little later in the play, in a rebuking exchange with Peter, her ex-husband's friend, who sees the kitchen house as 'nothing special', Marian remarks:

So why should Lily Mathews' home and hearth be less special than Lord Castlereagh's or the Earl of Enniskillen's? A whole way of life, a whole culture, the only difference being, that this home speaks for a far greater community of experience in this country than some transplanted feeble-minded aristocrat's ever could, have you looked at it, properly?[3]

In *Pentecost*, in stark contrast to the Anglo-Irish 'big house', Lily's tenement house, where '[e]verything is real except the proportions',[4] is the key to Parker's theatrical sense of the social and cultural reality of his characters: a 'whole way of life, a whole culture', 'this home [which] speaks for a far greater community of experience in this country'. And he has said as much in his non-dramatic writing about his background in Belfast while, incidentally, 'whole' and 'wholeness' are two of the terms Parker keeps coming back to, as in the following passage from his 'John Malone Lecture':

> There is a whole culture to be achieved. The politicians, visionless almost to a man, are withdrawing into their sectarian stockades. It falls to the artists to construct a working model of wholeness by means of which this society can begin to hold up its head in the world.[5]

This sense of both the broken and fragmented *lack* of vision in the present, set against future possibilities, is grounded in Parker's rendering of his own family's past, and their 'place' in the wider historical scheme of things. In a wonderfully evocative portrait of his paternal grandfather, 'An Ulster Volunteer', originally published in the *Irish Times* in March 1970, Parker takes the reader back to the life of a Belfast factory worker in September 1912, when at 'twenty-nine [he] signed the Ulster Covenant in the Belfast City Hall'. As Parker relates, this 'small man, spry and upright', had been:

forced to shuffle a little by the enormous wounds in his thighs and calves. He chuckles a lot … shy, proud and alone. And all his life he has thought of Roman Catholics as a feared and deadly enemy. When I quiz him about the past, I feel like a hapless, insatiable detective, cross-examining the victim of a vast crime.[6]

The physical wounds his grandfather carries (and the end of a promising football career) were 'decorations awarded in the vicinity of the Passchendaele Ridge and Hellfire Corner' during the First World War, as the one-time east Belfast UVF volunteers are 'metamorphosed into the 8th Battalion Royal Irish Rifles'.

In 1917, as Parker's dramatic account continues, 'the rifle spring[s] out of his [grandfather's] hands when the shell exploded near him, the two corpses in the trench beside whom he was placed, the awful noise of the support artillery passing over his head, the officer who covered him with a "Jerry coat" because he was shivering. At the dressing station the surgeon left him till the end, taking him for a German on account of the coat.' Making his own way back, 'wearing carpet slippers, with blood oozing through the dressings, [his grandfather] somehow made it to Liverpool and got the boat to Belfast, to his wife and seven children'. Through this unfolding portrait of his grandfather, Parker imagines him 'and his cronies' as 'earnest young men, full of certainties and zeal, readers of books like *Thrift* and *Self Help* by Samuel Smiles, not wishing to ape the gentry but respecting its superiority', and in a phrase that could summarise the life of Lily Mathews in *Pentecost* (if a life can ever be summarised), Parker continues: 'wishing merely to elevate their family's station from a kitchen house to one with a parlour, scullery and pantry too, and an inside lavatory; which my grandfather did'.[7] Soundings here of a comment Parker would make twelve years later, in 1982, about how his mind 'was framed by an urban neighbourhood, a working-class family struggle towards petit-bourgeois values, a recoil from home and church and country, an appetite for exile'.[8]

In one of the last things he wrote, his 'Foreword' to the History plays, Parker identified the 'ancestral wraiths at my elbow' as '(amongst other things) Scots-Irish, Northern English, immigrant Huguenot … in short the usual Belfast mongrel crew'.[9]

Anatomising this background from his own insider–outsider perspective, Parker could show, better than most, the inner realities of such a Protestant upbringing in the industrial heartlands of east Belfast. From the 'doleful moans of foghorns from ships coming up the lough' and the 'street cry' – the 'folksy sound that will now most effectively reclaim that submerged landscape of childhood' – to the 'bell of the church', Parker's recollection in *The Green Light* (a radio broadcast of 1971) on the Belfast world and lifestyle of the 1940s and 50s, now almost completely vanished, is well worth recounting:

> There seemed to be dozens of hawkers then, all with ponies and carts. Women would come out in their slippers with the hearth brush to sweep up the horse's droppings for garden manure. There was the rag and bone man, the herring man, the balloon man with his hordes of plastic windmills and those paper rolls that squawk and snake out when you blow into them. I can whip up a feeble and foolish nostalgia for all this now. Not so for the coalbrick man, though, flying past covered in black dust, surrounded by the steam curling from the coalbrick he sat on, like a devil rising from the pit.[10]

The 'feeble and foolish nostalgia' that Parker warns against here is framed by what he calls, in a review of the (Canadian folk artists) McGarrigle sisters in one of his 'High Pop' columns of 1976, 'a profound sense of genuine rootedness with a high level of sophistication. Which is rare indeed.'[11] But it's precisely the sophistication and rootedness that Parker himself displays at every turn. No surprises then in registering that in *The Green Light*, from which I have been quoting – the recovery of which I owe to Marilynn Richtarik – it is F. Scott Fitzgerald's masterly novel *The Great Gatsby* that provides both title and exit lines, and also engineers the imaginative context for Parker's retrospective vision:

> What was left from the gone years was the desire to penetrate the heart of the mystery. I hadn't been able to name the vision that had drifted before me all through childhood and adolescence. I still have it and I still can't name it. But I feel its nature most poignantly in the closing sentences of *The Great Gatsby*, Fitzgerald's great novel. These words are my only excuse for making this excursion into personal history: *Gatsby believed in the green light, the orgiastic future that year by year recedes before us. It eluded us then, but that's no matter – to-morrow we will run faster, stretch out our arms further … and one fine morning. So we beat on, boats against the current, borne back ceaselessly into the past.*[12]

In the same script, as Parker returns to his grandfather and family life, no punches are pulled:

> The Twelfth was fairly exciting, what with collecting wood for the bonfire and waving at my Uncle and Grandfather in the procession. All in all my self-centredness was almost impregnable. At the same time, the accompanying introspection made me aware of the poison in the Ulster system and saved me from growing up to be that palsied surgeon, the liberal Unionist.[13]

Parker's battle with ill-health[14] from an early age – a 'sickly constitution' as he recalls in *The Green Light* – turns him into 'a raving ornithologist' by the time the family had 'climbed the raised beach and forsook Sydenham for the more rarefied air across the Holywood Road': 'Suddenly, we were semi-detached and suburban, and a piece was no longer a piece but a packed lunch. But we were also adjacent to green fields, to a sports club and the estates of the landed gentry.'[15]

From Boy Scouts to 'being filled up with Byron, Shelley and Keats at grammar school',[16] Parker's retrospective view of his life growing up in east Belfast renders the plays all that more poignant outside of the stage, which is of course where they truly belong. But it is useful to find in this non-dramatic writing, which he so obviously enjoyed producing, after all, *corroboration* for what Parker achieved on stage:

> I did chemistry experiments in the kitchen, learnt magic tricks and practical jokes, embroidered tray cloths for a time, and having driven my parents to distraction, I then went to a Baptist tent mission and got saved and started conducting revivalist meetings in friends' garages. […] I started a skiffle group called The Troubadours which performed at one or two church hall dances. Inevitably, my long suffering father got implicated. I pestered him for a guitar until he finally built one for me. It was a vehicle of long hours of adolescent world-weariness up in my cold bedroom.[17]

So the intently rhetorical flourishes of *Northern Star* and *Pentecost* have a root in that earlier east Belfast life – and which would cause consternation in some critical circles, such as the dialogue between Ruth and Peter in *Pentecost*, as they exchange lines about Pentecost Sunday – as surely as the music-making and song writing of *Catchpenny Twist* (1977) started back in his youthful life in east Belfast.

And surely this typical experience of his generation, fifteen or so years later, would lead to Parker writing (between 1970 and 1976) the pioneering 'High Pop' column for the *Irish Times* – an extraordinarily witty ('Narcissism is the last word in boredom' he remarks in a Wildean moment), lithe, urbane, knowledgeable, well-researched, energetic and critically ahead-of-its-time reading of popular music, not just of the 1970s, but throughout the twentieth century.[18] As Lynne Parker remarked, Stewart 'had a poetic sensibility, an academic training and a historian's mind',[19] effortlessly revealed in *High Pop* through Parker's mix of ironic and comic anecdote with sharp-eyed cultural commentary. In his astute commentary on the fundamentalism of American country music, his reflection on the transmission of the American west coast of The Beach Boys to the windy strands of Portrush, and in his sense of 'political' songs and the 'capacity of our available art forms to cope with contemporary political realities'.[20]

Music and music-making, fun and laughter were part and parcel of Stewart Parker's artistic make-up, as much as they were features of his temperament. This is the Belfast poet Robert Johnstone's recollection of meeting Parker:

> I met Stewart Parker around 1970. I'd just left school. He was 29 or 30, he'd been to America, one or two of his plays had been on local radio, and Festival Publications had published *Maw* [a poetry pamphlet] … His flat seemed slightly hippy, in the fashion of the time, and I thought him an exotic figure, with his soft caps and big cigars. He was reviewing records for the *Irish Times*, and was delighted with all the free albums. He was friendly, polite and probably indulgent to what must have been a callow youth.[21]

While Brian Cosgrove, a contemporary of Parker's at Queen's University somewhat earlier, writes in his memoir, *The Yew-Tree at the Head of the Strand*, of how 'Stewart had a great love of music; and we discovered that we had in common a growing interest [as students at Queen's] in forties' swing, including Glenn Miller.' In this richly evocative recollection, Cosgrove continues:

> One abiding memory I have of Stewart is his rendition one night, with all the appropriate imitation of the orchestral instruments, of 'Tuxedo Junction', in which, I think, I eventually joined. He dearly loved the obvious syncopation, and, as his walking-stick leaned on the chair beside him, his one good leg moved up and down to the time of the music.
>
> I should take this opportunity to correct any false impression which may have been given with regard to relations between Protestant and Catholic at university level. There was indeed social interaction between us. Stewart was, as I knew (and alas we in the North always made it our business to know), a Protestant; but that simply did not feature as a factor in our acquaintance.[22]

Given what we know about the obsession with music in Belfast of the 1960s, *all* kinds of music, and the breaking free from his sense of the somewhat inhibited possibilities of the North of the time, it is no surprise that Parker should have yearned, as Lynne Parker describes it, to 'enlarge the frame'.[23] Yet Parker's background and his understanding of it and other backgrounds in Ireland, North America and Britain, still proves to be a critical stumbling block in appreciating his achievement.

In 'Belfast Women: A Superior Brand of Dynamite', a spirited piece on the reasons why he first left Belfast and the reasons for his return, Parker doesn't mince his words about growing up in the city during the 1940s and 1950s:

> It was like growing up in outer Greenland. We were supposed to be British, but when you visited 'the mainland' (an insult in itself) they took you for a Canadian or a Scot. We were supposed to be Irish, but when you went over the border to Dundalk or Dublin, they treated you humorously, as an exotic alien. We didn't have any country, we just had a Province. A very, very provincial Province – politically corrupt, culturally bankrupt, full of aggressive inferiority, sectarian, self-obsessed, and utterly dreary. I fled far from it to America ... Instant gratification ... I found myself inexplicably ruminating about Belfast. There was the other side to the old hometown, the rootedness, the sense of community, the way every conversation gets handled like a one-act play. And the pubs. Right from birth I'd been carrying on a private internal war with the place, and I need to come to terms. So in August 1969, I went home.[24]

In what he called his 'tangled involvement with Belfast' Parker could see other parallels; with fellow east Belfast playwright Sam Thompson (1916–65), whose plays he prepared for publication;[25] with the mentoring presence of the great liberal educationalist John Malone, with the exhilarating examples of Bertolt Brecht and Beckett, with the intellectual stimulus of Dutch philosopher of history Johan Huizinga and, specifically, with the one writer whom Parker valued above all others, James Joyce. In his witty and irreverent hymn of praise to Joyce, 'Me and Jim', Parker states the case succinctly:

> I knew from an early age that writing would not merely be a passion, that I would be making a life sentence out of it. The

later experience of reading *Dubliners*, *A Portrait*, *Ulysses* and [Richard] Ellmann's *James Joyce* was a form of confirmation. There was so much that was familiar. In the tenacity of his emotional ties with Dublin, the possessive love mingling with the obsessive execration, the struggle over the years to annex the place to the realm of his own imagination, I saw mirrored my own whole tangled involvement with Belfast.[26]

In almost everything Parker wrote – for stage, radio, television, newspaper, journal – Belfast, its history, people, streetscape and architecture, and what he called its 'plain, lean language' was paramount, primal and perpetual.[27] Parker knew what he was talking about, in Henry Joy McCracken's words.

In the mid-1960s, Stewart Parker gave a special class at Orangefield[28] on the poetry of Sylvia Plath. Afterwards, I spoke to him and confessed that I wrote poems. His smile was encouragement enough to a 15-year-old. Barely twenty years later, his untimely death robbed Irish literature of one of its most liberated and articulate voices. When I saw *Catchpenny Twist* in the Peacock in 1977, the idea of Parker's liberating creative intelligence struck me, and again, with even more force, when I saw *Northern Star* in the Lyric Players' Theatre in 1984. Field Day's production of *Pentecost* in Derry in 1987 showed Parker as a great playwright, and with Rough Magic's production of *Pentecost* (1995), this realisation came back with renewed conviction.

Pentecost is a contemporary classic, as central to Irish experience as *Translations*, *Double Cross*, *Bailegangaire*, *Observe the Sons of Ulster Marching towards the Somme* and *The Mai*. Yet responses to the play point towards a kind of cultural blind spot (to put it at its least contentious) when writing out of the Northern Protestant experience is addressed. The play takes place in east Belfast (Ballyhackamore) during the Ulster Workers' Strike against the Sunningdale Agreement between the British and Irish governments. The strike was in particular directed against the Council of Ireland dimension to that Agreement. The strike lasted from 14 to 29 May and was successful. It brought down the power-sharing Executive.

Pentecost begins in February 1974, moves into April, and focuses upon two weeks, from Sunday 19 May, Saturday 25 through to 2 June. Pentecost (Acts: 2) is a religious convocation marked in Christian churches on the seventh Sunday after Easter, Whit Sunday. Belfast in 1974 was a ghost town; the workers' strike turned it fleetingly into a bizarre disconnected state-let. I was sitting my final exams that May and June and recall my stepfather driving me through roadblocks from east Belfast, stopping to get petrol at which the UDA guy in a balaclava, carrying a stick, flagged us on, and wished me good luck in the exams. '[T]housands of hooded men with clubs,' as Parker has it in the play, but there was no widespread display of guns, contrary to conventional wisdom.

In the five years of the Troubles up to 1974, there were 1,000 dead, 620 of the victims in Belfast alone. Within the next year or so, 25,000 houses had been destroyed. In the first two weeks of May 1974, there had been eleven killings and thirteen bombs had gone off. Sectarian warfare was engulfing Belfast: republican paramilitaries were destroying the civic life of the city with terrifying rigour. To go out and about, people took their lives in their hands. The loyalist response was nightly assassinations, bombing pubs and sacking streets.

It is important to remember what the people of Belfast actually went through at this time. Caught in a historical trap not of their making, their fate was to play out some undisclosable finale, defined and ultimately determined by the extremes of political demands. As W.A. Maguire remarks in his study of *Belfast*:

> in the first four years of the Troubles somewhere between 30,000 and 60,000 people in the Greater Belfast area were driven to leave their homes, at that date possibly the largest enforced movement of population in Europe since the Second World War.[29]

Homes were burnt down; people were intimidated from their own houses and squatters moved in under the protection of one of the various defence committees. This is the backdrop to *Pentecost*. Precious wonder, then, that Parker referred to the play being written in a form of 'heightened realism' and certainly not 'the conventions of a broadly realistic piece' by which it has been described. Parker makes his intentions clear in the stage directions: 'Everything is real except the proportions. The rooms are narrow, but the walls climb up and disappear into the shadows above the stage.' The atmosphere of the entire play, inhabited as it is with ghosts and ghostly figures of dead and haunted men, lost children, ominous shouts, scuffles, helicopter searchlights, jegs of broken bottles on the yard wall, drumming – these all create a claustrophobic and surreal world.

Moving through the five acts are five characters: two Catholics – Lenny (to whom the house has been willed) and his estranged wife, Marian (who wants to buy the house); their two Protestant friends – an old college pal, Peter Irwin, who has returned to Belfast from Birmingham, and Ruth McAlester, the evangelical friend of Marian. The shade of the sitting tenant, Lily Mathews, custodian of Belfast history ('1900–1974. This house was her whole life,' Marian remarks) and in whose house the entire play takes place, enjoins a cast of unseen figures: Lily's own husband, Alfie, 'a good man'; Alan Ferris, the English airman and lodger, with whom Lily has had an all-too-brief affair, and a baby which she has given up, 'in the porch of a Baptist Church [to] ... moneyed people'; Ruth's demented RUC husband, who ends up in a mental asylum after repeatedly beating Ruth and turning upon himself; and the little baby of Marian and Lenny, Christopher, who lived for only five months.

The play is suffused with references to Protestant churches, Sunday school, hymns (Lily's singing of 'Rock of Ages' ironically corroborates the victory hymn of the Workers' Council); gospel (Lenny playing 'Just a Closer Walk with Thee'); mythologised Northern Protestant experience of the First World War, the shipyard, the landscape and street names of east Belfast (Lily refers to her lover buying her a dress in 'Price's Window', a famous store on the Newtownards Road).

There is also a depth-charged link, easily mislaid in hastily formulated interpretation, between the significance of the play's title and the reality-altering vision that pervades and ultimately transforms the character's lives:

> *Marian*: Have you never considered that if one of us needs treatment it might be you?
>
> *Lenny*: I never know how you do this, I start off trying to help you, and within ten minutes, I'm a villain, I'm a deviant, I'm the one in need of help, in the name of God just face reality!
>
> *Marian*: Which reality did you have in mind?
>
> *Lenny*: Your own, Marian, your own reality, you've been talking to yourself, you've been counting spoons, you've been babbling

in tongues in the middle of the night! … What are we *supposed* to think?

Marian: Don't think, Lenny. Don't think anything at all. Don't even try. It doesn't agree with you. Here's what we're doing. I'm staying here with my tongues – and you're going home with your trombone. That way we're all quits. Okay?

One of the most powerful elements in the play is the way Parker dramatically assimilates the apocalyptic, biblical vision (the babbling of tongues as the presence of the Holy Spirit) into the psychology of pain and loss which characterises the lives on stage, particularly the women's lives. Parker has also convincingly conceived women characters such as Marian and Lily, and, less centrally, Ruth. While their childlessness becomes a subdued focus in the play, the dramatic metaphor of 'the house' as home and refuge becomes both moral and mystical shelter, when 'good' means 'washed' and spotless; without blame:

Lily: Four of you's now, in on me, tramping your filth all over my good floors.

Within the house, Marian discovers Lily's diary as if it were a testament; while the christening gown of Lily's child, trimmed with lace and ribbons, merges naturally with the ceremonial white robes of Whit; and even Peter's awful bag of muesli can be seen half-seriously as a token of first-fruits. Be that as it may, the theatrical symbolism of the house is everywhere in the language of these broken characters. For 'house' read 'home-place', which means Belfast, Peter's Lilliput; whatever tensions surface, they revolve around possession, of being 'at home'.

Having fled violence in her own home, Ruth attacks Peter for losing touch with his own people:

> *Ruth*: You don't know what's been happening here. What the people have gone through. How could you? You got out.

The moral weight of 'You *got* out' doesn't stop Ruth and Peter making love, but it hangs over the play like an indictment. Leaving or staying, homesick or sick of home, taking over a place or being evicted from it, the seesawing of the arguments between Ruth and Peter, Marian and Lenny – and which also include the infamous Harold Wilson broadcast in which the British prime minister denounced the unionist reaction as 'sponging on Westminster and British democracy' – all are based inside Lily's parlour house, 'eloquent with the history of this city', as Marian describes it.

It is a history that is class-conscious too, as Marian points out to her disenchanted trombone-playing husband: 'Well away you and explain all that to your Uncle Phelim [a psychiatrist], if you can track him down in his underground bunker, it's somewhere up Fortwilliam way, isn't that right?'

The Catholic upper middle class retreated towards the upper reaches of the northern side of the city; previously such districts had been the preserve of predominantly wealthy Protestant and Jewish communities. What ensues in this exchange between Lenny and Marian shows the extent to which Lily's house earths the dramatic force of Pentecost. Marian starts to sound like Lily, and, at the age of thirty-three, she is Lily's age when Lily was most alive. Addressing Lenny, Marian says:

> *Marian*: I'm seeing this through. That's all. On my own terms. For Jesus' sake just leave me in peace, the whole shower of you,

I'm sick of your filth and mess and noise and bickering, in every last corner of the house, I've had enough … You find a refuge, you find a task for your life, and then wholesale panic breaks out, and they all come crowding in the door, her [Ruth] and you [Lenny] and that trend-worshipping narcissist [Peter].

Lenny: It's beside the point, you're in terrible danger, we've all got to get out of here. The last thing I ever intended or needed, me and you under the same roof, it was another one of his lame jokes (Gesturing skywards) okay, we move out, we go our separate ways to our respective families. I don't like to see you in the state you're in. You're just not fit to be left on your own.

(*Marian slowly turns on him*)

Marian: What are you getting at?

Lenny: I'm talking about what's going on!

Marian: Such as?

Lenny: What have we been having this entire conversation about?

Marian: You consider that I'm cracking up?

Lenny: When did I say that?

Marian: Not fit to be alone?

Lenny: In this house, that's all!

The talk is all about the place, at-home-ness: 'in every last corner of the house', 'refuge', 'door', 'roof' and so on. Throughout *Pentecost* the notion of belonging and of sustaining relationships with one another and to one place ramifies with similar terms of reference. But it is no longer 'just' the house; it is with living and being; or to use that desperate old Cold War jargon, 'co-existing': man and woman, Protestant and Catholic, the living and the dead; past and present.

The history of this possibility – of redemption, self-belief and common bonds, of sharing – is clearly established in the third act of *Pentecost*. Peter and Lenny are talking in superficial, blunt male terms about Marian:

> *Lenny*: It's the state she's in … totally obsessive, don't ask me what the story is … some weird syndrome, you know how it is with women. I'm just thankful she's finally agreed to a divorce.
>
> *Peter*: Would it still be losing the kid, maybe?
>
> *Lenny*: That? – oh, she took that in her stride … didn't she … no problem. Anyhow. It's five years now.
>
> *Peter*: Can't be.
>
> *Lenny*: Near as dammit. August '69.
>
> *Peter*: A Vintage month.

August 1969 remains the watershed in many Northern minds, particularly for those in their late teens and twenties living in the city, jockeying back and forth to London, caught up in the music of the time. It was the symbolic breakpoint, because after that date the North entered the nightmare; beforehand, it felt like an Indian summer of endless parties and club land.

Pentecost is a hymn to the self-consciousness of that lost time. Written as part of a triptych of history plays in the mid-1980s when the cycle of violence seemed unbreakable, Parker found in *Pentecost* a form for exorcising what he called the playwright's 'gift or sentence' which is 'to function as a medium, half-hidden in the darkness, subject to possession by the ghosts of other voices, often truer than his own'. What formed Parker's own voice is neatly summed up by himself in the bright and witty piece 'Me & Jim',[30] already referred to, and coincidentally, a list of priorities which neatly contextualises the themes of *Pentecost*:

> My own mind was framed by an urban neighbourhood, a working-class family struggle towards petit-bourgeois values, a recoil from home and church and country, an appetite for exile.

I may be deluding myself, but the voice of Stewart Parker that I hear has a faint American inflection and the style of the man links him immediately with my own generation. As Robert Johnstone remarked in his *Honest Ulsterman* tribute, Parker 'was only a couple of years younger than Michael Longley or Seamus Heaney, but he seemed to belong to a later generation, whose style was more optimistic and playful'. Throughout the years of the Troubles, the sanity, wit and guile of Parker's plays logged the dismay, devilment and anguish of a generation, which could not believe that what was taking place in its home place was actually happening. The belief and conviction that we were all one, irrespective of religion, if not of politics, was shattered. That sectarian violence and the lurid respect and support it received from so many, often-distant, sources had become a sickening reality that was poisoning every hope and expectation.

Pentecost plays out this tragi-comedy with a series of stories that are neither ponderous nor self-serving. In the powerful, concluding moments of the play, Parker captures the crazy contradictory energy of his characters and the cultural world they know inside out:

> *Marian*: I'm clearing most of this out. Keeping just the basics. Fixing it up. What this house needs most is air and light.

And as they tell one another stories – Marian and Lily's night of passion; Lenny recalling seeing 'a gaggle of nuns, real nuns, stripping off' and swimming, 'experiencing their sex'; before Ruth reproves him for not understanding what 'Christianity' is about:

> *Ruth*: You don't even know what day it is now, the meaning of it.
>
> *Peter*: You tell them, Ruthie child. Pentecost Sunday.
>
> *Lenny*: So what?

What follows is an extraordinary moment in Irish theatre and probably one of the most misunderstood scenes as well, which clearly caused critical unease. As the stories interweave, Ruth and Peter recite between them, 'The day our Lord's apostles were inspired by the Holy Spirit', to which Marian responds by talking about Christopher, the child she has lost. The scene runs a great risk of falling like O'Casey into pathos, but the energetic and disciplined performances of both Eileen Pollock (in the original Field Day production) and Eleanor Methven (in the Rough Magic production) maintained the religious rhetoric with a strict and passionate delivery:

> *Marian*: Personally, I want to live now. I want this house to live. We have committed sacrilege enough on life, in this place, in these times. We don't just owe it to ourselves, we owe it to our dead too … our innocent dead. They're not our masters, they're our creditors, for the life they never knew. We owe them at least

that – the fullest life for which they could ever have hoped, we carry those ghosts within us, to betray those hopes is the real sin against the Christ, and I for one cannot commit it one day longer.

This speech, and Ruth's opening of her Bible and reading aloud of the second chapter of Acts, is a metaphorical resolution, completely in keeping with the heightened realism of *Pentecost*. 'Thou hast made known to me the ways of life; thou shalt make me full of joy with thy countenance' leads into Lenny's playing 'a very slow and soulful version' of 'Just a Closer Walk with Thee' before Ruth opens the window, echoing Marian's earlier comment about what the house 'needs most is air and light'. I cannot think of a finer tribute of commemoration than this.

The ethos of *Pentecost*, taking into account its fun and laughter, and the caustic wit that sparks off between the couples, challenges certain kinds of (almost) subconscious critical categories in Ireland and Britain. While *Pentecost*, particularly through Peter, condemns the lack of political generosity within the 'so-called Protestants', the underlying picture defies easy notions of cultural stereotyping. The play takes Lily as its defining point of reference and dramatically explores the complexity, limitations and connectedness of Protestant culture within Northern Irish society. It takes that society as culture, not solely as prejudice, and cuts against the grain of received wisdom with a deeply human portrait of a stratum of a society in crisis. Parker was well aware of what he was doing, and in the Introduction to his *Three Plays for Ireland* he remarked about how his cultural inheritances had 'contrived between them to entangle me in the whole subject for drama which is comprised of multiplying dualities: two islands (the "British Isles"), two Irelands, two Ulster, two men fighting over a field'.[31]

Many writers and critics of Irish writing have problems with this reality and ignore it. Indeed, its critical invisibility until comparatively recently[32] is worth noting. For instance, in that most impressive and sweeping historical survey on literature and drama in Ireland, Declan Kiberd's *Inventing Ireland: The Literature of the Modern Nation* (1995), Stewart Parker's name does not appear once, not even in a passing reference. Yet I cannot think offhand of another playwright who, in the space of roughly a decade between the mid-1970s to the late 1980s, offered more light specifically on the various historical Irelands that inhabit the island of Ireland.

Parker was nothing if not switched-on to the here-and-now, the present, whether that be in his dramatic writing, such as the charade of *Catchpenny Twist*, the poignant insights of the television play *I'm a Dreamer, Montreal*, or in the three plays which he saw as forming one historical meditation, 'a common enterprise' as he called it, closing with *Pentecost*. As Parker said in his John Malone Memorial Lecture, 'Dramatis Personae' (June 1986):

> New forms are needed, forms of inclusiveness. The drama constantly demands that we re-invent it, that we transform it with new ways of showing, to cater adequately to the unique plight in which we find ourselves. For those of us who find ourselves writing from within a life-experience of this place, at this time, the demands could not be more formidable or more momentous.

Forms of inclusiveness? There is still a long way to go in being able to live up to Stewart Parker's comment about *Pentecost* when he remarked, 'for my own generation, finally making its own scruffy way onto the stage of history and from thence into the future tense'. *Pentecost* is about the everyday experience of political change. The play also marks the beginnings of significant cultural shifts and (ironically) the demise of political hegemony, at the very point when the Protestant working and farming classes exercised its self-confidence most forcefully in political action. Until that point in May–June 1974, Belfast was a unionist city and its cultural ethos was Protestant. It is not that any longer

Ten years after the setting of *Pentecost*, in 1985 Parker wrote 'Signposts' for *Theatre Ireland*.[33] In this important article, Parker traced the troubled history of getting his play *Spokesong* on stage and the often fraught path to his work being recognised and produced in Northern Ireland. He also noted how officialdom – cultural and political – simply did not want to know as horizons narrowed to the tried and tested. Much more significantly, Parker put his finger on the very core of the problem that remains at the centre of the social, public and emotional life of Northern Irish society. It is one of the clearest expressions of an imaginative artist of the first rank reflecting upon their own society at a critical moment in its history:

I was possessed then, as I am now, with the challenge of forging a unifying dramatic metaphor for the Northern Irish human condition. I take it as given that the tribal, sectarian malevolence in this society is the deepest, most enduring and least tractable evil in our inheritance: not the border, nor the discrimination, nor the corruption, not any of the other repellent *symptoms*. In my view, sectarian exclusiveness is the First Cause, for our purposes – however much you may care to argue about its historical origins. All the rest is predicated upon it. I see no point in writing a plea for unity between prods [Protestants] and taigs [Catholics]. What use has piety been? I can only see a point in actually embodying that unity, practising that inclusiveness, in an artistic image; creating it as an act of the imagination, postulating it before an audience. There have been political visionaries in our shared but fractured tradition who have like the grandparents in *Spokesong* briefly sustained such an image in the past – Henry Joy McCracken being one.[34]

There is much else in Parker's background and in the various different backgrounds his writing life has come out of and to which it returns. But above all else it is important to stress one fundamental point about Parker: that somewhat like John Millington Synge, shadowed by illness and pain and experiencing spasmodic tension at a time of social upheaval and historical change, he was, in his own words, 'a strong adherent of fun' as he said in his powerful John Malone lecture.[35] His aphoristic wit, his critical intelligence, the imaginative prowess, the delight and pleasure in writing well, is abundant in everything he wrote. The sheer zest for life pours through his stagecraft and his playing with language reveals an enduring curiosity in what makes things work and lives better. But it is Parker's distinctive ability to draw together both a highly tuned literary sensibility with an unerring instinct for the authentic note in popular culture which makes him a writer to treasure:

Remember how, in the 1960s, we were always being bombarded with 'new faces'? Face was a key word. Having face was having style, being utterly of the moment – with it – on display, acting David Hemmings photographing Jean Shrimpton posing on the set of Julie Christie's new film. The Mods called their pop idols 'faces,' and one of their groups responded by naming themselves the Small Faces. It all referred to the primacy of appearance, image, the media being the messages, just as in the Elizabethan comedy of humours. Today's lurid narcissists, like David Bowie and Marc Bolan, are the Jacobean fag-ends of the movement, a degeneration into sexual melodrama, vapid and joyless. But some heroes of the 1960s have matured into serene survivors, and amongst them are Rod ('The Mod') Stewart and his Faces. Maybe elegance is not quite the word for a man with the hairstyle of the Greater Crested Grebe and the Voice That Smoked A Thousand Cigarettes. Even so, in the gloss of the music, in its seemingly effortless panache, there is a considerable degree of deliberate fastidiousness, finesse ... style in fact.[36]

Whatever one thinks about his judgements of the time, what Stewart Parker had in abundance was 'style in fact'.

CHAPTER NINE

DAYS OF BURNED COUNTRYSIDE: EAVAN BOLAND & EILÉAN NÍ CHUILLEANÁIN

*I*n 'A Final Thought',[1] her fond and neatly thought-out epilogue to the sixtieth anniversary of *Icarus*, the well-known student literary magazine from Trinity College Dublin, Eavan Boland cast her mind back to her years as an undergraduate in the early 1960s, publishing her first poems:

> I wasn't active in getting out [*Icarus*], or distributing it. Other students, some of them friends of mine, did all the heavy-lifting. I was much more a prowler at its margins, eager to see the poems in it, and occasionally pleased to see my own.

Describing the magazine of the time as 'elegant', Boland considers to 'this day, however, nameless or not, I remember how that font set off poems that might have looked ragged and unofficial without it'. The sense of authorisation, of the first telling steps into a public endorsement, something every poet recalls with both excitement and trepidation, is etched in the epilogue's recollection of each physical detail of how the poems *looked* on the page, 'in the graceful slant of those particular block capitals or printed stanzas, every lyric looked as if it had landed safely'.

Following on from the impressions of the appearance of her poems in *Icarus* (in 1964), Boland reflects on her own literary self-consciousness as a young student-poet: 'I don't think I had the slightest idea … what it means to have a College magazine with its own strong, vivid and established literary tradition.' Nor the 'particular hard-to-define sense of esteem it hands out to fledgling poets and yearning talents. On the contrary, I took it for granted.' It is an important point of realisation, for as the established and much praised senior poet writing in 2010 looks back fifty years, the phrase that resonates here is surely 'took it for granted'. If Boland's development as a poet is characterised by anything as directly definitive as a 'theme', it is surely in her *not* taking anything for granted. For Boland as poet and essayist is driven by an overriding critical desire to challenge, revise, revisit and (eventually) restore much that is or was taken for granted in Irish literary terms and circles of the 1960s and 70s.

Perhaps this is what she means when, in summarising 'A Final Thought', Boland admits that:

> Maybe the fact that I am writing this at a distance means that some fraction of the value and privilege did get through to me. I was – in this I might have been in the majority of students – not at all sure what part of me would be confirmed or denied by my education. I was certainly unsure what place my hit-and-miss but nevertheless stubborn determination to be

a poet would have once I went through Front Gate. Like other students I looked for signs and guarantees that the world of knowledge would not frown on the world of imagination – however unformed the second might be.

Icarus, the student magazine, provided 'one of those signs, one of those guarantees' and 'even across so many years, I'm still grateful for that', Boland concludes. Naturally only so much can be read into an epilogue to an anthology produced for a commemorative celebratory anthology; nonetheless, there are several important underlying 'signs' in Boland's short prose piece which bear thinking about. Simply put, the 'prowler at' the 'margins' was much more at the centre of things,[2] even while recalling the general vulnerabilities of 'esteem' which were to remain central to Boland's 'stubborn determination to be a poet', a determination that brought into its ambit Boland's private and public interrogation of the role of womanhood and the suburban places of self-definition in Ireland, as well as the pressures on and of female sexuality in the tragically protracted separation of the morally dominant Catholic Church from the civic and cultural institutions of the Irish Republic. Often overlooked, however, is Boland's initiating engagement with and opening-up to the political and ideological conflict of the Northern 'Troubles', which erupted only a few years after her graduation from Trinity in 1966. She anticipated as much as participated in these difficult and, at times painful, challenges.

It is beyond the remit of the present chapter to do justice to each and every one of these important early influences on Boland's personal and poetic development. I would, however, like to connect these general introductory remarks to my own understanding of Boland's substantial contribution to what could be called 'the debates' of the 1970s and 80s as a kind of historical sketch by a younger contemporary who was greatly impressed by the focus and intensity of Eavan Boland's early collections: *The War Horse* (1975), *In Her Own Image* (1980) and *Night Feed* (1983). Most of the dedicatees of these publications are drawn from Boland's time at Trinity College[3] and the Dublin-based poets she met during the sixties. Eamon Grennan ('The Pilgrim'), Michael Longley ('Migration'), Derek Mahon ('Belfast vs. Dublin') and Brendan Kennelly ('The Flight of the Earls') feature alongside Philip Edwards,[4] David Norris[5] and her long-time friend, Mary Robinson.[6]

This sense of an identifiable literary college community is nothing new but it is clear from her later reflections, published in *Object Lessons*,[7] that Boland was very aware of the non-academic literary world and practice taking place in the local pubs and cafés, the 'inner city', which was becoming a home from home within a few paces of Trinity:

> Dublin was a coherent space then, a small circumference in which to be and become a poet. A single bus journey took you into college for the day. Twilights over Stephen's Green were breathable and lilac-coloured. Coffee beans turned and gritted off the blades in the windows of Roberts' and Bewleys. A single cup of it, moreover, cost ninepence in old money and could be spun out for hours of conversation. The last European city. The last literary smallholding. Or maybe not.[8]

After spending much of her girlhood and teenage years in Britain and the United States, she returned to Dublin as a 15-year-old and the city became her home. By the time she was an undergraduate at Trinity, she also had to find room for herself in the city's literary culture. Portraits of Patrick

Kavanagh[9] and Padraic Colum[10] paint a telling picture of the young poet's difficult attempts to connect with the city. 'On reflection,' her contemporary Derek Mahon remarked in 1993,[11] 'I now realise that she was struggling to assert herself in what she correctly perceived to be a male-dominated literary culture. Was it, for her, a necessary struggle? She had only to look at a door and it flew open.' Boland's first substantial volume, *New Territory*, appeared in 1967 when she was twenty-three. In the eight years which led into the publication of *The War Horse* (1975), the Irish poetry landscape was increasingly viewed (at least from outside) through the perspective of what would become known as 'Northern Poetry', with the 'Belfast Group' as its incubator.[12]

The second, third and fourth volumes of Longley, Mahon and Heaney were appearing[13] alongside the work of older contemporaries, including John Montague, John Hewitt, Roy McFadden, Robert Greacen and Padraic Fiacc, among others. By the time *In Her Own Image* and *Night Feed* appeared, in 1980 and 1982 respectively, the sense of a literary 'movement' in the North had gathered both critical momentum in the media and cultural definition, with the publication of Frank Ormsby's wide-selling and definitive anthology, *Poets from the North of Ireland*, the first edition of which appeared in 1979. And 'the North' as a cultural category and critical definition seemed to be underpinned in the Anglophone literary world by the controversial reception for Seamus Heaney's fourth collection, *North* (1975).[14] Heaney's inclusion and central presence in the talismanic *Penguin Book of Contemporary British Poetry* (1982), along with five[15] fellow Northern poets and the well-charted reactions to that, including Heaney's 'An Open Letter', point to the heightened 'tensions' of the 1970s and 80s. The laid-back optimism that people experienced with the late arrival of 'the sixties' in the Irish Republic, had to be quickly (and reluctantly) readjusted to the starkly local ('Northern') crises of the seventies. Its destabilising spill over into the Republic, when huge numbers of refugees evacuated from the sectarian mayhem of Belfast and other cities in the North sought emergency housing along the border, was a chastening reminder of what the future might hold.

Eavan Boland was a key artistic presence in urging publicly that certain elements of Irish national public discourse needed to be recalibrated in order to match the radically changing conditions of Irish political reality; a call for revisionism not at all common at the time. With the foundation of Field Day (1980) – a response to these political challenges and the perceived need to engage with them – and the ideological and cultural discussions at play in a journal such as *The Crane Bag* (1977–85) and a feminist imprint, Attic Press, reflected an intellectual ferment of revisionism, nationalism and feminism which suggested that the legacy and lifestyle of Patrick Kavanagh's generation, never mind W.B. Yeats and the Literary Revival, was fast breaking up. What was taking its place was the question.

Boland's role in focusing these discussions in the southern state fulfilled the role of what would be called today 'the public intellectual'. Boland wrote trenchant reviews for the *Irish Times*, presented her *Poetry Anthology* and *Poet's Choice* radio series, and made numerous television appearances on the national broadcasting network RTÉ, as well as giving many readings and moderating workshops throughout the Republic; it was by any standards an exceptional contribution.

Her characteristically robust review in the *Irish Times* of the first flush of Field Day pamphlets was deeply questioning for the time and proposed an integrating view of the island of

Ireland, rather than deferring to the partitioned and divided states it had, in many ways unwittingly, become:[16]

> A new Ulster nationalism is not my idea of what Irish poetry needs, but I would be quite willing to lay aside this prejudice if the new nationalism contained all the voices, all the fragments, all the dualities and ambiguities of reference; but it doesn't. Judging by the Field Day pamphlets here in front of me, this is green nationalism and divided culture.

While concluding her review of Seamus Heaney's poem 'An Open Letter', the second of the three pamphlets, Boland declared:

> Poetry is defined by its energies and its eloquence, not by the passport of the poet or the editor; or the name of the nationality. That way lies all the categories, the separations, the censorships, that poetry exists to dispel.

Six years later, six more years we should recall of 'The Troubles' and the dreadful daily toll of violence visited upon ordinary life in the North, Edna Longley's response to Eavan Boland's 1989 pamphlet, *A Kind of Scar: The Woman Poet in a National Tradition*,[17] chastises her for 'not questioning the nation'[18] and 'was surprised that *A Kind of Scar* … ignored the extent to which the North has destabilised the "nation". Boland holds to unitary assumptions about "a society, a nation, a literary heritage". Troubled about "the woman poet", she takes the "national tradition" for granted.'

A few years previously, in 1982, I had tried to represent the shifting of these poetic grounds in an anthology I edited, *The Younger Irish Poets*.[19] The book opened with three 'southern' poets – Paul Durcan, Eavan Boland and Richard Ryan – in an effort to exhibit what else was going on throughout the country, as well as the resurgence of poetry in and from the North. The anthology sold remarkably well and went into three reprints in 1983 and a little later in 1985 before going out of print.[20] Boland was represented in the anthology by six poems – 'Belfast vs. Dublin', 'The War Horse', 'Child of our Time', 'Conversation with an Inspector of Taxes about Poetry', 'Solitary' and 'A Ballad of Beauty and Time'. The poems, drawn from her three books to date, had their own story to tell; at least that was my intention.

I had met Eavan in the late 1970s as a raw graduate poet from Belfast living in Galway, grappling with the fall-out of the Northern violence and the accompanying political storms. There had been some exchange of views and I was greatly taken by the tension in her work between the public voiced concerns of *The War Horse* and the demeanour of family life and the contained impressionism composed in the 'suburban' poems of *Night Feed*. I had also made an intermediary connection between the poet and the artist Constance Short for an interim broadsheet publication featuring some of the poems which ultimately became *In Her Own Image*. Boland's independence and dedication was impressive, but there was a kind of fearlessness too which, in those intensely focused years, set her apart from the often sentimentalised responses or bewildered indifference in the Republic to what was going on 'up North'.

Looking back over three decades since that anthology was first published, the selection of Boland's poems seemed to reproduce a distinctive meta-narrative all its own. From the somewhat stylised opening poem of 'Belfast vs. Dublin' through the poignant and moving poems 'The War Horse' and

'Child of our Time' to the deft translation from Mayakovsky's 'Conversation …' and to the much edgier tones of 'Solitary' and the confident dramatisation of 'A Ballad …', it looked as if this introductory sample of Boland's poetry revealed a fascinating movement, a 'mini'-inner history. Between the stereotypically freighted inherited past of 'Belfast vs. Dublin' to the shocking disclosure of 'Solitary' and its scene of masturbation, within these (unstated) parameters sat centre-stage one of the finest Irish poems of the 1970s, 'The War Horse':[21]

> But we, we are safe, our unformed fear
> Of fierce commitment gone; why should we care
>
> If a rose, a hedge, a crocus are uprooted
> Like corpses, remote, crushed, mutilated?
>
> He stumbles on like a rumour of war, huge
> Threatening. Neighbours use the subterfuge
>
> Of curtains.

I think the poem's conclusion bears the rhetorical flourish in mind on this occasion with justice:

> That rose he smashed frays
> Ribboned across our hedge, recalling days
>
> Of burned countryside, illicit braid:
> A cause ruined before, a world betrayed.

In *Object Lessons*, Boland reflects, 'I wrote the poem ['The War Horse'] slowly, adding each couplet with care. I was twenty-six years of age. At first, when it was finished, I looked at it with pleasure and wonder. It encompassed a real event.'[22] However, her sense of the poem altered over time as she relates some twenty years later:

> In a time of violence it would be all too easy to write another poem, and another. To make a construct where the difficult 'I' of perception became the easier 'we' of a subtle claim. Where an unearned power would be allowed by a public engagement.[23]

But the political poem was not what Boland was after; the gesture was wrong-headed: 'I would learn that it was far more difficult to make myself the political subject of my own poems than to see the metaphoric possibilities in front of me in a suburban dusk.'[24] And of course this is precisely what *Night Feed* records in its atmospherics of surprise, at-homeness and an amazed joy while coping with the fissures of a self divided from these very stabilities which drive the fragmented lyrics of *In Her Own Image* into a form of despair. No one else writing in Ireland carried these contrary and contradictory pulses in their poems. The scrutiny that Boland entered into of what constitutes a soulscape of contemporary womanhood was relentless and, one can only assume, costly in its emotional and psychic draw.

But the wonder of these poems has never left them: 'How my flesh summers,/How my mind shadows,/Meshed in this brightness.' Such engagements were bound, eventually, to produce a reaction both within the work itself and in its reception. Risks are run in such self-consciousness too, of tracking the poetic pathways to self-construction, although it could be said that Boland was following a pattern laid down well before her by W.B. Yeats in his *Autobiographies*. But this transparent 'angle of approach' has been questioned by, among others, Caitríona O'Reilly in her review[25] of Boland's follow-up publication to *Object Lessons*, *A Journey with Two Maps: Becoming a Woman Poet*:[26]

> given that Boland has declared that her approach is self-rather than fact-based, what critic can feel comfortable about contending directly with Boland's narratives of her own poetic development and the necessarily partial version of literary history propounded through those narratives? The precise validity of this method is open to debate.

Indeed it is; but given O'Reilly's injunction that, 'One of the main problems with Boland's approach is its basic ahistoricity', it might be all the more necessary a requirement to see the poet in the contexts of *her* own time; in other words, the historicity of Boland's early achievement. It may also be the case, as Caitríona O'Reilly justly remarks, that Boland's 'habit of continually checking her pulse by submitting all threads into her narrative of personal witness becomes, by its very insistence, a distraction'.[27] In contrast, Boland's 'compelling' account of translating the German poet Elisabeth Langgässer and her 'empathetic and illuminating' reading of the German-Jewish writer Else Lasker-Schüler show Boland at her less 'self-centred best'.

However, there are the risks of what O'Reilly sees as 'false witness and intellectual fuzziness'. This is often the fate of post-war recollections, it has to be said. Indeed, Boland notes as much in the 'Introduction' to *After Every War*,[28] the anthology of her translations from nine German poets:

> During the Troubles in Ireland the political life of the island was endlessly on view – violent, oppressive, and often cruel.

> Gradually, act by murderous act, a country I had once known, once understood to have existed, disappeared. With that disappearance, a world of familiar signs – of memories and explanations – was displaced.

> What's more, as that land disappeared there was little enough to register its previous existence. The delicacy and actuality of a place in its time can quickly be overwritten.

She continues with a poignant and moving resolution that, while not intending to 'compare what happened on one island to the mid-century cataclysm', states:

> the violation of our island went so deep, was so toxic, that the private could no longer find shelter from the public. Everything was touched. Nothing was spared: A buckled shoe in a market street after a bombing. A woman looking out of window at an altered street – they were all emblems, images, perhaps even graffiti of the new reality. Overnight, so it seemed, the division between the public and private imagination ceased to be meaningful. Both were interchangeable ways of grasping and rendering a new reality. The political poem became a map of dissolving boundaries.

The achievement of Eavan Boland resides in the courage and willingness she demonstrated to say the things she said as poet and critic in a much less liberal and liberated Irish society than the one we currently live in; an advance and advantage that she and other women of her generation made possible, including fellow poet and Trinity College professor emeriti, Eiléan Ní Chuilleanáin.

In her review of Paul Muldoon's poetry collection, *One Thousand Things Worth Knowing* (2015), Eiléan Ní Chuilleanáin responds with a telling rebuttal to critics 'who often focus on Muldoon's talent for weirdness and his technical games'[29] and continues: 'It is hardly the main business of poetry to be normal, though this poetry turns out to be fit to take on the weight of normal life when called on.' In many ways, Eiléan Ní Chuilleanáin could be reflecting upon her own poetry, particularly when she discusses the 'pleasure' Muldoon's poetry gives: 'It is language itself, its multiplicity and its straining after meaning that is illuminated by his work.' For what Ní Chuilleanáin and Muldoon share is precisely this fascination with 'language itself, its multiplicity and its straining after meaning', set at times (though not *necessarily* so) within the parameters of 'normal life'.

More often than not, Ní Chuilleanáin's poetry travels in time and location out of the here and now, crossing cultural borders of language and epochs to chart an imagined terrain unspecified and transcendent. This elusiveness produces an extraordinary shadowland of suggested landscapes, hinted-at conversations, real and imagined journeys retold by a crystal-clear poetic voice; once heard, never forgotten.

Eiléan Ní Chuilleanáin was born in Cork in 1942, daughter of Professor Cormac Ó Cuilleanáin and the novelist Eilís Dillon. She was educated at University College Cork (BA in English and History 1962, MA 1964) and at Lady Margaret Hall, Oxford (1964–6) before commencing her full-time academic career at Trinity College Dublin in 1966, where she lectured in Medieval and Renaissance English for forty-five years up until her retirement as a Professor of English in 2011. Elected Fellow of the College (1993), her many and varied contributions to College life include acting as Head of the Department of English (1997–2000) and as Dean of the Faculty of Arts-Letters (2001–5). Her distinguished contribution to Medieval and Renaissance studies has occasioned a festschrift,[30] published to mark 'the breadth as well as depth' of Ní Chuilleanáin's scholarship, that scholarship 'notable for the effortless ease with which it has negotiated the often precarious balance between text and context and the clarity with which it has identified the general in the particular without compromising the historical specificity of the text'.[31]

Depth, effortless ease, clarity and precarious balance are qualities that equally characterise Eiléan Ní Chuilleanáin's eight collections of poetry. From the initial volume *Acts & Monuments* (1972) to her most recent single collection, *The Boys of Bluehill* (2015), Ní Chuilleanáin's poetry has an unmistakable poise that seems at times on a cliff edge between revelation and disappearance and loss. Her manifold imagination is drawn towards the light-filled landscapes of Italy – a central influence on her later volumes – and the intimacies of a local home, be that the recollected streets and houses of Cork or Dublin. This sense of quite literally moving from place to place, and translating one place or time into another, is a key to Ní Chuilleanáin's poetry as a whole. It begins in 'Home Town':[32]

> The bus is late getting in to my home town.
> I walk up the hill by the barracks,
> Cutting through alleyways that jump at me.
> They come bursting out of the walls
> Just a minute before I began to feel them
> Getting ready to arch and push. Here is the house.

Throughout these journeys in time and across different landscapes and languages, Ní Chuilleanáin characteristically establishes representative lives of family and friends, often women (for example, Katherine Kavanagh, the wife of the poet, Agnes Bernelle, actor and singer, and Leland Bardwell, writer) to carry the emotional significance of what is *not* being said, such as in the elegy 'At My Aunt Blánaid's Cremation':[33]

> But your face looks away now,
> And we on your behalf
> Recall how lights and voices
> And bottles and wake glasses
> Were lined up like the cousins
> In a bleached photograph.

The commemorated experience of religious life is similarly figured in poems to Saint Margaret of Cortona, the Anchoress and the Magdalenes, among several other poems which present a complicated picture of female sexuality, institutional power and how women find themselves often isolated from a living and embracing community. It is a point Aingeal Clare emphasised in her *Guardian* review of *The Boys of Bluehill*:[34]

> The collective noun for nuns is a 'murmur', which captures wonderfully the secret histories that echo through Ní Chuilleanáin's work, not to mention the ubiquity of nuns in her poems ... Among the attractions of nuns for Ní Chuilleanáin is the cloistered social space they occupy[.]

So do apparitions, litanies and a host of pilgrims bring the reader into a deeper sense of wondering otherness.

The atmospherics of Ní Chuilleanáin's individual collections merge a spiritual world with the everyday particulars of looking out a kitchen window; sensing animal life stirring in the countryside; negotiating imaginatively the seas, as in the splendid sequence of four poems 'The Sun-Fish' (glossed as

'*Basking shark, An Liamhán Greine, Cetorhinus maximus*') which opens with 'The Watcher':[35]

> The salmon-nets flung wide, their drifted floats
> Curve, ending below the watcher's downward view
> From the high promontory. A fin a fluke
> And they are there, the huge sun-fish,
> Holding still, stencilled in the shallows.

The sense of the spectacular nestles under the surface of the poem 'stencilled in the shallows' but also under the surface of so much of Ní Chuilleanáin's verse. Seamus Heaney's remark, quoted in Eiléan Ní Chuilleanáin's essential *Selected Poems* (2008), captures this magical seeing:[36]

> There is something second-sighted … about Eiléan Ní Chuilleanáin's work, by which I don't mean that she has any prophetic afflatus, more that her poems see things anew, in a rinsed and dreamstruck light. They are at once as plain as an anecdote told on the doorstep and as haunting as a soothsayer's greetings.

It is a balance explored in detail in recent publications dedicated to Ní Chuilleanáin's achievement as poet and translator, primarily from Irish, Italian and Romanian. A special issue of the *Irish University Review*,[37] edited by Anne Fogarty, is a good place to start, along with Guinn Batten's fine essay in *The Cambridge Companion to Contemporary Irish Poetry*.[38] Justin Quinn's lucid and contextualising study, *The Cambridge Introduction to Modern Irish Poetry*[39] identifies the cosmopolitan and European roots of Eiléan Ní Chuilleanáin and her contemporaries, while Patricia Boyle Haberstroh published a pioneering study in 2013.[40]

Recipient of several important honours since the *Irish Times* prize for poetry in 1966, recognition of Eiléan Ní Chuilleanáin's achievement was further enhanced when *The Sun-Fish* was awarded the distinguished Griffin International Poetry Prize in 2010 and in 2017 she was elected to the Ireland Chair of Poetry. She is a member of Aosdána, the assembly of Irish artists, and is one of the founding editors of *Cyphers* (1975), the long-established Irish literary journal which has done so much to bring younger and less established names to a wider audience, as well as critically maintaining a connection to an older generation of poets and prose writers, including Pearse Hutchinson and Dermot Healy.

Eiléan Ní Chuilleanáin's other writing includes a fascinating range of engagements with various literary and social issues. She edited the pioneering anthology *Irish Women: Image and Achievement: Women in Irish Culture from Earliest Times* (1985); *As I was Among the Captives: The Prison Diary of Joseph Campbell, 1922–23* (2001) and *The Wilde Legacy* (2003), based upon the international symposium held at Trinity College to mark the opening of the Oscar Wilde Centre in the School of English. Her work as a translator is also a central part of her writing life, with volumes co-edited and/or co-translated, including Nuala Ní Dhomhnaill, *The Water Horse* (with Medbh McGuckian, 1999), *Verbale/Minutes/Tuairisc* from the Italian of Michele Ranchetti (with Cormac Ó Cuilleanáin and Gabriel Rosenstock, 2002) and *After the Raising of Lazarus: Poems by Ileana Mǎlǎncioiu* (2005).

In one of her finest poems, 'Studying the Language',[41] a chastening reinvention of the solitude of poetry-making, as much as a depiction of the hermetic life, Ní Chuilleanáin seems to have disappeared into language itself, a remarkable ego-less act of self-belief and conviction in the power of scene and inference to set up in the reader's mind an emblematic meaning, as mysterious as the poem's setting:

> On Sundays I watch the hermits coming out of their holes
> Into the light. Their cliff is as full as a hive.
> They crowd together on warm shoulders of rock
> Where the sun has been shining, their joints crackle.
> They begin to talk after a while.
> I listen to their accents, they are not all
> From this island, not all old,
> Not even, I think, all masculine.
>
> They are so wise, they do not pretend to see me.
> They drink from the scattered pools of melted snow:
> I walk right by them and drink when they have done.
> I can see the marks of chains around their feet.
>
> I call this work, these decades and stations –
> Because, without these, I would be a stranger here.

The taut sentences, though almost ghostly, mask the poem's inner legacy to a Gaelic idiom as if in translation from a previously imagined world view of which we are afforded just a glimpse – of 'these decades and stations' belonging to another time. 'An Information', which opens Ní Chuilleanáin's *The Boys of Bluehill* (2015), is also a poem of revisitation, but on this occasion the journey back is more immediate and identifiable:[42]

> I returned to that narrow street
> where I used to stand and listen
> to the chat from the kitchen or parlour, filtered
> through rotten tiles. I thought

the rough walls seemed higher than before.
My cheek against the stone, I noted the new door
Since last I'd been there, began to count the years,

to count the questions I couldn't ask now[.]

The conversational tone, the casual flow of mid- to end-half rhymes (*parlour, higher, before, door, there, years; tiles, walls; street, chat, count*) seems almost overlooked as the poem conveys its displaced yet clarifying sense of reality. The recollection and the present coexist, to quote the poem's concluding lines, 'where' reality 'is hidden again when found'. The bounty of life 'outdoors', and *lived*, makes *The Boys of Bluehill* a collection full of nature. But the collection is probably most noted for its sense of the past being present in unexpected ways, random occurrences, and journeys taken.

Ní Chuilleanáin's poetry, without any sign of self-regarding anxiety, carries an authority all by itself and there is little sense of questions over where we are to 'place' the poet or her findings. Her poetry is at ease and confident with being in the world – of languages learned and used, of literatures read and absorbed, of cultures experienced over time and of family life with its joys (marriages, births) and anguishes (deaths of loved ones) such as one finds in *The Boys of Bluehill*. In the pitch-perfect quasi-sonnet 'Passing Palmers Green Station', which recounts a journey on the London Underground that brings back to the poet's mind an earlier journey with her mother to visit 'her younger daughter/among the dying' the transposition of the concluding two lines is both heart-breaking and releasing:[43]

The train dips
under the ground, and for the last stage

of this journey I am close to them, to the gap
that resembles the dark side of the moon in Ariosto,
where Astolfo flew on the hippogriff, and discovered
that everything lost on the earth can again be found.

Eiléan Ní Chuilleanáin's powers of suggestion can take us on a simple journey on the London Underground, yet it is one that also, naturally enough, includes the legendary winged horse with an eagle's body, the hippogriff, and the magical world of Ludovico Ariosto, the sixteenth-century Italian poet. She is one of the very few poets writing today who can make us believe that not only is this possible but that, also, more importantly as the poem implies, nothing is ever 'lost'.

CHAPTER TEN

STORY OF THE REPUBLIC

*I*n Neil Jordan's story 'A Love', which concludes his collection *Night in Tunisia*, the narrator, Neil, returns to Dublin to meet again the older woman with whom he has had an affair and who is recovering from cancer. The reunion, which takes place in 1975 against the backdrop of the state funeral of Eamon de Valera, has curious echoes of James Joyce's masterful story 'The Dead'[1] and of *A Portrait of the Artist as a Young Man*, echoes that Seán Ó Faoláin, reviewing the collection, was quick to spot:

> [Jordan] is intensely concerned with things of the mind and spirit rather than with the social world in which most of us spend most of our busy lives, but he is also tremendously responsive to all things, people, surroundings and influences that have affected him as a youth – which is precisely how one would also describe the relationship of Joyce to his world in [*A*] *Portrait of an Artist as a Young Man*.[2]

Certainly in 'A Love' there is a Joycean sense of taboos being broken, sexual as much as social and cultural. Neil looks back with Stephen Dedalus-like self-absorption to his illicit relationship as a 15-year-old boy with an older woman friend of his father's. In *A Portrait*, the symbolic disdain that Stephen shows for his father, Simon, is represented in 'A Love' with Neil's failed act of parricide, while Stephen's intensifying distancing between himself and his family and friends in *A Portrait* culminates in Jordan's story with a physical conclusion of sexual release. Neil views the state funeral, and the social and moral associations that attend it, with the cool and unflinching gaze of an outsider. It is as if Stephen Dedalus has returned by time-travel, sixty years on from his anticipated soul journey into silence, exile and cunning:

> Outside I could hear the brass band coming nearer, louder like the slowed step soldiers use in funerals. I knew I was out of step, it was all militarism now, like air in a blister, under the skin, it was swelling, the militarism I had just learned of before, in the school textbooks … And I felt the nostalgia of the emigrant, but it was as if I was still away, remembering, apart from it.[3]

The sense of estrangement is important because if one reads 'A Love' emblematically, Neil sees history itself as being buried behind him – 'We passed a TV sales shop where a crowd of people were staring at a white screen, staring at the death being celebrated behind them' – along with the actual funeral of Éamon de Valera, the once all-powerful revolutionary turned statesman: history is 'an animal that was huge, murderous, contradictory'.[4] It is nationalist Ireland or, to be more exact, the foundational orthodox nationalism of the Irish Republic, from which the young narrator is estranged, living his somewhat seedy life in London: 'And I wondered whether I'd rather be out of step here [in Dublin] or in step in London, where the passions are rational.'[5]

Jordan was in his mid-twenties when *Night in Tunisia* first appeared and, like many of his contemporaries, he had attended University College Dublin. This generation, born in the 1950s in what was still very much a recognisably traditional nationalist society: Catholic, deeply conservative, patriarchal and self-consciously Irish, was beginning to stretch its artistic muscle. De Valera was viewed as 'a joke' and belonged to a distant generation, while his successor as Taoiseach, Seán Lemass, dressed in the style and had the bearing of 'our fathers' age'.[6] The traditional sense of distance between generations had clearly reached critical mass by the late 1960s and early 1970s, and the writing registered this change in tone. The UCD 'group' had published in a college magazine, *St Stephen's*, edited by Kieran Kehoe among others, or had appeared as poets in *UCD Poetry Workshop Broadsheet*, originally established in 1968 by one-time lecturer and future diplomat, the poet Richard Ryan, and in the 'New Irish Writing' pages of the *Irish Press*, founded and edited by David Marcus, and very much the standard bearer in the 1970s for the emerging generation of Irish writers. A few of the young fiction writers would establish the short-lived but critically significant publishing breakthrough, the Irish Writers Co-Operative, out of which several would go on to develop substantial national and international reputations in literary and other artistic fields, including journalism, with the pioneering *In Dublin* edited by John Doyle (a far cry from the current version) and in *Hibernia Fortnightly Review*.

Some or all of the UCD generation of writers – poets, fiction writers and playwrights – starting to make a name for themselves in the mid- to late-1970s will be familiar to Irish readers: Harry Clifton, Gerard Fanning, Des Hogan, Neil Jordan, Richard Kearney, Conor Kelly, Patrick King, Aidan Mathews,

Frank McGuinness, Éilís Ní Dhuibhne, Dennis O'Driscoll, Fintan O'Toole, Lucille Redmond, Ronan Sheehan, Colm Tóibín and Caroline Walsh, among others. While this Dublin-based generation, who came from various parts of the country,[7] marks a significant moment in Irish literary history, rarely has its achievement been viewed collectively. One of the main reasons for this critical oversight, which may now be in the process of readjustment, is the international recognition accorded during the same period of writing from Northern Ireland. When Irish writing, contemporary Irish writing, that is, was considered in the British, European and North American scholarly and popular media, more often than not the attention was focused exclusively on what was happening *north* of the border.

The unique generation of Northern Irish poets who were associated with the Belfast 'Group' at Queen's University was in full stride.[8] There was an increasing and substantiating sense that the cultural initiative, the creative pulse of Irish writing, had swung unquestionably northwards. The notion of 'Northern Writing' assumed critical authority and, by the decade's end, Frank Ormsby's *Poets from the North of Ireland* (1979) had effectively set the seal on a powerfully articulated view of Irish literary achievement in the preceding fifteen years as being Northern. Sebastian Barry, responding to this view, was to remark a few years later in his anthology, *The Inherited Boundaries* (1986):

> the work of the younger Northern poets has received a (due) prominence, partly because of its excellence, partly because of The Troubles, and partly because of Faber and Faber; and they have come to be seen, in England and probably elsewhere, as the full story, or most of it. They are a fine part of the story of an island, but they are no part of the story of the Republic.[9]

I recall the time well, and its confusions. Northern Irish writers, who published in Belfast and/or London to overwhelmingly positive audiences, both popular and critical, were honoured and feted throughout Britain and farther afield in a manner relatively few, if indeed any, of their southern contemporaries had experienced or could even expect. Realignments were taking place at different cultural and political levels alongside the forging of new reputations. It was not simply a question of critical visibility, media interest, and publishing opportunities. There was in the Republic a sense that the 'old' issues of nationalism and identity, which had been so pivotal a point of cultural convergence during the foundation of the *southern* state, were re-emerging in the North in a particularly virulent fashion fifty years on. These issues threatened to overtake the cultural and literary landscape, and not just in Ireland. For in regard to expectations about *what* Irish writers *should* be writing about, there was a sense of 'back to the future': Ireland equals 'Troubles'. Incipient civil war, mounting sectarianism, nationalist struggle, anti-imperialism, political conflict and repression became the key phrases through which literary writing was being parsed – in other words, *via* the politics of the Northern conflict.

Certainly, when one moved outside the country, and increasingly, too, during the 1970s within Ireland, it seemed that Irish writing had become synonymous with Northern poetry.[10] Yet things were actually changing on the ground in the Republic, with the younger generation of writers whose work appeared in journals such as (the brief spell of) the *Mongrel Fox* (1976) and the *Crane Bag* (1977–85) clearly questioning – in different forms of creative writing and critical discourse – not only the legacy of Irish nationalism in the Irish state, but also taking a hard critical look at the country of their birth and the post-1960s world they had inherited.

The critical mood, which public intellectuals such as Conor Cruise O'Brien had produced,[11] was also finding a new imaginative level in the younger generation. This was a generation who clearly found it incomprehensible to imagine an Ireland cut off from the rest of the modern Anglophone world, who were hyper-literate in all aspects of popular culture, imaginatively hungry for the kind of personal experiences that a freer, more mobile, open and less domineering society could provide (even if their lifestyles remained relatively secure at home), both during their college years but also soon afterwards in the working lives they established for themselves, mostly in Dublin.

They travelled (to London, various Spanish cities and also, of course, New York), read widely, listened to the great singer-songwriters such as Bob Dylan, Neil Young, Leonard Cohen, Joni Mitchell, Van Morrison and the great jazz artists such as Charlie Parker – again, Ó Faoláin was quick to identify 'the hero of the central story' in *Night in Tunisia* as 'American jazz music'[12] – saw all the new films as they came out, particularly the auteur work of Truffaut, Godard, Scorsese and Bergman, and generally prospered in the cultural challenges that this widening cosmopolitanism brought in its wake. This liberated view keenly influenced their view of nationalism itself, and of the dominant Catholic morality of their parents' generation.

The often-heard Northern incomprehension that verged at times on hostile dismissiveness interpreted this critical independence of the young southern intelligentsia as self-absorbed and soft-centred in their 'free state' mentality. A mentality that became even more pronounced as those in the Republic saw the Troubles take root and the violence perpetuate itself; no longer a malfunctioning symptom of an unjust (if somewhat foreign and benighted relative) Northern state, but as a contagious cause, spiralling out of control, threatening to engulf the entire island and drag it backwards to its bloody beginnings.

My own sense of the opening up of southern Irish society was from the perspective of the west of Ireland, where I moved in 1974 – a 22-year-old research student who, as an undergraduate at the fledgling University of Ulster, had published and broadcast some poems – to University College Galway. I had not been part of the Belfast Queen's 'Group', either of the older 1960s generation of Seamus Heaney and Michael Longley, or of the younger emerging poets of the 1970s, also from Queen's – such as Paul Muldoon, Ciaran Carson, Medbh McGuckian and Frank Ormsby – although several would become friends in later years.

When I left Belfast, I knew almost nothing about the realities of Irish cultural life, north or south. Slowly, I started to identify with this younger generation of southern writers through contact with the UCD-educated poet Gerard Fanning, publishing like them in 'New Irish Writing' in the *Irish Press*, and subsequently in *St Stephen's* and *UCD Broadsheet*, edited by Fanning, while maintaining contact with developments when I was back home in Belfast. It struck me at the time that there was a kind of sublimated, 'partitioned' mentality abroad, or at least, wrapped within the inherited assumptions of 'Irish Literature' as a Yeatsian unity.

Indeed, there were quite strong currents of disaffection and mutual suspicion, and unquestionably a lack of understanding in the Republic, about the complex nature of what was happening in the North. There was also an unwillingness, or lack of interest, in the North to see the subtle indications of change taking place under the surface of Irish cultural life, and in particular in the minds of the (then) younger generation of writers. Changes that I had naively tried to draw attention to in a series of articles published in *Fortnight* magazine in Belfast, and elsewhere in a couple of essays,[13] as well as in the first edition of an anthology I edited, *The Younger Irish Poets* (1982), in which I had declared, rather portentously:

> the poets presented [in the anthology] are finding ways to liberate themselves, their art, and, by implication alone, their readers, from the literary conventions and literal expectations that have been handed down from the past. Present, I feel, in their best work is a need to unburden themselves of the past through whatever means, traditional or experimental, that sustains their own imaginative responsibilities.[14]

'[Unburdening] themselves of the past' seems to be, looking back, a grand rhetorical flourish, yet, when one tracks the writing that many of these young writers of the time subsequently produced, the term 'unburdening' might be appropriate after all. Jordan's second book would be called *The Past* (1982) and would deal explicitly with the fallout from the bloody Irish civil war. Colm Tóibín's innovative and challenging personal narrative *Walking Along the Border* (1987) and first novel *The South* (1990) clearly expressed a desire to explore the inheritance of the past in geo-cultural and emotional terms. The poetry of Tóibín's UCD contemporaries and friends, such as Fanning and Clifton, reveals a very assured engagement with the Irish past and landscape, secure and stable.[15]

The defining note is not one of anxiety but rather one of confidence and a steadiness, uncompromised by any need to prove their literary credentials from outside sources; the note, in other words, of being to the manner born. This self-belief expressed itself in many ways, not least in the conviction that the writing life was a feasible one in the first place, but perhaps, most significantly, in the quality of realism and the sparse and unflinching attitude of personal witness found in Tóibín's unfolding writing style. This is how I read the following representative moment from Tóibín's *Walking Along the Border*. The writer is in Strabane, County Derry, registering the impact of the ongoing terror campaign of the preceding six or seven years:

> All the pubs were Catholic pubs; most of the people were Catholic in Strabane. There had been one Protestant pub, which served the security forces, but that had been bombed. The town also had the highest unemployment rate in Western Europe: over fifty per cent of the male adults were officially unemployed. In the 1970s the IRA had blown the town to bits; most shops had suffered. I sat in one pub where the old photographs on the wall of what Strabane looked like before the IRA campaign: sedate, almost pretty, Victorian.[16]

The authority of this passage, the unequivocal sense that no sub-textual apology is in the offing, no extenuating circumstances drawn to excuse 'the IRA campaign', provoked in many reading *Walking Along the Border* a too simple response to a far deeper set of problems and the cat's cradle of political right and wrong. Tóibín's confidence, though, indeed his bravery, bearing in mind the murderous tensions and threats of the time, is a clear marker of a distinctive cultural shift then gathering momentum in the Republic. For nationalism was no longer viewed as the automatic cure, or catch-all, for political ills; rather than continually laying the responsibility elsewhere – on history, on 'England' – Tóibín's generation, witnessing the first signs of the benefits that might eventually accrue from European confederation, insisted that some other kind of social and economic freedom was needed *in* the Republic if the situation in the North, and the unpredictable economic and vulnerable social conditions of the Republic, were to be addressed and redressed.

The imaginative and intellectual realisation of these issues is part of the Tóibín generation's achievement. They also played an important part in creating a different modernising view of the country *outside* the island – be that *via* his own and his contemporaries' stellar achievements, such as (to focus on the UCD 'group' alone) Neil Jordan and Frank McGuinness, in both film and stage, the diligent imaginative light cast by the poetry of Fanning, Clifton, Mathews and O'Driscoll, in the philosophically probing revisions of Richard Kearney and in the critical dynamism of Fintan O'Toole. An achievement that was no mean feat, given the extent to which southern Irish writers of the late 1950s and 1960s, from Austin Clarke, Patrick Kavanagh, Flann O'Brien and Brendan Behan, to those utterly forgotten or neglected, had largely been side-lined or parodied out of existence.

In this regard it is equally important to acknowledge the overseeing presence of Thomas Kinsella, the mediating example of John Montague and John McGahern, the creative and critical influence of the faculty at UCD, such as Seamus Deane, Thomas Kilroy and Denis Donoghue, and the 'folk memory' of preceding UCD poet-figures such as Charles Donnelly, the young undergraduate poet who had fought and died in the Spanish Civil War.[17] The key influence of Richard Ryan also deserves mentioning since, at a time when there seemed so little contemporary *Irish* poetry around, he introduced to the younger student poets at UCD early books of Derek Mahon, and was himself published by Dolmen,[18] 'Ireland's Faber and Faber'.[19]

The UCD generation of the 1970s makes for a fascinating story in its own right. Indeed, the wider 'role' of this 'younger' generation (and of course the many other writers of the time, not associated with UCD) in forcing the developing readership in the Republic to reimagine itself, to get in step with the rest of Europe, and to think through the political, moral and cultural implications and achievements of its own history, played a decisive part in pushing forward a new agenda and creating the different kind of Ireland which was to emerge by the mid-1990s in the ground-breaking presidency of Mary Robinson, the increased recognition of women's rights and later, in the legal and political scrutiny of (particularly) the Church's authoritarianism and abuse of power in Ireland.

In his chapter on 'Enniskillen and South Fermanagh' in *Walking Along the Border*, Tóibín meets John McGahern and the encounter leads Tóibín to recall a lecture McGahern had given on 'Ireland in the early days of Independence':

> The true history of the thirties, forties and fifties in this country has yet to be written [McGahern declares]. When it does, I believe it will be shown to have been a very dark time indeed, in which an insular church colluded with an insecure State to bring about a society that was often bigoted, intolerant, cowardly, philistine and spiritually crippled.[20]

In revisiting John McGahern's spirited recollection of *his* own youth and early manhood, growing up in post-Independence Ireland, Tóibín sees through this mirroring hall of reflections *his* Ireland taking shape, the Ireland of today, and the never-ending story of literary history being made before his eyes. It is in making a story out of a different kind of upbringing, yet one that shared much with traditional Ireland, that makes one of Tóibín's contemporaries, Hugo Hamilton's fiction and memoir writing special.

Born in Dublin in 1953 of Irish–German parentage, Hamilton's home language was Irish (on his father's instructions) and German (his mother's first language). Author of eight novels, of which *Surrogate City*, *The Last Shot* and *The Love Test* are set in Germany, while the Coyne thrillers, *Head Banger* and *Sad Bastard*, take place in Dublin, Hamilton has also published a collection of short stories, *Dublin Where the Palm Trees Grow*, in which appears 'Nazi Christmas', a first outing of the idea that was to blossom into the international bestseller, *The Speckled People*.[21]

One of the most significant works by an Irish writer in some time, *The Speckled People* is a fictionalised memoir that has enjoyed the kind of popular and critical impact as *Reading in the Dark* by Seamus Deane, or Joseph O'Neill's *Blood-Dark Track* – the latter a book that Hamilton has cited as a significant example for his own work. Hamilton has also alluded to the influence of the European tradition in Elias Canetti; the first volume of whose autobiography, *The Tongue Set Free*, provides *The Speckled People* with its epigraph: 'I wait for the command to show my tongue. I know he's going to cut it off, and I get more and more scared each time.'[22] There are also tentative parallels to be drawn between the narrative voice of *The Speckled People* – a young boy's – and the mesmeric tone of Oskar in Günter Grass' masterpiece *The Tin Drum*.

The Speckled People is a story about finding a home in language; a cultural located-ness in the place where one lives, even though there are other powerful and countervailing influences pulling one away to somewhere else. What those influences may be are varied, though in Hamilton's account they are immediate and pervasive. His Irish language-speaking activist father is an authoritarian figure who represses certain elements in his own English-speaking upbringing in Cork; his own father, for instance, has served in the British navy. He has instead opted for a particular form of nationalism which passionately, on occasion brutally, believes in the strict faith in an imagined Ireland, its religion and its Gaelic roots. A sort of fundamentalism, in fact: simultaneously understandable, grim and grotesque.

The propagandist father (along with his close circle of friends) yearns for a distinctive, independent Irish culture which shuns the materialistic, heathen superficiality of mid-twentieth century Anglo-America – a worldview that threatens to contaminate his 'Ireland'. The radio threatens with its popular music; singing of any 'English' songs, even entertaining thoughts that the father considers transgressive of his priorities, leads to punishment. Yet the father is no narrow-minded or stereotypical chauvinist. His idealism, his passionate beliefs, are revealed in Hamilton's writing with an engaging understanding; a shocking realisation of the father's emblematic 'lost-ness' closes the memoir. But in deference to those who have not yet read *The Speckled People,* I think it best if I leave the particular ending of the father's story undisclosed. It is one of the finest pieces of writing in the book.

Hamilton's mother survived the Second World War in Germany. Her middle-class Catholic German family survived not only the horrendous wide-scale violence of war, but she had overcome the particularly gruesome aspect of her German life at the hands of her boss, a Nazi creep. Her story runs like a geological seam through *The Speckled People* as a counter-force to the father's often ludicrous antics. One history of past local colonised grievance (the Irish struggle for independence) is set alongside another epic history of intense, apocalyptic destructiveness (Germany and the Second World War).

The cross-cutting of these contrasting time zones and geopolitical sensibilities is the bedrock upon which the master narrative unfolds, because in the middle of 1950s and early 1960s Ireland, with Europe in recovery and Ireland in denial, the family are taken out of the real world of the here and now. Instead, they live in the intersection between their father's messianic hope for the future and their mother's keenly private yet haunting sense of her own dislodged past – a lost past.

Speaking Irish to the father, German to the mother and conceding to English only when the public occasion warrants it, the young narrator is caught between the life lived indoors in the family home in south County Dublin and the expectations, misunderstandings and changes taking place outside the front door. A door that repeatedly (and symbolically) slams, as do other doors throughout the house, in the increasingly desperate drama of the father as he struggles to preserve his little 'Ireland' by keeping out the world beyond his control. The children are seen as 'soldiers' in a language war and they pay for it. Local lads turn on the young narrator, his brother and sister and call them 'Nazis', subjecting them to a mock execution.

The young growing personalities are split between loyalty to their father and mother and bewilderment at the treatment meted out to them by their own peers. 'As a child,' Hamilton has observed, 'the overwhelming predicament for me was the linguistic predicament – but the clash of histories also preoccupied me. When you're called a Nazi on the street, you tend to become aware of history very quickly.'[23] The clash exists literally at every level of *The Speckled People*. Counting the stairs in German, English and Irish, Hamilton portrays the home as both a refuge and a prison house of language. His brother's nose is broken by the father for using English because outside 'is a different place',[24] 'not even one of their [English] words enters into the hall'.[25] It seems that at every turn the maturing children are caught in a web within which they struggle to become conscious of their individual selves, while the complexities of the past are seemingly reduced to one overarching story in which they are actors.

On a trip to their mother's family in Germany, the in-laws remark on how the German that the children speak 'was different, softer, more like the old days'.[26] After the mandatory holidays in the Connemara Gaeltacht and the concentration on speaking Irish within the home, the teenage narrator is applauded at school for the quality of his Irish – a true Gael. The father's realisation ultimately becomes a parable in itself:

> We are the new Irish. Partly from Ireland and partly from somewhere else, half-Irish and half-German. We're the speckled people, he says, the 'brack' people, which is a word that comes from the Irish language [...] It means speckled, dappled, flecked, spotted, coloured.[27]

The dog on the shoreline that barks until it is hoarse, the marvellous comic scene of the family sitting down to eat a cow's tongue, the liberating silence of swimming, when the outside world is closed off and one hears nothing, the tap-tapping of the mother at her typewriter as she records her own story for her children, and many other scenes, bring the reader back, consistently, to the core theme of this brave book.

What is it that makes us who we are? How is 'identity' generated if not from the inherited codicils of the past, of what has been honestly faced and revealed, of how much has been repressed or wisely forgotten, unceremoniously dumped or lost sight of in the wider familial, political or cultural exigencies of private and civic life? These are the issues that *The Speckled People* dramatises with such unsolemn energy. The ghostly presences in *The Speckled People* of the old Gaelic traditions, legends and the recurring image of the dead talking, of a culture vanishing, remind us of how ancestral voices play their own unpredictable role in contemporary self-projection. That, if you like, the past never dies, even though in *The Speckled People* the father's death implies the death of his vision. Yet there is also the mother's release and the almost Lawrentian-like gesture of the young narrator, who heads for home having faced down his aggressive accusatory peers, seekers of their own conforming orthodoxy:

> When I looked into the shadows under the trees it was so dark that I could see nothing there either. When you're small you know nothing. I know the sea is like a piece of silver paper in the sun. I can see people walking along the seafront with ice cream cones. I can hear the bells and I'm not afraid any more of being German or Irish, or anywhere in between. Maybe your country is only a place you make up in your own mind. Something you dream about and sing about. Maybe it's not a place on the map at all, but just a story full of people you meet and places you visit, full of books and films you've been to. I'm not afraid of being homesick and having no language to live in. I don't have to be like anyone else. I'm walking on the wall and nobody can stop me.[28]

The politics that subsists within this splendid book is a topic all to itself, as is the fine imaginative recreation of different times and places. And the remarkable sleight of hand that Hamilton achieves in *The Speckled People* (and in his other German-based novels) of convincing us that we are hearing a foreign language while reading English is a form of Friel-like trickery. *The Speckled People* is a tragi-comic work of fiction and a memoir of often heart-rending simplicity. It is also a powerful liberating challenge to the standard critical categories that operate both internally and externally when the phrase 'Irish Writing' is brought to mind. Critical expectations, that is, which can stunt a writer and narrow the scope of 'our' literature. For Hamilton reminds us that 'Irish' is no monolithic, self-evident cultural or political entity; that the emigrant, refugee and diverse ethnic, religious and cultural roots of this island are, as well, a vital and necessary part of the country's historical narrative. All too often these stories (which are at the core of *this* book) have been marginalised or self-repressed, since individuals felt either ashamed or embarrassed by their family's 'non-Irish' past. While the more visible and predominant Anglo-American social and cultural realities and the enabling values of the Gaelic traditional past (Ulster-Scots as much as Irish) come into greater critical focus, it is important that the multiculturalism of Ireland's own past (limited as it may be) is brought into view, along with the rapidly developing diversity of today.

In this sense, Hugo Hamilton's *The Speckled People*, along with the work of other writers of his generation based in Ireland and elsewhere, points out possibilities for a fresh, critically open engagement with the meanings of Irish writing. His memoir might well mark a significant step for those of us who wish to see not only Irish writing, but Irish life, interpreted in a much more radical way than the time-locked comfort zone of Anglo-centric familiarities and introverted two-way stereotypes, or in the rash of recent loosely generalised nostrums of nativist 'Celtic creativity'.

In this way, the cultural diversity of Irish society, reflected by multi-faceted imaginative voices, both today and historically, would find an adequate critical recognition and pedagogical response. Unless I am completely off-track, buried deep in *The Speckled People* is a kind of echoing parable. Listening to the story of his mother's family's experience of war and her sister Marianne's bravery in the face of Nazi totalitarianism, the young narrator reaches a clarifying point of self-awareness, a breakthrough in consciousness. While Hamilton's reconciliation with his father and what he stood for is clear from the altering, distancing images of the man, it is this conclusive resolution of his mother which strikes me as the most potent in the entire book. And a lesson for us all:

> My mother says you can only really be brave if you know you will lose. And the silent negative is not like any other silence either, because one day you will say what you're thinking out loud with your arms folded, like Marianne. You can't be afraid of saying the opposite, even if you look like a fool and everybody thinks you're in the wrong country, speaking the wrong language.[29]

CHAPTER ELEVEN

ETHNA CARBERY IN H BLOCK

On 9 March 1981, Bobby Sands, the IRA commanding officer, was twenty-seven years old and heading into what would become known worldwide as the Irish Hunger Strike. Various communications – basically smuggled letters and notes – from and to himself, his fellow prisoners in 'H Block' of the Maze Prison and the Sinn Féin leadership outside, were published in 1987 by David Beresford in his book *Ten Men Dead*.[1] It may or may not come as a surprise that the former 'apprentice coach builder' from Rathcoole, outside Belfast was, according to his own record, 'very much involved in soccer, athletics, swimming and about ten thousand other sports' but 'not really in any Gaelic football club. By the way, I used to run for Willowfield Temperance Harriers (real black [Protestant] place) in all the leading races in the north for boys.'[2] Sands then goes on to describe 'the first time' he was caught, as an 18-year-old, 'in October 1972':[3]

> I was then 18 and very naïve. Got bad time in [police] barracks and I did sign a statement which was basic (i.e. not bad). Was

convicted by a Judge Higgins late March, early April '73, to five years for possession of 4 shorts [pistols] which were stored in a place I was staying ... Also was done with two or three petty robberies which were fashionable in them days. I refused to recognize [the court] etc.

The communication explains how four years later, Sands 'was snared again' in October 1976 'outside a furniture showroom in Dunmurry in which were four ticking bombs. You'll get all the crack on that somewhere, it was pretty fierce – two or three comrades were shot, I was caught in a car with three others and a gun.' A little later he remarks, 'I've no criminal record, I'm a great admirer of your dog and Ethna Carbery' and the note concludes with 'I'm fairly fluent in Gaelige' and in brackets '(big head)'.

In the ensuing few exchanges (or 'comms' as they are referred to in *Ten Men Dead*) reference to Ethna Carbery (real name, Anna MacManus, née Johnston 1866–1902) recurs several times:[4]

I was wondering (here it comes says you) that out of the goodness of all yer hearts you couldn't get me one miserly book and try to leave it in: the *Poems of Ethna Carbery* – cissy. That's really all I want, last request as they say. Some ask for cigarettes, others for blindfolds, yer man asks for Poetry.

With the visible deterioration of his health as the hunger strike took its toll in its relentlessly eviscerating way, Sands, according to Beresford, issued a valedictory note, quoting John Keegan Casey's famous Fenian poem: 'The day will dawn when all the people of Ireland will have the desire for freedom to show. It is then we'll see the rising of the moon.'[5] In barely two months' time, on Tuesday 5 May 1981, one of the Belfast leaders of the Irish Republican Army would be dead, his name broadcast around the globe. In the immediate period leading up to his death, other communications refer to Sands's passion for poetry:[6]

> Bob was pleased you managed to get that book for him … But you know that while we were in H6, during 1979, he sent up to me and told me after reading some of Ethna [Carbery's] work that he had written her a wee note and 'you never know', sez Bob, she might just do something on the block. Did he take a red face when I informed him she'd been dead for more than 10 years [she actually died in 1902]. He has been extra careful what he says to me since then. Anyway, will you do your best to get some more stuff like that for him. He's mad about poetry as you know …

Who can tell whether Sands really did not know the biographical details of 'Ethna Carbery', the nationalist poet born in 1866 in Ballymena but who grew up off the Antrim Road in 'Glencoe', near Cave Hill, an upper middle-class suburb of north Belfast, sharing the Scottish names of the well-heeled neighbourhoods, Fortwilliam, Duncairn and Glandore; and, as the crow flies, no distance from blue-collar Rathcoole, where the young Sands had lived and socialised and, by most accounts, from where he and his family had been intimidated as Catholics and fled to what became known as West Belfast. Carbery would have a significant impact on Irish nationalist circles at the turn of the last century, and also well beyond that community through the extensive popular readership for her romantic and patriotic poems, reminiscent of Jessie Pope. While Sands's response in Beresford's account might be fictionalised, is it possible that one of the poems the IRA militant had in mind was 'In Glengormley', a suburban village on the upper north side of the city. This is an example of Carbery's seven stanzas:[7]

> Though prison walls should sunder
>> Our hands, that clasped, *a stór,*
> Though lonely years should weigh me down,
>> And you come back no more;
> Though our bright dreams be unfulfilled,
>> No shameful tears shall rise
> To mar the memory of the smile
>> That lit my love's brave eyes.

> I'd rather see you cold, love,
>> Beneath the shamrock screen,
> Than know you traitor to your God,
>> And traitor to the Green!
> I'd rather see your dear, fair head
>> On spear-point of the foe,
> Than know when Ireland needed you
>> You never struck a blow!

One can probably also imagine how the romantic nationalism – which Seamus MacManus identified with his wife 'Ethna Carbery' and the widespread response, shortly after their marriage, to her early death in 1902 (at thirty-six) – might have distracted Sands from his own situation in prison and the grotesque downward spiral of the Troubles into ever uglier sectarian warfare. By the time of Sands's death in 1981, another decade and a half had to run its shatteringly divisive local course before some kind of political resolution could be found to stem the flow of seemingly self-perpetuating violence.

'While she lived,' writes MacManus in 'A Memoir of Ethna Carbery', originally written for the posthumous collection *Poems* (1918), 'she was a quiet strong nationalising force. Since she passed she has been every year an infinitely stronger nationalising force, she has won hosts of young Irishmen and women to nationality.'[8] Across the generations, 'nationality' would prove to be the ties that bound, as much as her kind of poetry, in the view of Carbery's husband:

> Even where it was unnoticed by the workers, the spirit of Ethna Carbery has been a leaven working in the mass of every National movement in the present [twentieth] century.

> A few of our leading literary men have assumed that literature is literature only when it serves no useful end – above all, no national end. If literature aided Ireland it then ceased to be literature – and ceased to be noteworthy. Ethna Carbery's work was designedly national – and only incidentally aimed at being literature. Yet I have little doubt that her work will, in Ireland, be prized as rare literature when the writings of the orthodox ones will be neglected.

(MacManus's understandably partisan views were not vindicated with the passage of time.) It is a curious yet telling point to reflect upon that in the years after 'the North began', and the partition of the country forced many families born and bred there to make some hard decisions and relocate elsewhere.

As Máire Mhac an tSaoi (Máire Cruise O'Brien), the Irish language poet born in 1922, daughter of the leading Belfast republican, southern parliamentarian and sometime poet, Seán MacEntee, alludes to in her poem 'Fód an imris: Ard-Oifig an Phoist 1986' ('Trouble Spot: General Post Office 1986'): 'I hear now the Northern accent/Of the elder man I loved with hard devotion.' Where this all leads to is at the core of her powerfully resounding conclusion to the poem in this version, translated by Louis de Paor:[9]

In later years, we tried again;
you learned to be charitable,
but we still had to tread carefully;
your intelligence and sense of justice
never practised deception;
I am the same age as the state[10]
and neither turned out as you wished ...
in this place, father, you are the unknown
youth who went missing –
neglect and awkwardness hide the key from my mind –
but I hear now the Northern accent
of the elder man I loved with hard devotion:
do you remember the rebuke you delivered
before it became fashionable?
You spoke thus:

I see no cause for rejoicing
that Irishmen once again
are killing other Irishmen
on the streets of Belfast!

The Belfast-educated Protestant friend of Carbery's, the fiercely anti-partitionist Alice Milligan (1866–1953), whose much longer life was in large measure defined by her early involvement with the national movement in Dublin from the late 1880s and 1890s to post-1916. However, in her poem 'Up the Falls: At the Rising o' the Moon', she recalls the harsh conditions of the Falls Road by sampling (as would Bobby Sands) the reserves of Irish nationalism's dramatic metaphors, this time, however, with a critically self-alert sense of distance, of how others may view *her*.[11]

> What can it be – I thought, as I came in view –
> they are staring at, and one is pointing to.
> What wakes them from their state of stupor now?
> A dog fight, or a vicious back-street row?
> But all seems quiet,
> and from the distance comes no stir of riot,
> yet from their wall-propped places
> they all turned eager, forward-looking faces,
> perhaps at some companion who has sunk
> to the ground, dead drunk.
> Whatever it is he points to, and they see,
> would scarcely edify me,
> in this rapt, exalted poet's mood.
> I'd better cross the street for fear they should
> spit as I pass, or curse, and I should hear them[.]

Of the Northern literary voices of this earlier generation of political activists born in the 1860s, 70s and 80s, whose lives were in many ways framed by their journeys south, undoubtedly the best-known outside of scholarly and political circles is Joseph Campbell (1879–1944).[12] His songs were as popular as Tom Moore's in the drawing-room soirées, church hall stages and public broadcasting programmes of Northern Ireland and farther afield. Eileán Ní Chuilleanáin points out in her introduction to *'As I was among the Captives': Joseph Campbell's Prison Diary, 1922–1923*:[13] his 'nationalism, like that of many of his colleagues was lofty, poetic, with a cult of heroism and a faith in the destiny of the Gael which has been seen as proto-fascist, but was often combined with a respect for democracy and a dislike for dictators'.

Campbell's literary influence is, however, largely uncharted, as is generally the case with the heterodox nature of Northern nationalism and its contradictory, complicated relationship to both states in Ireland and to the British state. It should not pass us by that the educational and class origins of a Milligan, Carbery and Campbell (and Mac an tSaoi's) is in stark contrast to that of Bobby Sands and the mainly working-class republican movement for which his death, along with nine others, would have such a transformational effect upon the political fortunes of Sinn Féin and recruitment into the IRA in the years following 1981.

Joseph Campbell's traces are apparent at every turn in *By the Black Stream*,[14] the first book-length collection by Padriac Fiacc (b. 1924), a poet heavily identified with the poetry of the Troubles. Like so many others before him, including Campbell, Fiacc's IRA father had emigrated to the United States in the wake of the failed revolution of the 1920s; a failure that dogged their emigrant lives in New York and led eventually to Fiacc's return to Belfast in the 1940s; indeed, to a temporary family life in Glengormley.[15] While Campbell's poems sometimes give off the whiff of supremacist rhetoric, such as in 'The Planter'[16] – 'The grey past is dead/for you, as Beauty is. Your head/ is but a block, your filmed eye/blind to the vision and the mystery/of Man's progression thro' the Northern Land/Since the first Niall threw the Bloody Hand' – the characteristically *imagistic* Campbell is much more convincing as a poet. In 'The Ploughman', Joseph Campbell's poetic can be heard as clear as a bell – a tone, landscape and nuance that masks his upper middle-class east Belfast Catholic upbringing, as surely as the

Irish Volunteer Leader Eoin MacNeill's nephew, Brian Moore (1921–99) slid back the shutters from that world in his novels such as *The Lonely Passion of Judith Hearne*, *The Emperor of Ice Cream* and *Lies of Silence*.[17] (Like many before and since them, both Campbell and Moore, as members of the solid Catholic middle class, attended St Malachy's School, close by where Moore had grown up in north Belfast.) The moral, artistic, political and cultural lives of the Catholic nationalist community *in* the North,[18] its wider migrations and fate in the fledgling new Irish Free State (but also in Britain, North America and farther afield) is a fascinating history of adaptation and adoption as much as restlessness and disaffection. While that story has yet to be comprehensively told, it is interesting to see how elements of it play through the writing of writers from a Northern Catholic background, such as in the somewhat strained religio-mythologising of Campbell's 'The Ploughman', particularly in its concluding quatrain:[19]

> The ploughman ploughs the fallow –
> Smoking lines
> Of sunset earth
> Against a clump of pines.
>
> A flock of rooks and seagulls
> Wheel and cry
> About him, making music
> In the sky.
>
> Wings black and silver
> In a sky of grey,
> Like shadows folding
> Between night and day.

Thro' the pine-branches
Lights a dying gleam:
The swingle creaks,
The ploughman turns his team.

Not for himself he ploughs
The hill land tho';
He offers sacrifice
For me and you,

Of earth, that in its time
Will break to bread,
The sacramental veil
Of Godlihead.

In contrast, Brian Moore's Belfast novels explore the inner workings of Northern nationalism's middle-class roots and self-expression and its alignment with Catholicism after the 1920s. The various exchanges between anti-hero narrator Gavin Burke, his sister Kathy and their father in *The Emperor of Ice Cream*, set during the Belfast Blitz of 1941, illustrate generational tension. Fired-up by a growing frustration with what Gavin perceives to be the introversion of his family and class, cutting themselves off from the wider world and more immediately, bemoaning their separation from the nationality (and neutrality) of the Irish Free State, the following exchange between Kathy and Mr Burke captures the growing disenchantment with the Northern status quo:[20]

> 'I've said it before and I'll say it again: when it comes to grinding down minorities, the German jackboot isn't half as hard as the heel of John Bull. All this guff about Hitler being a menace to

civilization is sheer English hypocrisy. The things we've seen *them* do.'

'Oh, Daddy, let's not have the Troubles for breakfast. You're beginning to sound like Aunt Liz.'

To which Gavin reflects, '… a Jewish name discovered in an account of a financial transaction, a Franco victory over the godless Reds, a hint of British perfidy in international affairs, an Irish triumph on the sports field, an evidence of Protestant bigotry, a discovery of Ulster governmental corruption: these were his [father's] reading goals.' Gavin comes to the conclusion that his father was 'one of the most prejudiced, emotional, and unreasonable people … It was more than a year since he had decided there was no longer any point in arguing with [him]. Silence and silent rebellion were the only defence against his father's pious prate about Catholicism, his father's fascist leanings in politics, his father's literary pronunciamentos. His father's opinions were laughable. Or, perhaps, enough to make one weep.'[21]

In a sense, part of the novel's inner Joycean history reflects upon Moore's own family history and the cultural impact upon the Catholic middle-class *in the North* of the partitioning of what they had considered to be *their* country as well. As a result of the Belfast Blitz and the destruction of their own home, the Burke family relocate to in-laws in Dublin, but not before Gavin casts a final barb the father's way:[22]

'Another bomb', his father said. 'Somewhere over by the docks, I think. The shipyards must be a shambles. Ah well. I've said it before and I'll say it again. The German jackboot is a far crueller burden than the heel of old John Bull.'

To which the son retorts in disbelief, 'When did you say that? ... You never said anything of the sort.'

While Gavin remains in the partially destroyed city as an Air Raid Precaution warden, his father reappears towards the finale of the novel, and some form of reconciliation is achieved. Gavin's struggle to succeed in his Schools Leaving Certificate in the nearby Catholic grammar school had been a bone of contention between father and son; a marker of Northern Catholic ambition and social recognition.

The fictionalised school, based on St Malachy's on the Antrim Road, returns in Moore's later novel of the Northern Troubles, *Lies of Silence* (1990). The novel draws upon an experience Moore and his wife, Jean, had while staying in the Wellington Park Hotel, near Queen's University, where Moore was being awarded an honorary doctorate. They were 'rooted out of their bed in the middle of the night because of a bomb alert and found themselves in the street standing next to a group of elderly French tourists'.[23] Moore's biographer Patricia Craig extrapolates from this frightening experience the following:

> What if it had been a bomb, Brian thought, and these innocent French tourists had lost their lives without having the slightest understanding of the cause of the atrocity? From that point on, the idea began to grow on him of ordinary people caught up in a terrorist transaction ... the predicament of an apolitical protagonist coerced into participating in an outrage.

In the novel, Moore imagines a family being held captive during an IRA operation – a proxy-bomb which the lead character, Michael Dillon, is to deliver in his car. His wife, Moira, is taken hostage and turns on their IRA jailers in a dangerous rage: 'I don't know how we let you get this far' and then answers her own fallible and rhetorical question with a provocative grasp on how things would turn out, in real time:[24]

> 'If there was a vote tomorrow among the Catholics in Northern Ireland you wouldn't get five per cent of it. You're just a bunch of crooks, IRA or UDA, Protestants or Catholics, you're all in the same business. Racketeers, the bunch of you. There isn't a building site in this city or a pub that you or the UDA don't hold up for protection money. Protection money! Military operation, my foot! You've made this place into a bloody shambles and if it was handed over to your crowd tomorrow, lock, stock and barrel, you wouldn't have the first notion of what to do with it.'

To which she is told to 'shut your mouth', but Moira is not for stopping and, in a further rush of invective, addresses the 'faceless eyes in the woollen mask', her 'unblinking' captor:[25]

> 'The only thing you're doing is making people hate each other worse than ever. Maybe that's what you want, isn't it? Because if the Catholics here stopped hating the Prods, where would the IRA be? And the worst of it is, I'm wasting my breath talking to you because you're too stupid to know the harm you've done.'

Somewhat later, looking across at a neighbour, Mr Harbinson, going for a walk with his dog in the middle-class surroundings of north Belfast, Dillon:

> felt anger rise within him, anger at the lies which made this, his and Mr. Harbinson's birthplace, sick with a terminal illness of bigotry and injustice, lies told over the years to poor Protestant working people about the Catholics, lies told to poor Catholic working people about the Protestants, lies from parliaments and

pulpits, lies at rallies and funeral orations, and, above all, the lies
of silence from those in Westminster who did not want to face
the injustices of Ulster's status quo. Angry, he stared across the
room at the most dangerous victims of these lies, his youthful,
ignorant, murderous captors. What are they planning to do today,
what new atrocity will they work at to keep us mired in hate?[26]

Ferrying the lethal proxy-bomb in his own car, Dillon is
followed by the 'terrorists who could radio in an order to kill
his [hostage] wife' and 'in ironic procession, he would pass the
house where he had been born, the boarding school in which
he had been a pupil, and the university where he had written
poetry, edited a student magazine, and dreamed of another
life'.[27] The reference to the school is apt: 'the long tree-lined
avenue and, at its end, the red brick face of the Catholic school
where for eleven years he had been a boarder, a school where
teaching was carried on by bullying and corporal punishment
and learning by rote, a school run by priests whose narrow
sectarian views perfectly propagated the divisive bitterness.'[28]
The journey takes Dillon through a mental landscape as much
as a real one, past the Clifton Street[29] headquarters of the
Orange Order, and 'driving along the edge of those Protestant
and Catholic ghettos which were the true and lasting legacy
of this British Province founded on inequality and sectarian
hate'.[30] Against this portrait of a significant section of Northern
Irish society that had suffered most in the post-1920s conditions
of social deprivation, discrimination and political exclusion,
Moore's novel reveals another side to the story.

For on the Antrim Road, where much of *Lies of Silence* takes
place – an at one-time mixed area of working- and middle-
class Catholic and Protestant families – ordinary life goes on
undisturbed:[31]

People were out, strolling, shopping, bringing small children to the park, as though they were residents of a city thousands of miles away from bombs and guns. For most of them, these IRA events were what they saw on television, items on a daily disaster list of airline crashes, hostage-crises in the Middle East, guerrilla wars, hijackings. Even now, walking on the Antrim Road, none of them would ever think that masked men with guns and bombs might have been in their midst[.]

If *The Emperor of Ice Cream* explored the end of innocence for war-torn Belfast in the 1940s, *Lies of Silence* takes a stern account of the legacy of post-partition in Belfast. After all was said and done, what had the fifty years of nationalist struggle actually achieved or produced *in the North*? And how, even as late as the 1980s and 90s, the sectarian divisions in religious and political identity were not being reduced; far from it. They were instead shockingly reproducing mirror images of virulent terrorism in both republican and loyalist groups of paramilitaries with no discernible end in sight. The question is underlined by Moira's father, outraged at what has happened to his daughter but equally alarmed at the notion that she intends to pursue her captors further. He recalls the 1930s and 40s, 'back then the IRA was finished'. 'Sure, we had the same Troubles in those days, a Catholic would never get a job if there was a Protestant up for it.'[32] By the early 1970s the IRA had been resurrected and, as the tragic conclusion to *Lies of Silence* suggests, had become, within a matter of a decade, a much more deadly force.

Laurence McKeown, IRA volunteer and one of the survivors of the 1981 hunger strikes, was part of that new generation. As he remarked in an extensive two-page interview published in the *Irish Times* in 2016, the same school which plays such a central role in these two novels of Brian Moore, was to play a key part in his own real-life drama:[33]

> Laurence was a bright student with ambitions to be an architect. He went to St Malachy's College, a prestigious Catholic grammar school in north Belfast, but disliked it and quit to return to local education. 'It was very regimented,' he says, 'I left before they threw me out.'

McKeown's testimony is interesting because the pathway to violence seems to replicate a recurring pattern of the time, irrespective of class or home place, city or county. According to Gerry Moriarty, McKeown's interlocutor, 'McKeown describes his parents, Margaret and George, as Catholics who generally kept their heads down', like very many ordinary Catholics (and, it should be noted, Protestants) of the time:

> McKeown's desire to join the IRA wasn't the result of extensive political analysis. That would come later. 'I suppose it was a very simplistic thing of "Brits out" ... It was not about where you went to church on Sunday; it was about who had the power to carry a rifle and wear a uniform and stop me whenever they wanted to do it, which they did.'

As McKeown recalls his time in prison, 'a lot of our political naivety was stripped away'. Sands enters the picture: 'You felt he was one of the lads. He was a good singer, full of energy, always singing and talking and thinking. A bundle of ideas, good-humoured.' Admitting the early days were 'like some form of madness ... that was my choice', McKeown's view of the violence is worth quoting in full:

There was never a point where I thought we were wrong morally, because we did not think too much about it morally. State armies don't think like that, for that matter. We were going against the state, our church, our teachers. Republicanism was not very popular at the time … We were probably the most irreverent group of republicans. There is no mystical 'wrap the green flag around me' when you are living in sh*te.

The '"long-game" … violence and the campaign had nearly become a way of life'. As with fellow volunteers who had joined the Provisional IRA as teenagers in the 1970s, 'McKeown didn't reflect on the morality of a campaign for a united Ireland in which the IRA killed about 1,800 people' but what he did learn, according to Moriarty's interview, was that 'someone getting killed on the British army or RUC side is the same as someone on the IRA side or the loyalist side'.

Everyone has their story. We can tell ours, certainly, and we should tell ours, but there are going to be other stories. And for the RUC man his story was 'picking up bodies in plastic bags because of what [the IRA] were doing'. That's his truth.

Although what impact the death of the overwhelmingly innocent ordinary citizens (not the combatants, in other words) during the terrorist campaigns had on those conducting the violence remains abstract and averted from the actuality of individual personal actions:

McKeown knows that thousands of people were affected by the Troubles and the violence. But he says that he has no regrets about giving much of his life to republicanism and the IRA …

'We did what we felt we needed to do at the time. I am totally content with that.'

It is generally agreed that the 1981 hunger strike transformed the landscape for republican nationalism in the North, the main beneficiaries being Sinn Féin. At the time, Sands's self-reflections on the main reason behind the hunger strike and the physical conditions he was in make for disturbing reading. 'I will never bow to them or allow them to criminalise me,' he insists, before remarking how 'startling' it is to find himself being 'prepared to die first rather than succumb to their oppressive torture and I know that I am not on my own, that many of my comrades hold the same'. What follows is a kind of reverie that elides into political self-justification for the nationalist military campaign without any reference to the means used and the actual disastrous impact it had on ordinary Northerners:[34]

> My friends who had stood beside me one day and were dead the next. Boys and girls like myself, born and raised in the nationalist ghettos of Belfast to be murdered by foreign soldiers and lackey sectarian thugs. How many have been murdered at their hands throughout the occupied Six Counties. Too many! One boy or girl was one too many! How many more lives would be lost before the British had decided they had murdered enough and were forced to get out of Ireland forever? Inside and outside of gaol it was all the same – oppression bearing down upon you from every direction. Every street corner displaying an armed British soldier, every street having endured its share of suffering and grief at their hands.

As *Lost Lives* starkly reveals, the total *civilian* deaths of 2,074 during the Troubles far outweighs combatants, both in the number of paramilitary deaths (562) and army/police deaths (1,012).[35] In this grim numerology of the Northern conflict, the various republican groupings, of which the IRA was by far the most dominant paramilitary force, were responsible for more than 2,000 deaths, many in the most gruesome bombings, executions and shootings. The strange disjuncture between the realities of this military campaign, led by activists such as Bobby Sands, and his self-reflections, engrained with the sectarian realities of Belfast 'ghetto' life (and those bigoted unionist state functionaries), is transmogrified into the perverse world of the H Block. It is apparent at every turn of *Writings from Prison*:[36]

> '*Tiocfaidh ar la!*' I screamed out the door. One of the boys down the wing began to sing. A Nation Once Again resounded and echoed from behind every door and everyone joined in to break that ungodly silence, lifting our spirits and bolstering our shaken morale. The stench from the reeking urine streamed in through the door, flooding my eyes with tears and catching the back of my throat. The orderlies attempted a rendering of The Sash [*sic*], but were drowned out with an explosion of noise as the now empty pos rattled and battered the scarred doors in defiance and anger.
>
> '*Tiocfaidh ar la!* All right!' I said, 'and the sooner the better.'

It is also something of a shock, bearing in mind the condition of the men in the H Blocks, to read Sands's own poetry of this time – collected in *Writings from Prison* – as the fabling nationalist language of Ethna Carbery is so palpable an influence. In 'A Place to Rest', for example, the present IRA campaign merges into the populist and chaste Celticism of mainstream nineteenth-century nationalism with its 'gentle folk' and the romanticised landscape of 'whin bush' and Yeatsian 'linnets sing':[37]

> There's rain on the wind, the tears of spirits
> The clink of key on iron is near,
> A shuttling train passes by on rail,
> There's more than God for man to hear.
>
> Towards where the evening crow would fly, my thoughts lie,
> And like ships in the night they blindly sail,
> Blown by a thought – that breaks the heart –
> Of forty women in Armagh jail.
>
> Oh! And I wish I were with the gentle folk,
> Around a heartened fire where the fairies dance unseen,
> Away from the black devils of H-Block hell,
> Who torture my heart and haunt my dream.
>
> I would gladly rest where the whin bush grow,
> Beneath the rocks where the linnets sing.
> In Carnmoney Graveyard 'neath its hill,
> Fearing not what the day may bring!

It is hard indeed to reconcile this old-fashioned language of 'a heartened fire' where 'the fairies dance unseen' with the life and times of any switched-on, bright city boy of the late 1970s. Even more so for Bobby Sands, as a leader of the IRA, the other lexicon remained unavoidable: 'the black devils of H-Block hell'; for 'black' read 'Protestant'. Sands was obviously conscious of the wider world and how the image of the victim was central to the portrayal of the H Block campaign. In 'And so Life in the Living Hell Goes On', he identifies his plight directly with the Holocaust:[38]

> And I think of those long lines of naked, ragged Jews in the midst of a jungle of grey gruesome barbed wire and I can hear their feet, the almost silent, shuffling naked feet of wretchedness and inhumanity and the whispering, whimpering, weeping, shrieking, screaming sounds of torture and death and I hear them all right. They're screeching at me from all sides and the wolves of Dachau are no different from the wolves of this hell, and dearest Jesus, is this not hell?

The grotesque parallel between the millions who perished at the hands of Nazi Germany in the gas chambers of the Second World War and the (appalling) situation of paramilitary fighters on voluntary hunger-strike over political conditions in Long Kesh, might be connected to the young man's physical and mental being. There is certainly a descending sense of losing control:[39]

> I wonder do people really know and understand, for there is no relief or ease. And I keep seeing those lines of Jews and no one is listening to them 'cept I [*sic*], for I understand. And I am shaking as the door of my tomb flies open and the mass of black uniformed, howling wolves attack me, and I know this is the price of resistance, the price of freedom, and the Jews scream in my mind and are drawn by the screams and suffering of the naked political prisoners that surround me and their screams are dying to whispers.

An imaginary exchange with another inmate which Sands recounts in 'The Privileged Effort', while 'noting the sound of

the Dublin train passing by on the not-so-far-away railway',
points to the class aspect of their struggle against 'the whole
privileged side of the fence ... to oppress, to keep us down and
make sure that their wee slice of the British cake is secure' and
continues:[40]

'I wonder who's getting beaten up in Castlereagh [Detention
Centre] now?' says he as an afterthought.

'Well, it's no one from the Antrim or Malone roads,' says I.

'... and the not-so-funny thing about it is that just like the
peelers, civil servants, councillors, MPs or whoever, they'll never
be out of a job, 'cause to maintain their privileged positions, their
better and well paid jobs, their better housing and comfortable
lives and all the rest, they keep us down, keep us bottled up
in our ghettos, without work and in bad housing, in concrete
jungles like Divis and Unity Flats, deprive us, rob us, oppress us,
for they have a lot to lose but our misery and chains.'

It is a mixed-up conversation that sparks with resentment and
a baffling logic – 'when any of us attempt to change it we end
up here in the H Block, and in Milltown Cemetery'[41] – before
concluding wryly, '"Ah, well, on to the socialist Republic,"
says I. "The onward march of a risen nation," says the effort,
God help him, limping up and down the cell.'[42] Another
contradictory element that could well have complicated Sands's
interest in Ethna Carbery is the fact that she was indeed a
resident of the Antrim Road, and as the daughter of a very
successful businessman had spent many years in the splendid
privileged environment of the family villa, Glencoe, under the
famous Cave Hill.

The poetics of insurrectionary violence that are inscribed in modern Irish literary history, from mid-nineteenth century Fenianism through the various re-enactments of militant and/ or mainstream nationalism sweeping through so much of the popular ballad and broadsheet traditions and songs, have been collected in the excellent anthology *The Indignant Muse*,[43] edited by Terry Moylan. This material has its own important place in the cultural resources and political understanding of the country, but its relationship with the actual role such material played in augmenting a predisposition to violence in post-1920s Ireland – from the days of the Irish Civil War to the terrible decades leading into the Good Friday Agreement of 1998 – is a subject all to itself. It may well be the case that when in his poem 'The Flight Path' Seamus Heaney reimagines a conversation with an IRA activist – it is one of the very few times 'bad language' crept into his verse[44] – he had effectively drawn a moral and aesthetic line that remains contested to this day:

'When, for fuck's sake, are you going to write
Something for us?' 'If I do write something,
Whatever it is, I'll be writing for myself.'
And that was that. Or words to that effect.

CHAPTER TWELVE

FROM *DUSTY BLUEBELLS* TO *PARALLAX*

Some time ago I recall watching television presenter Mark Carruthers's weekly programme, *The View*, on BBC Northern Ireland. He was trying his best to interview four middle-aged Northern politicians. It was a depressing sight, no matter how one looked at it. Two unionist politicians bickering between themselves faced two nationalist politicians who had a cut at each other, but made little eye contact. The interviewer was physically and metaphorically in the middle, doing his best to find out the truth of the matter. The medium didn't matter; the message was that each of the four voices were addressing their own sectional interests. And it does not matter what the specific topic of 'debate' was that night, to be honest. The optics said it all: four professional politicians in suits, rattling against one another, those characteristically accusatory forefingers wagging away self-importantly amid accusation and counter-accusation.

All of these men had probably lived through and in ways suffered the years of 'The Troubles'. Their heated discussion contained mini-histories linked to that past; at times in their narration, technically quoting from various political and quasi-judicial reports that the ordinary citizen has long since either forgotten or care about. The moral zone of their arguments were based around different community perceptions about the rights and wrongs of how the relatively small society of Northern Ireland slipped into such a downward spiral of violence over what was, to quote from Patrick Kavanagh's elusive sonnet, 'Epic',[1] a local row.

However, in the greater global context of previous historical conflict – the Holocaust, the Second World War, the ethnic and racial wars of Africa, the civil wars of Spain or Chile, the brutal de-colonialising struggles in Algeria – the present and future outlook for Northern Ireland is, comparatively speaking, positive and affirmative, certainly in terms of the past twenty or thirty years. When it comes to sorting out the nature of our past, the failure of the politics to make a real paradigm shift, it is clear that other ways have to be found through which the different realities of Northern Irish life and its history are conveyed to as wide a section of the population as possible.

The digital revolution is making this feasible in a way unimaginable when I was a young student in Coleraine during the early 1970s, at what was then known as the New University of Ulster. And there is added value to the freeing-up that comes with the digitised past because so much space is virtually available, literally digital memory, to allow for as complete a picture as is possible to be made available. For the internet is roomy and technically non-sectarian! Part of this process means that people can make up their own minds based upon a more complex understanding of the conflicting and competing versions of 'our' own past. If the language of conventional political dialogue is becoming ever more bankrupt, and if the political imagination needed to redress the pain and suffering many people feel in Northern society has seized-up, then this inertia can *only* be overcome by new ways of thinking, new ways of presenting truth, new ways of conveying the complications of the past. Intellectual inertia, a lack of vision, along with the endless recycling and repeating of stereotypes and prejudices, no matter how good the political spin, is in no one's interests; but certainly not in the long-term interests of this society *as a whole*.

It seems that this is a cultural problem and that it has a generational aspect. To rehearse the experiences of the past has become a dividing line between the younger generation of men and women who wish to *live* in Northern Ireland and, in some manner of means, to prosper, and an older generation – those, say, entering their late 40s and 50s, who carry in some part or other, emotional, moral and possibly physical burdens from the past. I see this as a metaphorical dividing line which that television discussion seemed to dramatise: the widening gap.

It is difficult, if not simply wrong, to prescribe any 'role' for the literary imagination in times such as these – post-crisis, post widespread violence, but pre-closure, pre-reconciliation. During the darkest years of the Troubles there was an ongoing debate about whether or not poetry (or fiction, or drama; art in general) should in some way 'engage' or be 'relevant' to the political and human tragedy that was such a daily part of Northern life. I certainly do not want to resurrect that debate, which produced much heat but, after all these years, shed very little light.

The burden of the past sits awkwardly alongside the need for growth and development in Northern Irish society. In the mediation of these different, almost contradictory claims, the question being asked is about what place or function should the creative imagination fulfil: does it promote (a tricky word, too) 'cultural awareness'? No sooner does one use a word like 'creative' in this context than doubts surface, certainly in my mind, about how the word itself has become part of a discourse that connects less with the quality and challenge of the imagination, and much more with 'creative arts', creative 'factors' – the alignment of creativity with cultural tourism and the like.

I am thinking of something quite different, something much more complex and much more physical: about how writing and the history of writing from the North of Ireland can itself be viewed as a template, or, if you prefer, an example of best professional practice from which others in leadership roles – in the political and educational spheres – can learn something tangible. Learn something not only about the making of literature, how art and poetry, for instance, have been so closely interconnected in the Northern tradition; or song. But also, on a wider frame, to show how the imagination, in releasing hidden energies, creates in itself a neutral zone within which deeper truths about society can be communicated, along with much else. And crucially without the intention of denial or seeking to 'do down' one another; to create a more exciting vision of Northern Ireland than the often hectoring tone of its official default culture of blame or the interminable hassle over flags and emblems which mocks the very traditions they are meant to venerate.

The differing critical perspectives on how 'this place' is to be known, described and/or defined – the Six Counties, the North, Northern Ireland, Ulster, the North of Ireland, the Province, and so on – used to bother people much more than it does today. The notion of 'Northern Poetry' and 'Northern

Poets' has been tracked at some length by several leading critics and proponents since the publication, almost forty years ago, of Frank Ormsby's era-defining anthology, *Poets from the North of Ireland* [2] in 1979. The history of poetry from Northern Ireland has, in the main, been dated from the mid-1960s, with much less public and indeed scholarly attention being given to earlier generations, such as (shall we call them?) the Hewitt Generation of the 1930s and 40s.[3] Many of these writers – Robert Greacen, Roy McFadden, George Buchanan, George Reavey, Charles Donnelly – lived fascinating lives, sometimes based in Northern Ireland, sometimes elsewhere – in London, or Coventry, New York or Dublin. All of them inhabited a rich and diverse literary world.

They travelled; they set up art galleries, poetry presses and magazines. They carried with them the distinctive accents of this place, inflected with the nuances and expectations, assumptions and experiences of their lives elsewhere. Their poems and journalism, their professional 'careers' and political interests make a great story out of the literary mainstreams of mid-twentieth century cosmopolitan culture, perhaps too rigidly interpreted in the past as outsiders in a region looking on, or in John Hewitt's memorable phrase, 'forever shuffling, cap in hand, to the Ministries in Whitehall, begging for alms' – 'an expression', Hewitt viewed, which is 'partly an expression of the ruling clique's inferiority complex'.[4] As Hewitt's *A North Light: Twenty-five years in a Municipal Art Gallery* clearly shows, he was a much-travelled, well-read, enthusiastic art lover with an independent spirit and sense of dissent that brings some surprise in its wake. Here, for instance, he recounts, as a 22-year-old, a trip to Paris in 1929. After listing the various paintings and sculptures he has seen and noted his (at times 'arch') responses, he continues, perhaps surprisingly:[5]

[Jacob] Epstein's flying Assyrian Memorial to Oscar Wilde, I sought for in Père Lachaise, but for the sake of the man whose *De Profundis* was my prose model just then.

It is interesting to point out that also in Paris in the same year – 1929 – Samuel Beckett would meet the Northern Irish poet and editor George Reavey and mark the beginnings of a relationship that would include the establishing of Europa Press. Reavey's pioneering collaboration with such leading figures in the modernist movement based in the city – from Picasso to Beckett – and his work with The British Council, in the Soviet Union during the Second World War, his life in London, New York and elsewhere since leaving Cambridge behind, tells its own fascinating if little-known story.[6]

In his introduction to George Reavey's *Faust's Metamorphoses* (1932), 'Foreword to a Sunken Continent', the editor and publisher Samuel Putnam made the following astute assessment of Reavey's significance:[7]

> There is, conceivably, such a thing as electing, and even eclecting, one's racial tradition. I know of no better example of this than George Reavey and [his] poetry ... I do not believe that any poet could be more European, more difficult for the average American to understand, or better worth an effort at trans-Atlantic comprehension. We who have no tradition, and who are endeavouring so painfully hard to discover or to create one, have here an opportunity to see what it means to assemble a new heaven, and a new earth, of one's own.

The brash individualism aside, Putnam's view is unerringly reminiscent of a comment made some thirty years later by Allen Tate and Robert Penn Warren, when, in introducing their edition of Denis Devlin's poetry to an American audience, they stated:[8]

> [T]here are almost no traces of Yeats's 'romantic Ireland' of the Celtic Twilight. Devlin was one of the pioneers of the international poetic English, which now [1963] prevails on both sides of the Atlantic.

Looking back, 'prevails' might well have been a somewhat exaggerated claim, certainly if one is looking back from an Irish perspective. Because it seems that, a little like Denis Devlin, the fate of George Reavey's poetry has been to merge into the shadows of critical attention, as public and academic focus remains firmly focused on those writers who are palpably part of *one* national tradition or another, and not, as Putnam suggests, of many. I suspect that is what he means when he refers to Reavey as being 'European' in a similar way that Penn Warren and Tate refer to Devlin as not being identifiable with the dominant Yeatsian legacy of poetry or as a precursor of the 'Northern' poetry revival.

Reavey is, from various kinds of critical viewpoints, a conundrum. Where does one *place* him? He does not fit in to the customary 'national' bases of poetic identification, a little like, for instance, the problematic way that David Gascoyne 'fits' into the English poetic tradition. Reavey's accomplishment as a poet therefore is more difficult to assess because, as we all know, achievement is at least in part measured by and through common critical and cultural grounds of acceptable understanding. So what happens if we turn to consider a poet with different priorities in mind, such as the 'transatlantic comprehension' to which Putnam alludes, or, more pressingly, in the context of a poet such as Reavey who is so 'European'?

As James Mays remarked of another poet who has encountered similar issues of critical category, Brian Coffey, 'to dismiss a writer's claim to be considered on his own terms in favour of assigning him a role in a predetermined scheme'[9] is effectively to isolate him or her, and that has been Reavey's fate, certainly on this side of the Atlantic.

The question is, of course, what it means when we use a phrase such as 'European' or 'transatlantic', in terms of a poet's standing, and his or her worth as a poet. Derek Mahon once memorably expressed it many years ago when the issue of the nationality of Louis MacNeice raised its head, 'Is he an Irish poet? An Anglo-Irish poet?'[10] should clear the room as promptly as asking how 'European' a poet is, or should be. But there is an unease or uncertainty still abroad, when critics who are much more at ease dealing with Anglophone literary cultures address those poets who, as with Reavey, are (or were) obviously indebted to non-English cultures – such as, in Reavey's case, Russian and French. Yet Reavey poses a fascinatingly contemporary perspective. What is the role of national traditions in a globalised world? What does 'hybridity' mean in relation to a poet such as Reavey, with his multicultural and multilingual background?

From a more localised point of view, what does Reavey say to us in Ireland today, about our understanding of the European-ness of our country, and the history of difference within the island – a history which spans several generations of ethnic, refugee and émigré stock, assimilated in cities, such as Belfast since the turn of the last century, and elsewhere in Ireland going back to the late eighteenth century. Reavey is in this sense an utterly modern man in so many ways; a harbinger of twenty-first-century Ireland, bringing a significant and substantial artistic and critical presence that predates the somewhat faddish and self-regarding concerns with Europe of more recent times – concerns, to be frank, generally economic in the main, rather than anything else. For Reavey, like his friend Samuel Beckett, identified with continental literary and artistic developments. This was not as a way of rejecting or becoming self-consciously distant from their Irish roots (in fact the reverse might be argued in Beckett's case), but of expressing that experience, such as it was, in a different way.

Beckett, like Reavey, translated for a living, and was deeply indebted to French, German, Italian and Mexican writing, both modern and classical. Like Beckett, Reavey was clearly aware of the social, political and historical sea changes that were taking place on the European mainland during the thirties and forties, before, that is, he left for America. We should not overlook his work in this regard as an anthologist and critic in, for instance, *Soviet Literature To-Day* (1946).[11] George Reavey's situation mirrors that of much better-known writers of his time such as W.H. Auden and Christopher Isherwood. And more potently, his life and writing has much in common with the great wave of émigré artists who arrived in New York during the war and post-war years, several of who would become his friends. When I think of Reavey at this time, though, I go back to the testimony of his college friend and contemporary Kathleen Raine.[12]

> He did not have the English undergraduate immaturity but stood apart – he also did not look like an English undergraduate or behave like one, or fit into the Experiment picture ... His appearance was very unEnglish and unCambridge – Paris and New York suited him much better.

Reavey's sense of himself – as poet, editor, translator and publisher – is indelibly linked to his vision of writing (in English) as a creative interchange and collaboration between various non-English cultures (literary and visual), which were all connected through the overarching cultural (or if you prefer, underlying) assumptions of Europe and of being European. Reavey also had, through his own childhood experiences of revolution and social violence, in the Soviet Union and in Northern Ireland, an instinctive understanding and insight into the realities of political struggle and the human cost of historical change. As Edna Longley remarks[13] about fellow Northern poet Louis MacNeice, his [MacNeice's] politics began 'in childhood because Irish politics begin with the family and not at voting age. Hence the deeper sedimentation of [MacNeice's] political awareness than was usual among English writers during the 1930s'.

In this, too, a parallel with Louis MacNeice is apt again in Edna Longley's comment that MacNeice 'was not only amused but, like Orwell, frightened by the surrender of intellectuals to totalitarian habits of mind, to strategic imperatives'.[14] A 'surrender' which Reavey stoically resisted as he came under increasing pressure in America during the Cold War to declare against the Soviet Union. The same deep-seated understanding of politics and the imaginative life permeate Reavey's self-awareness as an artist. We should be seeing in George Reavey – this highly sophisticated, polyglot Northern Irish-Russian-Polish poet and editor – a sociable, troubled man, sometimes overshadowed by family difficulties but also a survivor of revolutions and wars, the loss of friends, and the ordinary worries of getting by as a literary figure, displaced by time and place, indeed as a figure of displacement itself. We should see him as the embodiment of mid-twentieth-century realities, over which he tried to live and maintain a poet's life. I think his was a heroic accomplishment in itself, way beyond the often indulgent and fashionable terms of exile with which Irish writers today are often eagerly greeted. As Reavey commented in a note to his sequence of poems, *Nostradam*,[15] 'some connection between my emotive life and the world of historical experience' is not too far below the surface of his poetry, yet both the life and work remain largely hidden from the contemporary record.

I am responding here to the characteristic openness to experience of Hewitt's generation of Northern Irish writers, in stark contrast to the jaded historical caricatures of both themselves and their Northern literary culture as 'dour' and introverted. Think of the young radical intellectual poet Charles Donnelly,[16] originally from Tyrone, living his short life mostly in Dublin, then London before he was killed in Spain during the civil war in 1937; or the troubled emigrant world of Padraic Fiacc,[17] born in 1924, divided as much between Belfast and New York as between gender roles and cultural identities.

One begins to see the extent and scale of difference that lies behind the extensive and internationally recognised generation which would emerge in the North in the 1960s. So it occurs to me that one of the first obligations of a digital revolution in reassessing the history of poetry from 'Ulster' might well begin with this earlier generation who, through their own lives and writings, recast the possible meanings of Northern Irish society. And there are of course many others, some well-known, others almost entirely forgotten. As Frank Ormsby remarked back in 1979:[18]

[George] Buchanan and [Louis] MacNeice were sons of clergymen and their scepticism and vitality of response to the world are partly at least reactions against this background. The same may be said of the poetry of W. R. Rodgers, who was himself a Presbyterian minister for eleven years.

Buchanan, who had a significant career as a journalist with the London *Times*, was of Scottish Planter descent. Hewitt explored the religious, linguistic, civic and cultural roots of this Planter culture in Northern Ireland. Clearly these local inheritances sit alongside the cosmopolitan in a productive line of critical exchange and artistic dialogue; not as a matter of one *or* the other.

And there are critical absences as well. Where are the women poets? Going back further in time they are there – from the late nineteenth century – Alice Milligan, Rosa Mulholland, Amanda Ros, Moira O'Neill, Ethna Carbery – and the fascinating feature of how they identified with popular and populist nationalist traditions. However, in his 'Preface' to *Poets from the North of Ireland*, Ormsby acknowledged the absence of more contemporary names:[19]

> Of the Northern women poets born since 1900 – Barbara Hunter, Freda Laughton, Meta Mayne Read and Joan Newmann, for example – few have published in book form.

By the time the new edition of *Poets from the North of Ireland* was published in 1990, only one woman's name had been added – that of Medbh McGuckian, who would in effect open up the canon to a new generation of woman poets from Northern Ireland and indeed the rest of the country. The intersection of a more complete understanding of Irish poetry and poetry written by women has been valuably explored in the editorial and critical work of Lucy Collins, particularly in her ground-breaking (if under-recognised) anthology, *Poetry by Women in Ireland 1870–1970, a critical anthology.*[20] There has also been a growing understanding of further poetic territories which inhabited the geographical and cultural space of Northern

Ireland, as Ormsby notes: 'a body of work in Irish by poets from Northern Ireland, much of it as yet untranslated'.[21] In the quarter of a century *since* 1990, the nature of Ulster-Scots and its linguistic and cultural role would also become increasingly more acknowledged. Taking stock of all these factors is going to be quite some job.

Yet to my way of thinking this intellectual challenge represents a wonderful opportunity. For it is important to read all these 'local' influences, mini-histories and experiences and to do so alongside all the other ambitions and contexts that crucially flowed in and out of what had been – even in the difficult period of the thirties, the dark days of the 1940s, the economic crises of the fifties – a hybrid culture. It was just that no one was 'letting on'.

The dominant public culture, divided along sectarian lines and fraught with official deference to opposing ideologies, power structures and class hierarchies, led many such as Robert Greacen, and several of the more significant visual artists of the time, to simply move on. The critical mass which gathered around Belfast by the mid-1960s saw an extraordinary achievement recognised worldwide, with poets such as Seamus Heaney, Michael Longley and Derek Mahon. And we should not take for granted the significance of that achievement. Along with the younger 'group' of poets of my generation – Ciaran Carson, Medbh McGuckian, Paul Muldoon, Frank Ormsby, Tom Paulin – have now been joined by a further group of whom Leontia Flynn, Sinead Morrissey,[22] Jean Bleakney, Nick Laird and Gearóid Mac Lochlainn come to mind. Nothing comes from nothing.

It is the past that lies behind this powerful development and it is infinitely possible now to trace and recreate via digital form, not as a static archival text of history, done and dusted, but of the multicultural dynamic experiences, lifestyles and achievements of so many talented people from Northern Ireland. 'Here' is not frozen in time – though at times it feels like it, and sounds like it. Perhaps too much time is spent identifying Ulster with a place, or versions of this place, and not enough time de-territorialising the culture and asking other questions about attitudes, how we think and see each other, rather than seeking to find or maintain a monolithic, albeit divided, truth. There has been and there needs to be wider recognition of the flux and change in fortunes that characterises Northern Ireland as much as those features – often but not exclusively, the more negative – which remain the same. The educational division which underwrites the sectarian schism of this society is the most obvious.

In a sense, literature has been the weathervane, or changing metaphor, at the forefront, of altering images. While it is rooted 'here' it is important to recognise that this place, as its northern-ness, is variable; created out of many varieties of cultural expression: not, in other words, to state the obvious – one thing against which all others are viewed in some way or other alien, foreign, 'theirs', not 'ours'. The energy and diversity of the digital world is a perfect fit to overcome this monochromatic view of ourselves.

The multifariousness of knowledge and experience in each of the poets I have mentioned – from John Hewitt through to Sinead Morrissey, from Irish-Gaelic to Ulster Scots, from the cultural influences of English, American and European art and literature that plays through the poetry of Louis MacNeice, or Michael Longley, or Derek Mahon; from the particularly popular, indeed, populist roots of Northern culture to the, at times, spiky tensions *within* Irish literary culture (now mostly a thing of the past) – these forces and themes, as John Wilson

Foster's pioneering study of forty years ago called it,[23] can be honestly and practically made visible through new and exciting digital approaches.

There is an interesting admission that catches some of these reverberations in Hewitt's *A North Light*. In 1955, Hewitt returned to Dublin for a viewing of what was the latest Jack B. Yeats exhibition. Hewitt had been less than enamoured with some of Yeats's paintings but, as he says himself, 'making my report in the *Belfast Telegraph*, I set out my recantation with some relief'[24] and continues:

> The overwhelming effect is of richness of imagination, of human heartedness, of marvellous colour, and the masterly manipulation of a highly personal style. With my sceptical northern nature, it has taken me a long time to come to terms with the Yeats enchantment: now I have to admit that the man is a magician.

How fascinating it would be to reproduce some of this work – the original *Telegraph* column, the paintings of Jack Yeats to which it refers, some of the journal entries and the timeline of 1955 – to create a great visual entry into the history of Ireland of the fifties, north and south, while Hewitt's 'sceptical northern nature' is worth a study all to itself.

Framed within the visual art world of Europe and Britain and Ireland that he knew so well, Hewitt could move from the 'enchantment' with Jack Yeats to the ballads of the *Rhyming Weavers* and much else. Hewitt may well be, as the editors of his *Selected Poems*, Michael Longley and Frank Ormsby, remarked,[25] the forerunner, 'the prophetic predecessor of the so-called Ulster Renaissance' (which he was), but in the Hewitt Generation we see the strains and stresses of what Seamus Heaney described as 'those accurate, painful quests towards self-knowledge'.[26] It is from that point that we can best trace historical pathways to our own cultural situation today in the twenty-first century. From the disappeared street skipping songs of the past – 'In and out the dusty bluebells/Who will be my master?/Tippy-tappy tippy-tappy/On my shoulder/You will be my master' – to the self-confident orchestration of the prize-winning *Parallax*[27] by Sinead Morrissey, the first ever poet laureate of the city of Belfast. Think of what can be done to bring all this art-work to a wider audience.

It makes Northern Irish society a much greater and better place than the one bickering politicians seem to prefer. In this sense, and probably with a naïve but enduring belief, I see poetry as an alternative universe, a virtual reality, all to itself, open to all, with the click of a mouse. The application of digital skills to this complex, busy and exhilarating history, can act as a democratic and demographic remapping of how Northern society, as well as the rest of an interested world, will come to be known in the future. This is what 'parallax' means in theory: 'The effect whereby the position or direction of an object appears to differ when viewed from different positions, e.g. through the viewfinder and the lens of a camera.'[28] And this is what it all means in practice, in Sinead Morrissey's fine poem, 'Baltimore'[29] the final lines of which reads:

in the white space
between radio stations when no voice
comes at all and the crackling static
might be swallowing whole a child's
small call for help; even in silence itself,
its material loops and folds enveloping
a ghost cry, one I've made up, but heard,
that has me climbing the stairs, pausing

in the hall, listening, listening hard,
to – at most – rhythmical breathing
but more often than not to nothing, the air
of the landing thick with something missed,
dust motes, the overhang of blankets, a ship
on the Lough through the window, infant sleep.

CHAPTER THIRTEEN

Bashō, the River Moy and the Superser

*D*uring the early 1970s I used to spend a lot of time on the CIÉ coach between Galway and Ballina as my girlfriend was from the town. Occasionally I travelled by train from Athlone via the mysteriously named Manulla Junction. Ballina intrigued me. Especially the wonderful River Moy, but also the stories that attached themselves to various arts and parts nearby, including the stone-clad boat, the *Crete Boom*, the naming of Boher-na-Sup, and the story about Ardnaree, also known as Abyssinia, because it was the last place in the town for electrification.

Over the many years of spending summers and winters, springtime and autumn, it perplexed me that, so far as I knew, little had been written out of this terrain. Now it is different but back in time there seems to have been an absence, a little like the sense of absence that emigration brings in its wake. Often those who left towns in the west of Ireland like Ballina took a little of the imaginative light with them. I could certainly name several women as proof of this, including Ballina-born poet and artist Dorothy Molloy. Tragically, Molloy died in 2004, aged sixty-two, only a matter of days after *Hare Soup*, her first collection, was published by Faber and Faber. Two further collections were published posthumously – *Gethsemane Day* and *Long-Distance Swimmer*.[1]

Dorothy Molloy and her poems do not represent a loss. Instead her poems are a powerful statement of self-worth and self-confidence in being in the world at large. There is no self-pity here but rather a concentration on making out of what came her way – her roots, experience, education, travel, love, marriage, friendships, her tragic illness, her religious inheritances, her reading, her love of painting – of making out of all this fabric of living, a vivid and challenging form of literary art.

Her poems are full of the energy that comes from not sitting back but of embracing the world in all its multifarious reality; what Louis MacNeice famously heralded as 'crazier and more of it than we think/Incorrigibly plural'.[2] I hear this loud and clear in Dorothy Molloy's poems, such as in 'The dream-world of my pillow',[3] which opens:

> Things float in the dream-world of my pillow
> As I wrap my arms round the billowing sheets
> Of wind. But the storm escapes me,
> Rocking the ship of the house, the dry waves
> Bashing against the bricks and the glass
> Eyes and smoky funnels of home.

And in a later poem, 'Waiting for Julio',[4] the sense of history breaks down into an almost fable-like story of war and its varied victims such as Julio and Maria. The fine delivery of the domestic details of village life and custom simply shudder to a shocking halt as the traumatised soldier returns home:

He pushed past 'My Jewel', the baby, the bed,
and curled up in the cot;

plugging his ears with his whimpering hands,
he made soft sucking sounds

with his lips.

The physicality of Molloy's poetry – no matter where the
individual poem is located – takes on a substantially different
value when she confronts her own illness and the arduous,
protracted treatment which brings with it the consciousness of
likely death. These are poems of exceptional bravery but also
of wit and intelligence, notwithstanding the dire reality which
underpins them:[5]

Will I ever be ready, I muse today,
As I lie in my cozy bed,
Will I always be needing a little more time
To get things straight in my head?

The strength of Dorothy Molloy's poetry in each of the three
volumes is not so much the unfolding of a developing and
confident vision but rather that the poems seem part of an
imagined universe within which her life, loves and death form
part of an extraordinary intense experience that draws upon
other literatures and visual arts as well. It were as if Molloy
becomes what she is looking at, irrespective of historical period
or language culture. She has taken these experiences to be her
life and made them over into poems of unquestionable emotional
force and liveliness without ponderous self-regard. It is quite
some achievement, as in 'Ice Maiden',[6] quoted here in full:

I walk in my night-dress and slippers
along winter beaches in Finland.
My earrings of polished tin
flash at the Northern Lights.
I shovel up the sea.

But the cold is quick. Quick
as I crack open the rock
of the ocean with my axe,
it freezes behind me.
My task is endless.

The pity is that she did not live to see the flourishing of poetry from her native west of Ireland or indeed the significant critical response to her own poems, which will hopefully find a greater resonance in the years ahead, especially with the collected edition of Molloy's poetry due from Faber and Faber in 2019, a younger generation will come to her work and uncover its manifold stresses, strains and transcendences.

By the late 1990s, a host of women poets had emerged from the west of Ireland who would go on to produce volumes of verse with leading Irish and British publishers: Moya Cannon, Mary O'Malley, Eva Bourke and Rita Ann Higgins among them. Their success and the public attention they received was timely, given the relative lack throughout earlier decades of publishing opportunities available to Irish poets who were women.

Of those poets writing in English who started to publish collections more recently, Michelle O'Sullivan impresses me greatly as a poet of real artistic endeavor and concentration.

Her poems are tuned to the visible world but carry within marvellous, haunting refrains of absences, the working of lives intently observed or, at times, overheard, which make the sudden presences of her poetry so distinctive. It is the

Mayo landscape – rivers, mountainsides, livelihoods – that shapes her first collection of poetry, *The Blue End of Stars*,[7] published when the poet was forty, into such a stunning debut. But, as with the ending of 'Halcyon' where the poet imagines meeting the enchanting seventeenth-century Japanese poet Bashō, there is nothing taken for granted in this most distinctive of voices:[8]

> He gives me a pair of hummingbirds
> one for my pocket, one for my hand.

Indeed there is a Bashō-like clarity to much of O'Sullivan's writing. In *The Narrow Road to the Deep North*,[9] depicting Bashō's poetic journey through his beloved Japanese islands, the poet pauses upon a scene and meditates upon its fascinating strangeness:

> I noticed a number of tiny cottages scattered among pine trees and pale blue threads of smoke rising from them. I wondered what kind of people were living in those isolated houses, and was approaching one of them with a strange sense of yearning, when, as if to interrupt me, the moon rose glittering over the darkened sea, completing the full transformation to a night-time scene.

The sense of isolation, wonderment and the fixing of a particular landscape in the mind are all strong characteristics of O'Sullivan's poetry. Born in 1972, she was educated at the University of Hertfordshire, worked in England as a primary teacher, lived in Greece and the US, and now lives in Co. Mayo with her two children and works as a tutor. *The Blue End of Stars* was awarded the dlr Strong/Shine Award for 2013 while her second volume, *The Flower and the Frozen Sea*,[10] was a Poetry Society Recommendation. She is a recipient of a Patrick and

Katherine Kavanagh Fellowship and a Tyrone Guthrie Bursary from Mayo County Council.

Bartra, Nephin, the River Moy and its seasonal life, the estuary and the dramatic western Mayo coast which unfolds towards the Atlantic – all these feature in intense lyrics, fastened upon an emblematic frame of nature within which a domestic and interpersonal world is etched, shadowy, undeclared and tense. A parallel with the stark clarities of Ingmar Bergman's cinema comes to mind.

As Lucy Collins has remarked, O'Sullivan's 'intense scrutiny of the world yields insight into mutability and loss – the boundaries between entities become unstable, such as when earth meets water or smoke drifts in air. Liminal states demand concentration from the reader; these are the moments when unexpected realisations emerge.'[11] The feeling the poetry encapsulates is physical and unexplicated like 'salmon dreaming/ deep beneath the Moy',[12] and there is throughout both volumes of O'Sullivan's poetry to date what looks like a refusal to self-interpret (such a feature of much contemporary verse) or to foreclose meaning with resounding lines of conclusion. The poem, if I read O'Sullivan correctly, has its very own key and does not require any secondary or ancillary source of explanation, as in the marvellous mid-section of the title poem, 'The Flower and the Frozen Sea':[13]

The birds are beginning to return, small arrivals
that will grow to modest; wind-voices warming
from ribcage to throat.

Across the meadow a bullock dissolves
in half-hearted mist. He's like a relic, his static
silhouette merges into the river's unmade bed.

If there is a hint of McGuckian in some of the 'merges' which take place between domestic life and the natural world of the countryside, it might be more coincidental than anything deliberate. As the poet points out in a note in *The Flower and the Frozen Sea*, there is a form of Japanese art, 'Kintsukuroi', which repairs 'broken pottery using resin mixed with precious metals such as gold, platinum or silver'.[14] This art of rehabilitation, the careful, intimate restorative act of making art, is both a telling source for the visual pre-eminence of much of O'Sullivan's poetry[15] but also, possibly, a useful insight into her own way of making poems:

> The field I take you to with the oaks –
> rain-brushed and clean as a high room in a green
> house; and the sea unrolling its blue lawn.

> Not sun-gold yet, a feldspar glow catches
> the water's cuffed edge, a fold of linen
> touched with frost dust.

To quote from Lucy Collins again, the 'aphoristic quality' of O'Sullivan's poetry 'heightens its philosophical aspect, but reminds us too that meaning may lie beyond even the power of language'.[16] If O'Sullivan is in all but name a Japanese poet, the landscapes of her home have a beneficent yet chastening presence throughout both of these impressive volumes.

It is revealing to compare O'Sullivan's intensely landscape-focused poems with her contemporary, Leontia Flynn, born two years after O'Sullivan in 1974 in County Down, Northern Ireland. Flynn's four collections,[17] beginning with her first, the highly regarded *These Days*, published in 2004 when the poet was thirty, have been met with significant critical acclaim and prestigious public recognition.

A Gregory Award winner, Flynn has also been awarded the Forward Prize for Best First Collection, the Rooney Prize for Irish Literature, the Lawrence O'Shaughnessy Award for Poetry, the AWB Vincent American Ireland Fund Literary Award, a Major Individual Artist Award from the Arts Council of Northern Ireland, and the Irish Times Poetry Now Award, as well as featuring on the shortlists of the Whitbread Poetry Prize and the T. S. Eliot Prize. Named as one of the twenty 'Next Generation' poets by the Poetry Society, her third collection, *Profit and Loss*, was their choice for autumn 2011. Currently she is a lecturer in the School of English and the Seamus Heaney Centre at Queen's University Belfast.

If Dorothy Molloy's poems have a powerfully dramatic expressionistic dimension and Michelle O'Sullivan produces exceptionally emblematic and tacit images which seem to compel the reader inwards, Leontia Flynn's work lives out in the world of strange, exhilarating encounters – be that emotionally or imaginatively. The sheer volume of lived life that her four collections reproduce is – at times – breathtaking. From the life of her family – her poems to both her mother and the ever-whistling and singing father who succumbs to Alzheimer's[18] – are blissful, poignant and wise – to the erratic student pads (and some dodgy detritus), techie treats and teases, to the mixed joys of background music (The Bangles, Neil Young, Karen Carpenter, Patsy Cline, Foster and Allen), videoing what's going on in the many cities her poems visit while returning, allusively, to a Belfast both actual and imagined, troubled and post-Troubles, Flynn never lets up: 'Imagine being *thirty* …?'[19] Health 'issues' – such as Samuel Beckett's, George Orwell's, Elizabeth Bishop's, Marcel Proust's[20] – like language itself and how 'we' say things and mean what we say, are all decoded in her energetically *spoken* poems.

But behind these good vibrations is an abiding sense of the way we lose one another, how life is fragile and always passing. Mortality shows up, as accident, as suicide, but also as the bloody business of war and its leftovers. That there are lives we didn't live sits in the background, as in the moving poem 'Colette':

> Colette, Colette: your name is a hiccup of grief,
> And the hollow knock inside an empty closet.
> A seed of loss, it sprouts beyond the day
> We tuck your little shoes, now yellow with age,
> Like a breech birth in the soil of granny's grave.

But if the light at the intersection of rooftops has a distinctive Larkinesque tint ('Where our phone wires meet/over those terraces – look/the sky is still blue!),[21] not to worry, Larkin's presence and influence is completely absorbed and reformed. The wayward, misplaced and various bounty that comes from the most incidental of pleasures and memories acts as a strong antidote to despair and the foreboding that seems like a cyclorama to many of Flynn's bright-eyed poems.

Her poems are full of ordinary things invested with some kind of humane significance (such as mangles and cookers[22]) but, also, the symbolic eponymous and somewhat incongruous Superser:

> It was very ugly. With hindsight, was it quite safe?
> It looked like a cross between a TV robot
> And a roadside shrine in Italy or France.
> When I read how Lucille received the vision of hell
> I deliberately toasted my toes upon its grill
>
> Just like Catholics did in books, and then drifted back
> To *St. Elsewhere, Dallas* or *The Antiques Roadshow*

the upper atmosphere a roiling cloud,
our trade-off with the cold that tapped the glass,
with the shapes made out of dark – while our whole
stunned clan

slumped safe and half-stifled on some Sunday in the
 middle of an era.

The key is in the voice and if the reader cannot 'hear' that – the Frank O'Hara off-the-cuff delivery, the contemporary cultural references (middle-of-the-road television programmes, for instance), the self-ironising and wry wit of not taking one's self too seriously, whatever about the subject of the lines, and the surprising catch to many of her best poems (of which there are many), Flynn really has a unique and admirable range. The only downside is the rare lapse into whimsy and the occasional over-playing of the literary hand, reminiscent of Paul Muldoon at his most provocatively arcane. But taken together, Flynn's four collections add up to some of the very best in contemporary poetry in English. Certainly, her fourth collection, *The Radio*, confirms her substantial achievement in longer and more constructed poems such as 'Letter to Friends'[23] with the two title poems 'The Radio',[24] 'August 30th 2013',[25] 'Black Mould and Mildew: Obsessive-Compulsive Poem for Lawrence'[26] and most particularly the riskier dramatic sequence, 'Poems Conceived as Dialogues between Two Antagonistic Voices'.[27]

I can't help feeling, though, that notwithstanding the subtle playful imagining of these ambitious poems, the pulse of Flynn's imaginative flair is sourced in some part in 'Drive'[28], her poem paying tribute to her mother; of having the drive to write and to keep at it *at this level*:

215

                        (this last leg of this drive
leads back to the empty house which she takes as a sign)…
how does it work, she thinks, this little motor?
Where are its cogs, and parts and curly oiled springs
that make her now, improbably, the wellspring
of five full persons – out upon life's highroads:
a grown-up son, a gang of grown-up daughters,
prodigal, profligate – with 30 years on their clocks?
She doesn't know, and isn't one to assign
meaning to their ways, their worlds' bewildering drives –

though she tells this offspring she's nearing the end of the road
a clock ticks softly…the low pulse of some *drive*…?
My mother watches. She's waiting for a sign…

These three very different poets from different parts of Ireland
bring into formal control powerfully *imagined* worlds. At no
point do we get lost in self-conceit or predictable themes
because the poetry is first and foremost grounded in emotional
intelligence and lived experience which is open, accessible and
challenging. Such achievement is indeed rare and deserving
of widespread recognition, and whatever thoughtful critical
attention is available today should unquestionably attend to
the undoubted literary merit of Dorothy Molloy, Michelle
O'Sullivan and Leontia Flynn.

~

CHAPTER FOURTEEN

THE PRACTICE OF WRITING

*I*n April 1976, the playwright and novelist Thomas Kilroy
published an account of an experiment that had just
concluded in Galway.[1] The experiment was a ten-week course
for writers based in University College Galway (UCG, as it
then was known), the National Writers' Workshop, sponsored by
the Arts Council of Ireland and the first of its kind. According
to an earlier report by Michael Finlan, which had marked the
beginning of the venture in January that year, the idea for
the course had come from the novelist Eilís Dillon.[2] Future
moderators based at UCG would include Eoghan Ó Tuairisc,
John McGahern and Patrick Mason, and in many ways it was
the prototype for creative writing programmes in Ireland. In
his retrospective, Kilroy was of the opinion that the experiment
had worked:

> It is difficult to give an adequate impression of that discussion:
> explication, analysis, criticism, certainly but also the opening up
> and defining of the personality through the medium of highly
> personal work. We covered an extraordinary amount of material
> and in depth.[3]

Kilroy went on to generalise about his experience of the writers' group in terms that I think are possibly even more relevant today:

> As a writer I was interested in this course because of my belief in the importance of a critical intelligence operating within imaginative writing. Despite the exceptional imaginative energy in Irish writing, now and in the past, we have never had what might be called a critical tradition in our culture. The absence of a tradition of enquiry and analysis has influenced not only the shape of our art but the nature of our politics, our religious practices, our social habits, I believe, in a way that has seriously diminished their potential.[4]

In the thirty-five years that separate us from that early exercise, the situation has completely changed in what is now generally referred to as creative writing (a phrase absent from Kilroy's article). Apart from the pioneering work of The Poet's House, based at one time in Northern Ireland with a degree course accredited by a British university, Trinity College Dublin was the first Irish university to offer a Masters' programme in creative writing in 1998. Several other Irish universities have since followed on with fully accredited degrees in creative writing and/or publishing and editing, at both undergraduate and graduate levels. However, it should be noted that creative writing workshops had proliferated and developed from the 1960s and the early 1970s, both informally and formally.[5] The universities were merely catching up with developments already taking place in the wider society and responding accordingly.

My own anecdotal sense of this growth is aligned to initiatives in Irish state policy, with leadership from the Arts Councils in both parts of the island, in the form of the 'Writers-in-Schools' scheme, supplemented by the 'Writers-in-Prisons' scheme, established under the guidance of Brendan Kennelly.[6] Both initiatives flourished during the 1980s and 1990s and continue to play an important (if largely unheralded) role in Irish cultural life. The innovative drive of numerous women's groups is also a key part of this story, in that the hard-won struggle for various civic rights was responsive to a deep need for a breakthrough in establishing platforms for women's writing.

Since these developments took place, non-academic creative writing courses, based in literature centres and libraries, have sprung up all over the country, including Dublin, Cork and Galway, engaging with new important challenges in Irish society, such as the Fighting Words initiative in Dublin.[7] There are creative writing networks and dedicated writers' groups which meet in local neighbourhoods in numerous villages, towns and cities. Alongside which, there are now workshops attached to literary festivals and creative writing residential weekends. Creative writing courses are offered by national newspapers, literary magazines, and local versions of UK-based publishers have included in recent years academy-style programmes – many of which are run on commercial bases.

There is a lot of creative writing going on in Ireland today at all kinds of levels and with different scales of expectation and provision, obviously not just in the universities. There are some who find all this creative writing buzz less than convincing, being of the opinion that while it does not do any harm, it bears little critical relationship to actual literary production and achievement, or the essentially self-motivated, solitary and singular nature of the artistic personality. Others may be of the view that the *non-academic* creative writing experience is closer to ordinary reality and, as a result, more valid and praiseworthy as a form of individual or social expression, prioritising the building of self-esteem over other literary objectives.

Some consider that the involvement of the academy, through the accreditation of degrees in creative writing, will inevitably lead us in Ireland towards the kind of parallel universe in which students enrol primarily to become teachers of creative writing, rather than to become bolder and better poets, fiction writers and playwrights with working lives outside the creative writing hub. While there are academics and writers who remain less than enamoured of the creative writing project, the demand for such courses is steady and shows no sign of diminishing in the years ahead.

The question has to be asked: what is creative writing as an academic discipline? Is it literature, and if so, what criteria do or should we use to teach it, or assess it? There is also the seemingly unpreventable question that emerges when creative writing as a concept enters the air space of the media: is it possible to teach someone how to be a writer? This question seems – to me at least – to wilfully ignore the guilds and *ad hoc* groups and patronage systems through which artists, musicians, theatre practitioners and writers have for centuries past shared their practical skills. From another strictly educational viewpoint, questions can be raised about whether or not it is pedagogically sensible for a poet or novelist or playwright, who may have displayed little previous aptitude, appetite or skill, to be in charge of a class simply *because* he or she is a writer. And there is also the complicated situation of an individual writer who may well find the year-long business of teaching, assessment, administration and pastoral concerns a testing burden on the real work at hand – their own writing – and a difficult and sometimes stressful balance to achieve.

Then there is the consideration that while an individual artist may not indeed be a great teacher, their own depth of learning and range of experience as a writer brings its own lasting inspiration and educational value. It would be a pity if idiosyncrasy and unpredictability – often the hallmarks of the creative mind – were ruled out of the classroom in the interests of bland routine. Genuine creativity can be wayward, a point that can pass the cultural legislators by. There is too the wider history and culture of the writer based in the university creative writing system – a cultural history only beginning in Ireland, yet one that has fascinating historical roots. It is a system much influenced by the example and protocols of writing programmes in the United States.

An established and respected American poet, Louis Simpson, reflected in 1991 on his time teaching mainly in university poetry workshops:

> The students I had were amazingly ignorant. They wanted to write poetry because they were far more interested in their own feelings than in the feelings of other people ... They knew hardly anything of history, philosophy or religion. What they did know about was writing as a career – the names of successful poets were often on their lips, the ones who were awarded prizes and who frequently gave poetry readings. The writing students were blown about by every wave of fashion.[8]

I don't think this is where we are in Ireland, but it is a timely warning of where we could be heading unless different kinds of artistic and cultural motivations are fashioned in our own context to provide more complex and challenging educational experiences for generations to come. We obviously have to think here about quality and excellence, about critical and technical standards when we talk about creativity, as well as the issues of equality of opportunity and access in social terms.

The 'subculture' that Louis Simpson caricatures is something akin to a form of literary *X-Factor*[9] and it may not be completely unfamiliar to those involved in literary matters in Ireland. More pertinently, Simpson goes on to remark of the process of assessment: 'A teacher of creative writing is expected to encourage students [which is] a very different thing than giving honest criticism.'[10] Another American poet, Elizabeth Bishop, remarked in 1966: 'if *anyone* in that class uses the word "communicate" *once* more, I'm going to *scream*! I *hate* that word. Those students are *not* there to "express" themselves; they're there to learn how to write a *good poem*.'[11]

While these American considerations may not have the same voltage in the particular contexts of the Irish literary or academic world of creative writing, both Simpson and Bishop raise an important pedagogical issue about what it is creative writing *teaches*; or, to put this another way, what do we do when we teach 'it'. For me there is no mystery here, creative writing is a generic term that has international name-recognition for those who want to develop their skills at writing poetry, fiction, drama and non-fiction. But as a subject or academic discipline, it evaporates in my mind. I don't think it exists at all and I believe that the creative writing culture is something we should be very circumspect about building into a virtual reality distinct from the actual demands of the literary world. The whole point of teaching creative writing – in whatever setting – is to benefit the individual and strengthen their ability to read and see better what it is they are doing; to critically connect the reality of the poem or story or scene from a play with the aspiration of the writer; and to place in a revealing light what has or has not been achieved. Knowledge, example, comparisons that flow from the imaginative use of language are every bit as critical as the support and responses of encouragement and enjoyment. And we cannot exclude the pleasure principle in all this; otherwise, why bother?

In my opinion, the role of creative writing should not be the equivalent of a feel-good session of self-congratulation. Vigorous reading and revision have to be adjusted obviously to the particular setting, but my own sense of creative writing is that it is only about one thing and one thing alone: practice, the making of literary work. In order for this to be achieved, individuals – in community workshops as much as in seminar rooms – should think about what they are doing, and be challenged to do better, and to learn as much as they can about the making of literature from various traditions other than their own in time and place. This assumes a certain degree of enthusiasm, engagement, belief and knowledge, of course, but when it is matched with intrinsic talent and focus, the work will prosper. Whether this will add up to literary success is of course another day's work.

In terms of my own experience, it seems incontrovertible that best practice comes from the workshop when it is being conducted as precisely that – a *work*shop. Obviously this has to be supplemented for those who want their writing to become a way of life with a realistic picture of the publishing world, of the business (to quote Louis Simpson again) of 'making a name and getting ahead' and of the varied personal and professional pressures of 'being a writer'.[12] My sense of creative writing is predicated exclusively upon the individual's expectations, not upon the putative function of creative writing as a subject in itself. I find such intellectualising and problematising a sideshow. The delivery of the class – the pedagogy of what happens in creative writing workshops – is not structurally different from the rehearsal of a scene in a play, the practice of a pianist or dancer or, for that matter, the intensity of a good sophister or graduate literature seminar at full tilt.

Yet I would like to refer to two related articles on the subject of creative writing which in one way or another raise intellectual questions about the value and moral dimensions of long-established creative writing programmes in the United States. The first is a lengthy review article by Elif Batuman, published in the *London Review of Books*, to which the novelist Paul Murray drew my attention when he was Visiting Writer Fellow at the Oscar Wilde Centre at Trinity College Dublin.[13] The second is an essay by Louis Menand, 'Show and Tell: Should Creative Writing be Taught?' published in *The New Yorker*.[14] Both articles respond to Mark McGurl's study, *The Program Era: Postwar Fiction and the Role of Creative Writing*.[15] I think I am right in saying that the answer to the question posed by Menand is: yes, creative writing should be taught. But we have to watch out for the pitfalls, excesses and failures of critical judgement which Batuman identifies in the US system. She castigates the wound culture within which creative writing is all too often identified as a form of compensation and which questions the propensity of writers entering the literary market via distinguished creative writing schools as a form of self-commodification.[16] Batuman is particularly alarmed by what McGurl describes as the role of 'paradoxically *enabling* disablement'[17] and also challenges both 'literary production as social advocacy'[18] and 'fiction as a form of empathy training':

> Although there is nothing intrinsically wrong with writing about persecution, for either the persecuted or the non-persecuted, there is a genuine problem when young people are taught to

believe that they can be writers only in the presence of real or invented sociopolitical grievances.[19]

Elif Batuman queries how in the handbook-driven, manual-conscious, American environment of many deterministic creative writing programmes – understandably reacting in part to the more informal, therapeutic workshop – students and their teachers become obsessed by technique and writing exercises. She notes that the 'raw material hardly seems to matter anymore … The fetishisation of technique simultaneously assuages and aggravates the anxiety that literature might not be real work.'[20] The conclusive point that Batuman reaches is a somewhat absolutist, exasperated hope that creative writing programmes should 'teach writers about history and the world, and not just about adverbs and themselves'.[21] She does not seem to entertain the possibility that 'history and the world' might well be elliptically contained in an 'adverb'.

Batuman's view is corroborated by Louis Menand in his response to the McGurl book, which also provides a useful mini-history of the American experience, identifying many of its successes and strengths but also illustrating the psychological weaknesses, indulgences and ego-driven problematics that have obtained from time to time. 'Surely the goal should be,' Menand asks, 'to get people to learn to think *while* they're writing, not after they have written.'[22] In saying so, he stresses the key elements of 'revision', 'the importance of making things', 'a love of reading' and of 'moving in the world' before concluding in the workshop of his own remembering:

> I don't think the workshops taught me too much about craft, but they did teach me about the importance of making things, not just reading things. You care about things that you make,

and that makes it easier to care about things that other people make.[23]

If creative writing in Ireland 'makes it easier to care about things that other people make', then that is a very good place from which to start – which neatly brings us back to Thomas Kilroy's observations in 1976 about the need for a critical spirit to match the imaginative energy, to foster and guide writers through the courses that many gifted and committed authors and academics offer – creative writing programmes, workshops, call them what you will. Kilroy's emphasis on the role of critical intelligence and the need for enquiry and analysis are fundamental here.

In the period of time that separates us from Kilroy's original comments, the sheer volume of material in English that is now produced internationally – in printed books and online – make it near-on impossible to maintain any degree of critical focus in the public perception and reception of literary writing. The mass market book-selling world of wall-to-wall exposure and publicity book tours have brought literature ever closer to entertainment. Self-parody seems to merge with self-importance in the profiles that have largely taken the place of intelligent readings of a writer's work, while critical proportion and historical comparison are becoming much less secure or based upon shared literary values that are part of mature literary discourse.

Louis Simpson was unequivocal on this point as it related to the world of poetry that he experienced twenty years ago:

But then you have to think that poetry is an art, and that the poet aims to make it grow. If you conceive of poetry as entertainment, which is that reaching out for a wider audience requires, then by all means do everything you can to increase your audience. But will it be an audience for poetry or for theatrics – an attractive personality, a striking emotional delivery? The people who would rather have their poetry in performance are not lovers of poetry but of performance.[24]

Or maybe they are lovers of both? Either way, the overarching notion of celebrity in today's culture has weakened the moral authority of the writer and his or her place as a genuinely independent figure on the critical edge of the mainstream. Modern literature has always had its celebrities (think of Dickens) but they were better known for the views and visions their writing embodied than for their lifestyles and the foibles of their personalities, which is now increasingly more so the case. It is not the business of promotion that is at fault – the greater and wider access to writers and writing is a certain good – but rather the product that fits this process best tends to be based on what the market can sell rather than on literary excellence. The saturation of the media with populist notions of accessibility contrasts with the increasingly diminished role of literary reviewing as a form of critical filter and opinion-making. These influences have had a huge impact on how literary writing in Ireland, Britain and North America is viewed. As writing itself is turned more publicly into a lifestyle choice driven by the promise of some degree of commercial and/or emotional reward, being a novelist sounds roughly the same as being a chef.

It is in such circumstances as these that creative writing, both in the academy and without, finds its pedagogical, commercial and cultural *raison d'être*. Writing is seen more popularly as an option, and the inclusivity of creativity in the face of economic recession is portrayed as a key to innovation and self-esteem.

While writing as a cultural entitlement shifts the balance away from innate individual talent to something fostered as an access route (a journey) to self-expression – detached from the critical demands and difficulties of formal achievement in the use of language – the pre-eminent view of the social benefits of literature is equally promoted as a non-judgemental communicator of class, gender and ethnicity issues and regarded as valuable primarily in these terms alone, underscored by the rights and entitlements of civic equality.

These current characteristics have created in turn a different kind of readership with a different set of aspirations and expectations, a niche-market of genre writing, which has and will continue materially to affect the way literature is read and, of course, taught. It has always been this way – the history of literary fashion is scored with fads, as any research through the best-selling lists of the 1910s, 20s or 30s will show. But what has altered radically in the present is the rapid technological developments of e-books and Kindles, the upsurge in festivals and literary events, and the hugely influential role of marketing for publishing, bookselling and the contradictory and often merely self-serving benefits of social media. Those engaged in creative writing need to know just how much of the visibility of their writing will be utterly dependent upon the non-creative realities of publishing and that that 'reality check' can be chastening. Ironically, in this context, creative writing may become a crucial point of critical reference and relevance as the marketplace seeks ever more 'product' to *buy* and also as the pressure of selling grows increasingly influential in defining our literary culture, in much the same way as these factors have made an impact on other cultural sectors, such as popular music.

We are all in this world together – as writers both in and out of the academy. Maybe the academy, the much-derided ivory tower (a silly patronising phrase for intellectual and imaginative effort), will provide a productive space in the twenty-first century within which the artistic imagination finds time to develop and wherein the practice of writing will be able to thrive in a free if challenging atmosphere of genuine critical exchange – practices for which the great universities were originally designed.

EPILOGUE

FITTING IN

I'm going to finish with a look back to the ups and downs of literary life as seen by the wonderful eighteenth-century novelist and dramatist Oliver Goldsmith in an article he published in his short-lived magazine *The Bee*. Goldsmith had, John Lucas informs us, 'planned to issue [*The Bee*] … as a weekly paper, beginning in October 1759' but two months into circulation it 'died after eight issues and when printed in book form at the end of the year was coolly received'.[1] One rather rapid fall for the thirty-something Goldsmith, but it certainly did not halt Goldsmith's rising again and again.

Goldsmith exhibits a sharp eye on his contemporary world and it is clear to a non-eighteenth century specialist such as myself that Goldsmith was well capable of seeing through the fashionable literary games of patronage, favour and influence. He had an outsider's ability to nail with wit and scepticism the hypocrisies and double standards of his time. The text which I will come to shortly is no. IV of *The Bee* from 27 October 1759 and is entitled 'Miscellaneous'.[2]

But I want to fast forward a couple of centuries and refer to something another great 'Anglo-Irish' writer, the novelist

Elizabeth Bowen, wrote about what she saw as the achievements of Anglo-Irish writing. I know the term 'Anglo-Irish' is no longer in critical and academic fashion, but I am using it here strictly in the context of how it *was* used as a self-description by writers such as Bowen and by later writers on the subject of Irish literature. This is what Bowen wrote in *Pictures and Conversations* (1975):

> Accommodating ourselves to a tamer day, we interchanged sword-play for word-play. Repartee, with its thrusts, opened alternative possibilities of mastery. Given rein to, creative imagination ran to the tensed-up, to extreme situations, to confrontations. Bravado characterises much Irish, all Anglo-Irish writing: gloriously it is sublimated by Yeats. Nationally, we have an undertow to the showy. It follows that primarily we have produced dramatists, the novel being too life-like, humdrum, to do us justice. We do not do badly with the short story ... There is this about us: to most of the rest of the world we are semi-strangers, for whom existence has something of the trance-like quality of a spectacle. As beings, we are at once brilliant and limited; our unbeatables, up to now, accordingly, have been those who best profited by that: Goldsmith, Sheridan, Wilde, Shaw, Beckett. Art is for us inseparable from artifice: of that, the theatre is the home.[3]

Now it is interesting to note just how many times Bowen refers to 'we' and 'us' here – nine times I counted! Clearly what she was trying to explore within the tradition of Irish writing in English are the contours of *other* elements which – while being *part* of an Irish literary past – form themselves into different influences and finally inhabit a somewhat different cultural and religious space while remaining on the

Irish cultural map. The term she uses is really curious – 'semi-strangers, for whom existence has something of the trance-like quality of a spectacle'. The list that she names from Goldsmith through to Beckett also includes Yeats, and, as we know, Yeats spent much of his emotional and intellectual energy thinking and writing about these very matters of cultural integration and the place his Protestant forebears found for themselves *in* Ireland:

> How much of my reading is to discover the English and Irish originals of my thought, its first language, and, where no originals exist, its relation to what original did. I seek more than idioms, for thoughts become more vivid when I find they were thought out in historical circumstances which affect those in which I live, or, which is perhaps the same thing, were thought first by men my ancestors may have known. Some of my ancestors may have seen Swift, and probably my Huguenot grandmother who asked [for] burial near Bishop King spoke both to Swift and Berkeley.[4]

The 'may have' and 'probably' are the poet's licence to imagine more than the literal truths of history. In the poems Yeats published around this time Goldsmith features too, as a figure who links together provincial Ireland, Protestantism, Dublin and London; a network of contradictory and challenging imaginative pulses that Yeats recognised in his own writing life. These impulses involved Yeats, as his editors remark, 'in a search for his intellectual ancestry among the Anglo-Irish of the 18th century'. In 'Blood and Moon', Yeats has Goldsmith 'deliberately sipping at the honey-pot of his mind' and in lines channelling 'The Deserted Village', Yeats remarks in 'The Seven Sages':

Oliver Goldsmith sang what he had seen,
Roads full of beggars, cattle in the fields,
But never saw the trefoil stained with blood,
The avenging leaf those fields raised up against it.[5]

Poems and prose that indicate how Goldsmith, along with the other eighteenth-century Anglo-Irish writers, had played a critical role in helping Yeats to work out if, where and how he fitted in to the literary traditions of Britain and Ireland. At the same time reconciling himself as a poet, dramatist and as a polemicist who had been greatly excited by the separatist cultural nationalism of his early manhood and even later on into the turbulence of the new twentieth century.

What it means creatively to be part of this complicating 'tradition' is, as we have already seen, precisely what Thomas Kilroy explores in *his* critical writing on Irish drama, particularly in three central essays: 'Anglo-Irish Playwrights and Comic Tradition',[6] 'The Anglo-Irish Theatrical Imagination',[7] and 'The Literary Tradition of Irish Drama'[8] but also in other pioneering work on Synge, O'Casey, Yeats and Beckett.[9]

It is fascinating to see how one of the country's leading playwrights reads Goldsmith and his tradition, and from a different critical viewpoint to Bowen. Goldsmith, Kilroy writes:

> had an acute ear for the way in which language betrays a distortion of personality and a benevolent discernment of how metropolitan culture [London] produces such artificiality. The perspective from which [Goldsmith] perceived this is that of a figure off-centre, perfectly awkward in a society which measured correct bearing with calibrated accuracy, feckless in a society dedicated to thrift and efficiency.[10]

Kilroy quotes from a letter in which Goldsmith had recounted the difficulties 'he encountered in earlier days in London': 'left as I was without friends, recommendations, money or impudence; and that in a country where being born an Irishman was sufficient to keep one unemployed'.[11] It is a familiar complaint: of the writer in the capital trying to find his or her feet in a host society that often patronises the emigrant sensibility by either provocatively stereotyping with caricatures the experiences upon which the writer draws or exploits or patronises both for commercial gain. The route to find a just balance has led many a writer into dark nights of the soul as much as to the comparative well-being of recognition and fame.

The significance of Goldsmith's statement is central to Kilroy's argument in his essay, 'Anglo-Irish Playwrights and Comic Tradition'. Here Kilroy looks at the conventions of the eighteenth-century comedy of manners:

> the basic formula is that of the countryman or provincial ill-planted in the Metropolis and therefore an object of social and linguistic mockery. When the playwright is himself a provincial, arriving into the imperial Metropolis from Ireland this tension is assimilated into an artistic view-point, accounting in large part, it seems to me, for the peculiar, considerable contribution of Anglo-Irish playwrights to the genre. When we acknowledge, then, the contribution of Irish-born playwrights to the tradition of polite English comedy, Farquahar, Steele, Goldsmith, Kelly, Sheridan, Wilde and Shaw, we are inviting questions which range across colonial mobility and identity, class consciousness and consciousness of language as an instrument of measurement and discrimination.[12]

This is stirring stuff, but what I am interested in is the ambiguous, existential condition (if that does not sound too portentous) of those Irish-born, London-based, predominantly Protestant writers and of how their situation has been viewed. Not so much self-consciously, but intuitively, as an ironic contradiction that has marked out their literary intelligence and which they could play with; but also, critically, it was a condition that exercised their minds, teasing them, joking with them, at times, mocking them. On the one hand, acknowledged and 'accepted' for their writing as being 'English' or 'British' but, on the other hand, lacking levels of critical understanding they would never *really* enjoy or be completely recognised as such. That the host society viewed Goldsmith with a certain degree of recognition is obvious from the tributes paid on his death, to the tablet written by Samuel Johnson in his honour in Westminster Abbey.

Yet I think it is equally true to say that Goldsmith, and other Irish writers since, have never *felt* completely accepted; a condition that extends to other 'host' societies, including our own, when those viewed as being 'different' – in terms of race, sex or religion, or even simple regional cultural calibrations – were not fully accepted and elements of which continued to be present in Irish cultural life up until comparatively recently.

Thomas Kilroy's reformulation of Elizabeth Bowen's self-descriptions of an Anglo-Irish tradition into an interesting cultural and political context, will play in the background of what I want to move on to now – Goldsmith's article on the ups and downs, the falling and rising of literary fame and misfortune. The intelligence, wit and acute understanding of the literary world hold up well in Goldsmith's short article for *The Bee*, even though we are talking about over 250 years ago. It is a brief masterclass in the vagaries of the writer's life.

It fits, as a kind of critical and psychological bridge, between the literary achievements Goldsmith was about to secure as playwright, novelist and poet, and his (what shall I call it?)

outsider status in the society he has settled into in London; an outsider-insider, if you like. Based around two 'stories' which he uses as anecdotal touchstones in the article, he jokes about what he had 'once determined to throw off all connexions with taste' and, instead, 'address my countrymen in the same engaging style and manner with other periodical pamphlets, much more in vogue than probably mine will ever be'.[13] He got that right – 'not in never falling but in rising every time'.

The list of what he *should* be doing reads today like something from one of the broadsheet weekend supplements with their mantra of 'entertaining' and/or celebrating, with accessible lifestyle stories and effusively self-promoting journalism; what Goldsmith calls 'a proper stock of popular topicks'. The list is intriguing:[14] 'encomiums [*sic*] on the king of Prussia, invectives against the queen of Hungary and the French, the necessity of militia, our undoubted sovereignty of the seas, reflections upon the present state of affairs, a dissertation upon liberty, some seasonable thoughts upon the intended bridge at Blackfriars, and an address to Britons'. He also remarks on the self-congratulation that characterises other essayists whom he knows and reads; those who receive 'numerous compliments paid to them in the course of their lubrications; of the frequent encouragements they met to inspire them with ardour, and increase their eagerness to please'.

'Lucky them!' you can almost hear Goldsmith whisper under his breath. For on the contrary, the letters he receives are far from 'congratulatory' but rather 'not assuring me of success and favour; but pregnant with bodings that might shake even fortitude itself'. Responding to what he calls the 'denunciations' which he receives, Goldsmith is a bit tongue-in-cheek perhaps but his writing is laced with a wry and cool self-understanding, and a clear idea about the fortunes of writers like himself, who

question and challenge through their writing *style* the ethos
and conventions of their time.

There is, in other words, an edge to all this playfulness,
as Goldsmith points to those who surf the expectations and
prejudices of his here and now without sufficient detachment,
or, at the very least, of the necessary distance being placed
between the individual writer's conscience, the pull of the
marketplace (Grub Street) and the force of the state and/or
monarchy. It is all nicely allusive, but darting under the surface
of Goldsmith's prose, he is actually identifying some significant
issues of cultural worth, as opposed to market value, something
that clearly connects his time with ours – where celebrity,
manipulations of reputation and representation in much of the
popular media are all highly inflated while actual literary or
artistic worth often underexamined. Why is the latest novel by
X being hailed as a masterpiece? What actually makes this play
'radical' or 'controversial'? – that kind of thing.

Goldsmith rebukes the denunciations with an ironic turn
of phrase: 'I write partly to shew my good-nature, and partly
to shew my vanity; nor will I lay down the pen till I am
satisfied one way or another.'[15] His conclusion has a resounding
resonance to my way of thinking: 'For my part,' Goldsmith
writes, 'I am ever ready to mistrust a promising title, and have,
at some expense, been instructed not to hearken to the voice
of an advertisement, let it plead never so loudly, or never so
long.'[16] For as we know, we live in a world utterly drenched
in advertisements – self-advertisements, promotional material
of one kind or another that bestows 'value' on the principle of
that which can be consumed in the greatest volume, without
any previewed sense of critical filter or comparative perspective.

The online platforms of the twenty-first century, a quality
control-free zone, 'accepts' whatever comes its way as individuals

can claim for their work whatever they so desire; numerous television programmes, cynically based around the hopes and aspirations of many, produce a form of hollowed-out celebrity rather than actual achievement. While on the one hand this appears as democratic accessibility, in practice it is simply commercial business, and often on the cheap. Goldsmith's 'mistrust' is, in another way of stating it, a form of critical enlightenment and detachment from all the swirling claims and counterclaims of his time; it is a quality the like of which seems to be diminishing more and more in the culture of today. But, as I am suggesting here, it is instructive and valuable to note what happened to Goldsmith's writing, bearing in mind that he died at such a relatively young age – he was forty-five.

When one thinks of how literary fashion over the intervening centuries has not been (generally speaking) so interested in eighteenth-century achievement in comparison, say, with the unrelenting obsession with the Romantic poets, or the great Modernists of the twentieth century – or of course, much earlier, with the Elizabethan period of Shakespeare's monumental accomplishments – yet for all that, Goldsmith's work survives, alongside that of his more famous contemporaries and nationally identifiable peers such as Samuel Johnson. Goldsmith's plays are performed widely and regularly, his 'The Deserted Village' is known and well established in popular and academic terms, and, thanks to a younger generation of scholars, including Michael Griffin, whose study *Enlightenment in Ruins: The Geographies of Oliver Goldsmith*[17] sensitively unlocks the wider European cultural and philosophical contexts of Goldsmith's achievement.

For the non-specialist, such as myself, a poet and moonlighting essayist, Oliver Goldsmith is much more than the sum of his various parts. His independence, that outsider–insider, brings a sense of critical filtering to even his slightest prose works, including 'Miscellaneous'. He is an exemplary figure of contradictions, first and foremost, but he is also, crucially, a figure of creative style. There is an unflinching quality that glints under the easeful surface of sentiment and comedy in the drama, and the mellifluous harmonics of the poetry, just as there is, bizarrely, a hint of latter voices in his prose:

> instead of having the learned world apostrophising at my untimely decease, perhaps all Grub-street might laugh at my fall, and self-approving dignity might never be able to shield me from ridicule. In short, I am resolved to write on, if it were only to spite them.

Am I hearing Beckett's Malone in there somewhere? – 'Let me say before I go any further that I forgive nobody,' recites Malone, 'I wish them all an atrocious life and then the fires and ice of hell and in the execrable generations to come an honoured name. Enough for this evening'?[18]

No matter. 'Miscellaneous' turns the gaze back on to the reader with all the characteristics of a very un-illusioned and adult sense of parody, which is in fatally short supply today as well, given the currently dominant culture of self-obsession, 'over-sharing' as it has been called, along with the remorseless hunger for praise, approval and recognition. A parable to match the old adage of not believing everything you read in a newspaper, on the cover of a book, or that paper never refuses ink is neatly enfolded here in the final paragraph:[19]

> A countryman coming one day to Smithfield, in order to take a slice of Bartholomew-fair, found a perfect shew before every

booth. The drummer, the fire-eater, the wire-walker, and the salt-box were all employed to invite him in. *Just a going: the court of the king of Prussia in all his glory; pray, gentlemen, walk in and see.* From people who generously gave so much away, the clown expected a monstrous bargain for his money when he got in. He steps up, pays his sixpence, the curtain is drawn, when too late he finds that he had the best part of the shew for nothing at the door.

Oliver Goldsmith worked as hard as any of his contemporaries for advancement and acknowledgement, but what makes his life and his writing both poignant and challenging is that he did so knowing full well that he would never be *completely* accepted for what he was by the host society in which he lived most of his life; and that his having to cope with not 'fitting in' was the mark of becoming the great writer he was and whom we all cherish, for this and for very many other, quite different reasons.

ENDNOTES

CHAPTER 1

1 W.B. Yeats, 'Reveries over Childhood and Youth: xxxiii', *Autobiographies* (London: Macmillan, 1956), p. 106.

2 Terence Brown, *The Life of W.B. Yeats: A Critical Biography* (Dublin: Gill and Macmillan, 2001), p. 4.

3 James Knowlson, *Damned to Fame: The Life of Samuel Beckett* (London: Bloomsbury, 1996), p. 24.

4 D.E.S. Maxwell, *A Critical History of Modern Irish Drama, 1891–1980* (Cambridge: Cambridge University Press, 1984).

5 Katharine Worth, *Samuel Beckett's Theatre: Life Journeys* (Oxford: Clarendon Press, 1999) and *The Irish Drama of Europe from Yeats to Beckett* (London: Athlone Press, 1978).

6 Gordon Armstrong, *Samuel Beckett, W.B. Yeats and Jack Yeats: Images and Words* (Lewisburg, PA: Bucknell University Press/Associated University Press, 1990).

7 Enoch Brater, 'Intertexuality' in Lois Oppenheim (ed.), *Palgrave Advances in Samuel Beckett Studies* (New York: Palgrave, 2004).

8 Ibid. p. 40.

9 Samuel Beckett, *Waiting for Godot* (London: Faber and Faber, 1988 [1956]), p. 19.

10 Maxwell, *A Critical History of Modern Irish Drama*, pp. 33–4.

11 Samuel Beckett, *Happy Days* (London: Faber and Faber, 1981 [1963]), p. 43.

12   W.B. Yeats, *Collected Plays of W.B. Yeats* (London: Macmillan, 1963), p. 208.

13   Samuel Beckett, '… but the clouds …', *The Complete Dramatic Works* (London: Faber and Faber, 1986), pp. 415–22.

14   W.B. Yeats, 'The Tower', in Richard J. Finneran (ed.), *W.B. Yeats, The Poems: A New Edition* (London: Macmillan, 1984), p. 197.

15   Samuel Beckett, 'Walking Out', *More Pricks Than Kicks* (London: Faber and Faber, 2010 [1934]), p. 97: 'Indeed she was better than lovely, with its suggestion of the Nobel Yeats, with her jet of hair and her pale set face.'

16   Samuel Beckett, 'Recent Irish Poetry', *The Bookman* (August 1934), pp. 235–6.

17   John Pilling, *Samuel Beckett* (London: Routledge & Kegan Paul, 1976), p. 253.

18   Martha Dow Fehsenfeld, Lois More Overbeck, Dan Gunn, George Craig (eds), *The Letters of Samuel Beckett, Vol. 1:1929–1940* (Cambridge: Cambridge University Press, 2009), p. 518.

19   W.J. McCormack, *From Burke to Beckett: Ascendancy, Tradition and Betrayal in Literary History* (Cork: Cork University Press, 1994), p. 392.

20   Fehsenfeld et. al, *The Letters of Samuel Beckett, Vol. 1*, p. 351.

21   W.B. Yeats, *Oxford Book of Modern Verse 1892–1935* (Oxford: Oxford University Press, 1936).

22   Dorothy Wellesley, *Letters on Poetry from W.B. Yeats to Dorothy Wellesley* (Oxford: Oxford University Press, 1964 [1940]), pp. 82–3.

23   W.J. McCormack, *Blood Kindred: W.B. Yeats: The Life, The Death, The Politics* (London: Pimlico, 2005), p. 108.

24   Anthony Cronin, *Samuel Beckett: The Last Modernist* (London: HarperCollins, 1996), p. 63.

25   Deirdre Bair, *Samuel Beckett: A Biography* (London: Picador, 1980), p. 121.

26   Ibid.

27   Ibid. 'Notes', p. 659.

28   Anthony Roche, *Contemporary Irish Drama from Beckett to McGuinness* (Dublin: Gill and Macmillan, 1994), p. 15.

29   Richard Ellmann, *Four Dubliners: Wilde, Yeats, Joyce, and Beckett* (London: Hamish Hamilton, 1986), p. 98.

30   At the Beckett Summer School, Trinity College Dublin (11 August 2015), the actor Barry McGovern recounted a comment of Beckett's to the effect that he *had* indeed met Yeats.

31   Samuel Beckett, *Echo's Bones*, edited with an introduction by Mark Nixon (London: Faber and Faber, 2014), p. 75.

32   Anne Atik, *How It Was: A Memoir of Samuel Beckett* (London: Thames and Hudson, 2001), p. 127.

33   Ellmann, *Four Dubliners*, p. 97.

34   John Montague, *Company: A Chosen Life* (London: Duckworth, 2001) and *The Pear is Ripe: A Memoir* (Dublin: Liberties Press, 2007).

35   Ellmann, *Four Dubliners*, p. 97.

36   Gerry Dukes, *Samuel Beckett: Penguin Illustrated Lives* (London: Penguin, 2001), p. 136.

37   Ellmann, *Four Dubliners*, p. 100.

38   Yeats, *The Poems*, p. 193.

39   Fehsenfeld et. al, *The Letters of Samuel Beckett, Vol. 2*, p. 105.

40   Ibid. p. 623.

41   Ibid. p. 633.

42   Bair, *Samuel Beckett*, p. 526.

43   Atik, *How It Was*, pp. 60–1 and 67–8.

44   Wellesley, *Letters on Poetry*.

45   Atik, *How It Was*, p. 69.

46   James Mays, 'Samuel Beckett', *Field Day Anthology of Irish Writing* (Faber and Faber: Field Day Publications, 1991), p. 246.

47   Atik, *How It Was*, p. 117.

48   J.M. Synge, *Collected Works: Vol. 1. Poems*, edited by Robin Skelton (Oxford: Oxford University Press, 1962), p. 31.

49   Atik, *How It Was*, p. 124.

50   Ibid. p. 68.

51   Yeats, *The Poems*, pp. 199–200.

52   Atik, *How It Was*, p. 125.

53   Montague, *The Pear is Ripe*, p. 237.

54 Nicholas Grene, *Yeats's Poetic Codes* (Oxford: Oxford University Press, 2008).

55 Samuel Beckett, *Molloy* (London: Faber and Faber, 2009 [1951]), p. 29.

56 Brown, *The Life of W.B. Yeats*, p. 382.

57 Katharine Worth, *The Irish Drama of Europe from Yeats to Beckett* (London: Athlone Press, 1978), p. 253.

58 Terence Brown, 'Yeats and Beckett: The Ghosts in the Machines', in Anna McMullan and S.E. Wilmer (eds), *Reflections on Beckett: A Centenary Celebration* (Ann Arbor, MI: University of Michigan Press, 2009), p. 43.

59 Knowlson, *Damned to Fame*, p. 191.

60 Samuel Beckett, *Murphy* (London: Faber and Faber, 2009 [1938]), p. 66.

61 Ibid. p. 3.

Chapter 2

1 All quotations are from James Plunkett, *Strumpet City* (Dublin: Gill & Macmillan, 2013 [original edition London: Century 1969]), p. 300.

2 Examining the list of twentieth-century Irish writing would take up more space than available here – from Joyce's *Dubliners* to *Ulysses* through Samuel Beckett's early fiction (*More Pricks Than Kicks*, *Murphy* and his sequence of journeying poems, *Echo's Bones*), through to Patrick Kavanagh, Austin Clarke, Thomas Kinsella (whose *Nightwalker*, published the year before *Strumpet City*, is one of the great Dublin poems of the last century), to plays such as Sean O'Casey's Dublin trilogy and, say, Thomas Kilroy's *Talbot's Box*; as well as numerous poems *about* Dublin by long-time visitors here, such as Louis MacNeice and Philip Larkin, to long-time dwellers in the city such as Brendan Kennelly and Michael Hartnett. For a relatively recent perspective, see Maria Johnston, 'Walking Dublin: Contemporary Poets in the City' in Fran Brearton and Alan Gillis

(eds), *Oxford Handbook of Modern Irish Poetry* (Oxford: Oxford University Press, 2012). Readers might also like to consult Pat Boran and Gerard Smyth (eds), *If Ever You Go: A Map of Dublin in Poetry and Song* (Dublin: Dedalus Press, 2014).

3   Plunkett, *Strumpet City*, pp. 34–5.

4   Ibid. p. 271.

5   Ibid. pp. 272–3.

6   Ibid. p. 273.

7   Ibid. pp. 352–3.

8   Ibid. p. 422.

9   Ibid. p. 418.

10 Ibid. p. 419.

11 Ibid. pp. 419–20.

12 Ibid. p. 448.

13 Ibid. p. 539.

14 Ibid. p. 540.

15 Brown, *The Life of W.B. Yeats*, p. 200.

16 Plunkett, *Strumpet City*, p. 549.

17 Terence Brown, 'Dublin in Twentieth-Century Writing: Metaphor and Subject', *Irish University Review*, 8, 1 (Spring 1978), pp. 7–21.

18 Ibid. p. 9.

19 Ibid.

20 Yeats, *The Poems*, p. 109.

Chapter 3

1   John Hewitt, *A North Light: Twenty-five years in a municipal art gallery*, edited by Frank Ferguson and Kathryn White (Dublin: Four Courts Press, 2013).

2   Roy Foster, *W.B. Yeats: A Life. The Arch Poet, 1915–1939* (Oxford: Oxford University Press, 2003), p. 651.

3   Hewitt, *A North Light*, p. 185.

4   Foster, *The Arch Poet*, p. 657.

5   Hewitt, *A North Light*, p. 184.

6   Allan Wade (ed.), *The Letters of W.B. Yeats* (London: R. Hart-Davis, 1954), p. 613.

7   Hewitt, *A North Light*, p. 184.

8   W.B. Yeats, 'Man and the Echo', *The Poems: A New Edition*, p. 345.

9   Hewitt, *A North Light*, p. 185.

10   Ibid., p. 186.

11   Ibid.

12   Foster, *The Arch Poet*, p. 654.

13   Ibid. p. 657.

14   Hewitt, *A North Light*, p. 187.

15   W.J. McCormack, *Northman: John Hewitt 1907–87. An Irish Writer, His World and His Times* (Oxford: Oxford University Press, 2015), pp. 90–1.

16   Hewitt, *A North Light*, p. 187.

17   Guy Woodward, *Culture, Northern Ireland, and the Second World War* (Oxford: Oxford University Press, 2015).

18   Timothy Kearney, 'Beyond the Planter and the Gael', *Crane Bag*, 4, 2 (1980–1), p. 728.

19   John Hewitt, *Loose Ends* (Belfast: Blackstaff Press, 1983). The collection includes the poem 'In Recollection of Drumcliffe, September 1948', p. 48.

20   Frank Ormsby (ed.), *The Collected Poems of John Hewitt* (Belfast: Blackstaff Press, 1991), p. 304.

21   Ibid. p. 305. The Crossley tender was a militarised vehicle used in Ireland during the Troubles.

22   Ibid. pp. 443–4.

23   Ibid. 'Notes to Appendix 1', p. 651. Ormsby directs the reader to the Hewitt Archive, Notebook 9, p. 78, for the text of Hewitt's unpublished Connolly sonnet of 26 April 1929.

24   Roger McHugh, an academic, playwright and senator (1954–7) in the Irish Senate, was Professor of English at UCD and in 1966 was appointed the first Professor of Anglo-Irish Literature and Drama; H.O. White: Herbert Martyn Oliver White, was Professor of English Literature at Trinity College Dublin 1939–60; Kenneth Reddin's

claim to fame, other than writing a novel, *Another Shore* (which was turned into a well-known film of the same name [1948] featuring Robert Beatty, one of the character actors who featured in *Odd Man Out* [1947], the classic film about Belfast's IRA campaign), was as the magistrate who heard the case in Samuel Beckett's car accident in 1937.

25 McCormack, *Northman*, p. 83.
26 Ibid.
27 John Hewitt, 'The Colony', in Ormsby (ed.), *The Collected Poems of John Hewitt*, p. 79.

CHAPTER 4

1 Dominic Sandbrook, *Never Had it So Good: A History of Britain from Suez to The Beatles* (London: Abacus, 2006), p. 282.
2 See John Joseph Lee, *Ireland 1912–1985: Politics and Society* (Cambridge University Press, 1990), p. 377; James Ryan, 'Inadmissible Departures: Why did the Emigrant Experience Feature so Infrequently in the Fiction of the Mid-Twentieth Century?' in Dermot Keogh, Finbarr O'Shea and Carmel Quinlan (eds), *The Lost Decade: Ireland in the 1950s* (Cork: Mercier Press, 2004), p. 228.
3 Dermot Keogh, 'Introduction: The Vanishing Irish', *The Lost Decade: Ireland in the 1950s*, p. 18.
4 Terence Brown, *Ireland: A Social and Cultural History 1922–2002* (London: Harper Perennial, 2004), pp. 201–6. See also Tom Garvin 'Dublin Newspapers and the Crisis of the Fifties', *News from a New Republic: Ireland in the 1950s* (Dublin: Gill & Macmillan, 2010), pp. 61–77.
5 Thomas Kinsella, 'Nightwalker' in *Nightwalker and Other Poems* (Dublin: Dolmen Press, 1968).
6 Jonathan Bardon, *A History of Ulster* (Belfast: Blackstaff Press, 1992), pp. 569–74 gives a succinct portrait of the bombings and after effects. See also Bardon's definitive *Belfast: An Illustrated History* (Belfast: Blackstaff Press, 1983), pp. 234–45.

7   See Gerald Dawe, *In Another World: Van Morrison & Belfast* (Dublin: Merrion Press, 2017).

8   Brian Fallon, *An Age of Innocence: Irish Culture 1930–1960* (Dublin: Gill & Macmillan, 1998), pp. 263–5.

9   Brown, *Ireland: A Social and Cultural History*, p. 206. See also Clair Wills, *The Best are Leaving: Emigration and Post-War Irish Culture* (Cambridge: Cambridge University Press, 2015).

10 Brown, *Ireland: A Social and Cultural History*, pp. 206–7.

11 John Ryan, *Remembering How We Stood: Bohemian Dublin at the Mid-Century* (Dublin: Gill & Macmillan, 1975).

12 Anthony Cronin, *Dead as Doornails* (Dublin: Dolmen Press, 1976).

13 Eoin O'Brien, *The Weight of Compassion & Other Essays* (Dublin: The Lilliput Press, 2012).

14 Brendan Behan, *Borstal Boy* (London: Arrow Books, 1990 [1958]), p. 77.

15 Kenneth Tynan, *The Observer*, 27 May 1956. Quoted in Michael O'Sullivan, *Brendan Behan: A Life* (Dublin: Blackwater Press, 1997). For the review and the BBC interview, see pp. 208–11.

16 The Catacombs was a hub for writers and artists during the late 1940s, based in Fitzwilliam Square, Dublin.

17 J.P. Donleavy, *The Ginger Man* (London: Abacus, 1996 [1955]), p. 157.

18 John McGahern, 'The Solitary Reader', in *Love of the World: Essays* (London: Faber and Faber, 2009), pp. 87–95.

19 Ibid. p. 92. It is interesting to note that in his memoir of mid-1950s Ireland, *Irish Journal*, the German novelist Heinrich Böll remarked about how the 'utterly un-uniform unity that is Ireland has spoken to me most clearly of all through its literature. Beckett, Joyce and Behan – all three are intensely, almost outrageously Irish, yet each is far removed from the other, farther than Australia from Europe.' 'Epilogue', *Irish Journal* (Chicago: Northwestern University Press, 1967), p. 123.

20 Brian Friel, *Philadelphia, Here I Come!* (London: Faber and Faber, 1965), p. 68.

21 Ibid. p. 96; the penultimate line: 'God, boy, why do you have to leave?'

22 Ibid. p. 69.

23 John McGahern, 'High Ground', in *High Ground* (London: Faber and Faber, 1985), p. 102.

24 Patrick Kavanagh, *Self Portrait* (Dublin: The Dolmen Press, 1964), pp. 25–8.

25 Patrick Kavanagh, *Come Dance with Kitty Stobling & Other Poems* (London: Longmans, Green and Co. Ltd, 1960).

26 Louis MacNeice, *The Strings are False: An Unfinished Autobiography* (London: Faber and Faber, 1965), p. 212.

27 McGahern, 'Journey along the Canal Bank', in *Love of the World: Essays*, pp. 330–1.

28 Kavanagh, *Come Dance with Kitty Stobling*, p. 1.

29 Ibid. p. 33.

30 Brian Fallon, *The Age of Innocence: Irish Culture, 1930–1960* (Dublin: Gill & Macmillan, 1998), p. 262.

31 For the view of one of Ireland's leading younger writers, see 'The Interview: Paul Murray in conversation with Eoin Tierney', *Icarus LXIII.II* (School of English, Trinity College Dublin, 2013), pp. 20–8.

CHAPTER 5

1 McGahern, *Love of the World: Essays*, p. 6. All quotations from John McGahern courtesy of Madeline McGahern (The Estate of John McGahern) and Faber and Faber.

2 In conversation with Dorothea Melvin, who taught national curriculum subjects at primary and secondary levels at several schools in the west of Ireland during the late 1960s and early 1970s.

3 John McGahern, 'Bank Holiday' in *The Collected Stories* (London: Faber and Faber, 1992), pp. 350–65.

4 McGahern, 'Faith, Hope and Charity', *The Collected Stories*, p. 148.

5 McGahern, 'Doorways', *The Collected Stories*, p. 170.

6   McGahern, 'Strandhill, the Sea', *The Collected Stories*, p. 41.

7   Ibid. p. 43.

8   McGahern, 'Hearts of Oak and Bellies of Brass', *The Collected Stories*, pp. 33–4.

9   McGahern, 'Strandhill, the Sea', p. 43.

10 Ibid. p. 44.

11 Ibid.

12 McGahern, 'My Love, My Umbrella', *The Collected Stories*, pp. 66–7. The portrait of the poet is clearly based upon Patrick Kavanagh.

13 McGahern, 'High Ground', *The Collected Stories*, pp. 314–15.

14 McGahern, 'The Wine Breath', *The Collected Stories*, p. 185.

15 Hugh MacDiarmid, 'The Little White Rose', *The Complete Poems of Hugh MacDiarmid 1920–1976, Vol. 1* (London: Martin Brian & O'Keeffe, 1978): 'The rose of all the world is not for me./I want for my part/Only the little white rose of Scotland/That smells sharp and sweet – and breaks the heart', p. 461.

16 McGahern, 'The Recruiting Officer', *The Collected Stories*, p. 103.

17 McGahern, 'The Devil Finds Work for Idle Hands' republished in *Love of the World: Essays* as 'The Solitary Reader', pp. 87–95.

18 John Butler Yeats, *Letters to His Son W.B. Yeats and Others, 1869–1922*, edited by Joseph Hone. Abridged and with an Introduction by John McGahern (London: Faber and Faber, 1999).

19 McGahern, 'The Solitary Reader', *Love of the World*, p. 92. *Nimbus*, founded by Martin Green and Tristram Hull, was co-edited by David Wright (1955–6) during which time the 'little magazine' published nineteen poems by Patrick Kavanagh. These poems would form a central part of *Come Dance with Kitty Stobling*.

20 Kavanagh, *Come Dance with Kitty Stobling*, p. 17.

21 McGahern, 'Journey along the Canal Bank', *Love of the World*, pp. 330–1.

22 Ibid. p. 331. The poem was published as 'The Hospital'.

23 McGahern, 'The Bird Swift', *Love of the World*, p. 65.

24 This was 'The End or the Beginning of Love: Episodes from a Novel'. See Patrick Swift and David Wright (eds), *An Anthology from*

X: A Quarterly Review of Literature and the Arts, 1959–1962 (Oxford: Oxford University Press, 1988), pp. 153–63.

25 'His agitated presence had more the sound of a crowd than the single person sitting in a chair', McGahern, 'Bank Holiday', p. 358.

26 McGahern, 'Journey along the Canal Bank', p. 333.

27 Coincidentally, Patrick McDonogh (1902–61) – without the 'u' – was the author of five books of poetry, including *Over the Water* (1943) and *One Landscape Still* (1958). See Patrick McDonogh, *Poems*, edited and introduced by Derek Mahon (Oldcastle: The Gallery Press, 2001).

28 W.B. Yeats, 'Beautiful Lofty Things': 'Maud Gonne at Howth station waiting a train/Pallas Athene in that straight back and arrogant head:/All the Olympians; a thing never known again.' Yeats and Gonne had spent a day walking in Howth Head after his first unsuccessful proposal in 1891. A. Norman Jeffares (ed.), *Yeats's Poems* (Basingstoke: Palgrave, 1998), p. 421.

29 McGahern, 'Bank Holiday', p. 355.

30 Ibid. p. 357.

31 McGahern, 'Peaches', *The Collected Stories*, pp. 81 and 89.

32 McGahern, 'Bank Holiday', p. 357.

33 Antoinette Quinn, *Patrick Kavanagh: A Biography* (Dublin: Gill & Macmillan, 2001), pp. 298–9. McGahern's questioning attitude to Kavanagh's personality is also worth noting, p. 371.

34 McGahern, 'Bank Holiday', p. 358.

35 Ibid. p. 360.

36 Ibid. pp. 364–5.

37 Ibid. p. 365. The sonnets include 'Canal Bank Walk', 'Lines Written in a Seat on the Grand Canal, Dublin', 'October', 'Come Dance with Kitty Stobling' and 'The Hospital'.

38 John McGahern, *The Leavetaking* (London: Faber and Faber, 1974/ rev. ed. 1984), p. 168.

39 Ibid. p. 169.

40 Matthew Arnold, 'Dover Beach', in Lionel Trilling and Harold Bloom (eds), *The Oxford Anthology of English Literature: Victorian Prose*

and Poetry (New York: Oxford University Press), pp. 593–4: 'Listen! you hear the grating roar/Of pebbles which the waves draw back, and fling,/At their return, up the high strand,/Begin, and cease, and then again begin.'

41   Kavanagh, 'The Hospital', *Come Dance with Kitty Stobling*, p. 34.

CHAPTER 6

1   Saul Bellow, *It All Adds Up: From the Dim Past to the Uncertain Future* (New York: Viking, 1994), pp. 323–4.

2   John Montague, 'John Berryman: Henry in Dublin', in *The Figure in the Cave and Other Essays* (Dublin: The Lilliput Press, 1989), pp. 200–7 (p. 202).

3   Ibid. p. 201.

4   John Haffenden, *The Life of John Berryman* (London: Routledge & Kegan Paul, 1982), p. 89.

5   Berryman, in Peter Stitt, 'The Art of Poetry: An Interview with John Berryman', *Paris Review*, 53 (Winter 1972), pp. 176–207, reprinted in George Plimpton (ed.), *Writers at Work: The* Paris Review *Interviews* (London: Secker & Warburg, 1977), pp. 295–322 (p. 304).

6   Robert Lowell, 'For John Berryman', in Frank Bidart and David Gewanter (eds), *Robert Lowell: Collected Poems* (London: Faber and Faber, 2003), p. 737.

7   Eileen Simpson, *Poets in their Youth: A Memoir* (London: Faber and Faber, 1982), p. 239.

8   Montague, 'John Berryman', p. 202.

9   Ibid. p. 205.

10   Ibid. p. 206.

11   Ibid.

12   Robert Lowell, 'John Berryman', in Robert Giroux (ed.), *Collected Prose* (London: Faber and Faber, 1987), pp. 104–18 (p. 116).

13   Bellow, *It All Adds Up*, pp. 267 and 271.

14   Saul Bellow, *Humboldt's Gift* (New York: Viking Press, 1975), p. 118.

15   Bellow, *It All Adds Up*, p. 270.

16 Home to numerous mythological rock heroes such as Janis Joplin, who also died well before her time. Leonard Cohen's elegy on Joplin, 'The Chelsea Hotel', might serve as a moving coda to Berryman's own tragedy.

17 Haffenden, *John Berryman*, p. 419.

18 Ibid. p. 331.

CHAPTER 7

1 Ezra Pound, *ABC of Reading* (New York: New Directions, 1960), p. 32.

2 Derek Mahon, *Collected Poems* (Oldcastle: The Gallery Press, 1999), p. 147.

3 Ibid. p. 56.

4 Naomi Miki, *'We are seen by what we see': Derek Mahon and Japanese Literature*, unpublished MPhil dissertation (Dublin: School of English, Trinity College Dublin, 2004).

5 See Derek Mahon, *Theatre* (Oldcastle: The Gallery Press, 2013).

6 Hugh Haughton, *The Poetry of Derek Mahon* (Oxford: Oxford University Press, 2007).

7 Clíodhna Ní Anluain (ed.), *Reading the Future: Irish Writers in Conversation with Mike Murphy* (Dublin: The Lilliput Press, 2000), pp. 156–71.

8 Derek Mahon, *Harbour Lights* (Oldcastle: The Gallery Press, 2005), p. 61.

9 Ibid. p. 16.

10 Ezra Pound, *Selected Poems* (New York: New Directions, 1957), p. 99.

11 Mahon, 'Dawn at St. Patrick's', *Collected Poems*, pp. 169–71.

12 Mahon, 'St. Patrick's Day', *Collected Poems*, pp. 285–8.

13 Mahon, 'A Portrait of the Artist', *Collected Poems*, p. 23.

14 Mahon, 'Rage for Order', *Collected Poems*, p. 47.

15 Ibid. p. 68.

16 Matsuo Bashō, *The Narrow Road to the Deep North and Other Travel Sketches*, trans. by Nobuyuki Yuasa (London: Penguin Books, 1966), p. 33.

17 Mahon, 'A Refusal to Mourn', *Collected Poems*, p. 87.

18 Mahon, 'North Wind: Portrush', *Collected Poems*, p. 100.

19 Ibid. p. 109.

20 'Tractatus', *Collected Poems*, p. 120.

21 Mahon, 'Resistance Days', *Harbour Lights*, p. 18.

22 Eileen Battersby, 'Made in Belfast: An Interview with Derek Mahon', *Sunday Tribune*, 26 August 1990, p. 26.

23 Derek Mahon, 'shiver in your tenement', *The Yellow Book* (Oldcastle: The Gallery Press, 1997) pp. 18–19.

24 Derek Mahon, *Poems 1962–1978* (Oxford: Oxford University Press, 1979), p. 110.

25 Jimmy Kennedy was born in Omagh in 1902 but grew up in Portstewart. He died in Cheltenham, England in 1984.

26 Mahon, *Harbour Lights*, p. 57.

27 Seamus Deane, 'The Famous Seamus', *The New Yorker* (20 March 2000), pp. 54–79.

28 Gerard Fanning, personal correspondence to author. Tragically, Fanning died in 2017 after a protracted struggle with cancer. He was sixty-five.

29 Poets whom Seamus Deane has referred to in the past as influences include W.S. Merwin and James Tate. See John Brown (ed.), 'Seamus Deane', *In the Chair: Interviews with Poets from the North of Ireland* (Cliffs of Moher, Co. Clare: Salmon Publishing, 2002), pp. 97–107.

30 Seamus Deane, *Rumours* (Dublin: The Dolmen Press, 1977), p. 18.

31 Rosie Lavan, personal correspondence.

32 Personal correspondence.

33 Brown, 'Seamus Deane', p. 101.

34 Seamus Deane, *Gradual Wars* (Shannon: Irish University Press, 1972), p. 22.

35 See, for instance, Deane's essay, 'Walter Benjamin: The Construction of Hell', *Field Day Review*, 3 (2007), pp. 3–27.

36 Deane, *Gradual Wars*, p. 28.

37 Ibid. p. 25.

38 Ibid. pp. 15–16.

39 Ibid. p. 36.

40 In his review of *Gradual Wars*, Seamus Heaney identified this strain very early on: 'The tone is typically nervous, highly-strung, on the edge of violence or catastrophe, in the face or the aftermath of some climax … Love and death in a violent time, a time of killing, a time of terror and exhilaration, are the preoccupations of many of the poems.' ('Violence and Repose', *Hibernia Fortnightly Review*, 19 January 1973), p. 13. My thanks to Jonathan Williams for this reference.

41 Deane, 'Shelter', *Rumours*, pp. 50–1.

42 Seamus Deane, *Reading in the Dark* (London: Vintage Books, 1996), pp. 116–17.

43 Ibid. pp. 117–18.

44 Seamus Deane, *Foreign Affections: Essays on Edmund Burke* (Cork: Cork University Press, 2005).

45 Brown, 'Seamus Deane', p. 106.

46 Seamus Deane, 'Introduction', *Selected Plays of Brian Friel* (London: Faber and Faber, 1984).

47 Seamus Deane, 'History Lessons', *History Lessons* (Dublin: The Gallery Press, 1983), pp. 10–11.

48 Personal correspondence with the author.

49 Brown, 'Seamus Deane', p. 102.

50 Ibid. p. 103.

51 Deane, 'The Famous Seamus', p. 62.

52 'The Education of Seamus Heaney', *The New Yorker*, 20 March 2000, p. 62.

53 Seamus Deane, 'Reading Paradise Lost in Protestant Ulster, 1984', *Selected Poems* (Oldcastle: The Gallery Press, 1988), pp. 77–8.

CHAPTER 8

1 Stewart Parker, 'Northern Star', *Plays: 2* (London: Methuen, 2000), pp. 81–2.

2 Parker, 'Pentecost', *Plays: 2*, p. 192.

3 Ibid. pp. 207–8.

Endnotes

4 Ibid. p. 171.

5 Gerald Dawe, Maria Johnston and Clare Wallace (eds), *Stewart Parker: Dramatis Personae & Other Writings* (Prague: Litteraria Pragensia, 2008), p. 25.

6 Ibid. p. 35.

7 Ibid. pp. 37–8.

8 Ibid. p. 102.

9 Ibid. p. 122.

10 Ibid. pp. 65–6.

11 Stewart Parker, *High Pop: The Irish Times Column 1970–1976*, edited by Gerald Dawe and Maria Johnston (Belfast: Lagan Press, 2008), p. 353.

12 Dawe, *Dramatis Personae*, pp. 78–9.

13 Ibid. p. 73.

14 Parker, who was diagnosed with bone cancer at the age of twenty, had his left leg amputated. He died of inoperable cancer in 1988 at the tragically early age of forty-seven. See Marilyn Richtarik, *Stewart Parker: A Life* (Oxford: Oxford University Press, 2012), p. 31.

15 Dawe, *Dramatis Personae*, p. 69.

16 Ibid. p. 71.

17 Ibid. p. 74.

18 Parker, *High Pop*, p. 187.

19 Stewart Parker, 'Introduction', *Plays: 1*, p. x.

20 See Parker, *High Pop*, p. 359; p. 373; p. 126.

21 See Robert Johnstone, 'Playing for Ireland', *Honest Ulsterman*, 86 (Spring/Summer 1989), pp. 63–4.

22 Brian Cosgrove, *The Yew-Tree at the Head of the Strand* (Liverpool: Liverpool University Press, 2001), p. 183. I am indebted to Dr Maria Johnston for this reference.

23 Lynne Parker, 'Introduction', in Stewart Parker, *Plays: 1* (London: Methuen, 2000), p. xvi.

24 Dawe, *Dramatis Personae*, pp. 89–90.

25 Sam Thompson, *Over the Bridge*, edited with an introduction by Stewart Parker (Dublin: Gill & Macmillan, 1970). See also *Over the Bridge & other plays*, edited by John Keyes (Belfast: Lagan Press, 1997).

26 Dawe, *Dramatis Personae*, p. 104.

27 Ibid. p. 60.

28 Orangefield School (1957) was a well-known comprehensive located in the east of Belfast, and included among its alumni Van Morrison. As a result of local demographic changes it closed in 2014. See Dawe, *In Another World*.

29 W.A. Maguire, *Belfast: A History* (Lancaster: Carnegie Publishing, 2009), p. 234.

30 Stewart Parker, 'Me & Jim', *Dramatis Personae*, p. 98.

31 Ibid. p. 116.

32 See, for instance, Gillian McIntosh, *The Force of Culture: Unionist Identities in Twentieth-century Ireland* (Cork: Cork University Press, 1999), Gail McConnell, *Northern Irish Poetry and Theology* (Basingstoke: Palgrave Macmillan, 2014) and Adam Hanna, *Northern Ireland Poetry and Domestic Space* (Basingstoke: Palgrave Macmillan, 2015).

33 Stewart Parker, 'Signposts', *Dramatis Personae*, pp. 102–9 (p. 104).

34 Parker, 'Signposts', *Theatre Ireland* (Autumn 1985), pp. 27–9, reprinted in *Dramatis Personae*, p. 108.

35 Dawe, *Dramatis Personae*, p. 23. See also Parker's remarks on Brecht, p. 14.

36 Parker, *High Pop*, pp. 178–9.

CHAPTER 9

1 Eavan Boland, 'A Final Thought', in Dan Sheehan, Joanne O'Leary, Eoin Nolan, Anna Kinsella (eds), *Icarus:60 Years of Creative Writing from Trinity College* (Dublin: Dublin University Publications, 2010), p. 241.

2 Jody Allen Randolph (ed.), *Eavan Boland: A Sourcebook* (Manchester: Carcanet Press, 2007) contains a useful bibliography of 'Selected Articles by Eavan Boland', particularly relevant here, pp. 192–207.

3 Boland attended Trinity College between 1962 and 1966 and was appointed junior lecturer in English, a post from which she resigned in 1968.

4   Philip Edwards was Edward Dowden Professor of English Literature (1867) in the Department of English, Trinity College Dublin (1960–6).

5   David Norris: Lecturer in English at TCD (1968–96) and member of Seanad Éireann (1987–present).

6   Mary Robinson was Reid Professor of Law, TCD and subsequently president of Ireland (1990–7).

7   Eavan Boland, *Object Lessons: The Life of the Woman and the Poet in Our Time* (Manchester: Carcanet Press, 1995).

8   Ibid. p. 249.

9   Ibid. pp. 98–100.

10 Ibid. pp. 138–40.

11 Derek Mahon, 'Young Eavan and Early Boland', *Irish University Review: Special Issue – Eavan Boland*, 23, 1 (Spring/Summer 1993), p. 24. Mahon would recall these days in prose reminiscences, including 'Yeats and the Lights of Dublin' and 'Icarus in the Ignorance Age' in *Selected Prose* (Oldcastle: The Gallery Press, 2012), pp. 64–75 and pp. 241–3 and, on a slightly earlier frame of reference, in the sequence 'Decadence 4: shiver in your tenement', *New Collected Poems* (Oldcastle: The Gallery Press, 2011), pp. 201–2.

12 See Edna Longley's rebuttal of 'the origin-myth' in 'Encryptions', *The Yellow Nib*, 10 (Spring 2015), p. 55, a review of Stephen Enniss's *After the Titanic: A Life of Derek Mahon*.

13 From her Trinity College contemporaries: *Night-Crossing* (1968), *Lives* (1972), *The Snow Party* (1975) by Derek Mahon; *No Continuing City* (1969), *An Exploded View* (1973), *Man Lying on a Wall* (1976) by Michael Longley; *Acts and Monuments* (1972), *Site of Ambush* (1975) *The Second Voyage* (1977) by Eiléan Ní Chuilleanáin; and *My Dark Fathers* (1964), *Getting up Early* (1966), *Selected Poems* (1969), *Shelley in Dublin* (1974), *A Kind of Trust* (1975) by Brendan Kennelly, who had also edited *The Penguin Book of Irish Verse* in 1970 which included Boland as the penultimate poet: 'Her book *New Territory* put her with the leading younger poets of Ireland', ran the editorial note (p. 27).

14 A year before *North* was published, Boland moderated and published in *The Irish Times* (5 July 1974), 'The Clash of Identities', an important round table of discussions with poets, politicians and paramilitaries which, forty years later, deserves republication.

15 Andrew Motion and Blake Morrison (eds), *The Penguin Book of Contemporary British Poetry* (Harmondsworth: Penguin Books, 1982). The other poets from Northern Ireland were Michael Longley, Medbh McGuckian, Derek Mahon, Paul Muldoon and Tom Paulin.

16 The first series appeared in 1983: Tom Paulin, 'A New Look at the Language Question', Seamus Heaney, 'An Open Letter' and Seamus Deane 'Civilians and Barbarians'. Boland's review 'Poets and Pamphlets' was published in the *Irish Times*, 1 October 1983.

17 Eavan Boland, *A Kind of Scar: The Woman Poet in a National Tradition* (Lip Pamphlet, Dublin: Attic Press, 1989).

18 Edna Longley, *From Cathleen to Anorexia: The Breakdown of Irelands* (Lip Pamphlet, Dublin: Attic Press, 1990).

19 Gerald Dawe (ed.), *The Younger Irish Poets* (Belfast: Blackstaff Press, 1982).

20 A second edition, *The New Younger Irish Poets*, edited by the author was published by Blackstaff Press in 1991.

21 Eavan Boland, 'The War Horse', *New Collected Poems* (Manchester: Carcanet Press, 2005), p. 39.

22 Boland, *Object Lessons*, pp. 176–9.

23 Eavan Boland, *A Critical Companion: Poetry, Prose, Interviews, Reviews and Criticism* (New York: W.W. Norton & Company, 2008), p. 81.

24 Boland, *Object Lessons*, p. 179.

25 Caitríona O'Reilly, 'Notes to Self', *Irish Times*, 4 June 2011.

26 Eavan Boland, *A Journey with Two Maps: Becoming a Woman Poet* (Manchester: Carcanet Press, 2011).

27 See Gerald Dawe, 'The Suburban Night: On Eavan Boland, Paul Durcan and Thomas McCarthy', in Elmer Andrews (ed.), *Contemporary Irish Poetry: A Collection of Critical Essays* (London: Macmillan, 1992), pp. 168–93 and republished in *The Proper Word:*

Endnotes

Ireland, Poetry, Politics Collected Criticism (New York: Fordham University Press, 2007), pp. 276–97.

28 Eavan Boland, *After Every War: Twentieth Century Women Poets* (New Jersey: Princeton University Press, 2004), pp. 5–6.

29 Eiléan Ní Chuilleanáin, 'Rousing the Reader', *Dublin Review of Books*, 1 April 2015.

30 Helen Cooney and Mark Sweetnam (eds), *Enigma and Revelation in Renaissance English Literature: Essays Presented to Eiléan Ní Chuilleanáin* (Dublin: Four Courts Press, 2012).

31 Ibid. p. 9.

32 Eiléan Ní Chuilleanáin, *Selected Poems* (Oldcastle: The Gallery Press, 2008), p. 75.

33 Ibid. p. 116.

34 Aingeal Clare, 'The Boys of Bluehill by Eiléan Ní Chuilleanáin', *The Guardian*, 20 May 2015.

35 Eiléan Ní Chuilleanáin, *The Sun-Fish* (Oldcastle: The Gallery Press, 2009), p. 44.

36 Seamus Heaney's comment is included on the cover of *Selected Poems*.

37 'Special Issue: Eiléan Ní Chuilleanáin', *Irish University Review*, 37, 1 (Spring/Summer 2007).

38 Matthew Campbell (ed.), *The Cambridge Companion to Contemporary Irish Poetry* (Cambridge: Cambridge University Press, 2003).

39 Justin Quinn, *The Cambridge Introduction to Modern Irish Poetry 1800–2000* (Cambridge: Cambridge University Press, 2008).

40 Patricia Boyle Haberstroh, *The Female Figure in Eiléan Ní Chuilleanáin's Poetry* (Cork: Cork University Press, 2013).

41 Ní Chuilleanáin, *Selected Poems*, p. 89.

42 Eiléan Ní Chuilleanáin, *The Boys of Bluehill* (Oldcastle: The Gallery Press, 2015), p. 11.

43 Ibid. p. 54.

CHAPTER 10

1   At one point in 'A Love', the unnamed woman asks: '"Have you ever been to the West?" "No", I said. "You'll never understand this country till you have."' Neil Jordan, *Night in Tunisia and Other Stories* (Dublin: Writers Co-Op, 1976), p. 114.

2   Seán O'Faoláin, 'Introduction', *Night in Tunisia*, n. p.

3   Jordan, *Night in Tunisia*, pp. 105–6.

4   Ibid. p. 111.

5   Ibid. p. 105.

6   Gerard Fanning; in conversation with the author, 14 August 2007.

7   Tóibín is from Enniscorthy, Co. Wexford, McGuinness from Buncrana, Co. Donegal, the late O'Driscoll was from Thurles, Co. Tipperary, and Patrick King from Co. Galway, as is Des Hogan. Kearney is from Cork.

8   Rightly or wrongly, according to Derek Mahon, 'Modernist Poets', *Irish Times*, 16 July 1987, p. 9. The story of Northern Poetry has been told many times before, but for a fuller treatment of the subject readers might like to consult Heather Clark, *The Ulster Renaissance: Poetry in Belfast, 1962–1972* (Oxford: Oxford University Press, 2006), while the author's 'History Class: On "Northern Poetry"', in his *The Proper Word: Ireland, Poetry, Politics, Collected Criticism* looks at the critical genesis of the idea of Northern poetry.

9   Sebastian Barry (ed.), *The Inherited Boundaries: The Younger Poets of the Republic of Ireland* (Dublin: The Dolmen Press, 1986), p. 14.

10 Dawe, 'Anecdotes over a Jar', *The Proper Word*, pp. 107–16.

11 In works such as *States of Ireland* (1972), *Writers and Politics* (1965/76) and *Herod: Reflections on Political Violence* (1978).

12 O'Faoláin, 'Introduction', n. p.

13 See Dawe, 'Writers from the South of Ireland', *Fortnight* [Belfast] on: Thomas Kilroy, 176 (May 1980), pp. 19–20; Paul Durcan, 177 (July 1980), pp. 15–16; Neil Jordan, 178 (October 1980), pp. 19–20; Harry Clifton, 180 (March 1981), pp. 14–15 and 'One Stone for the Indifferent Cairn: The Southern Literary Scene', 181 (May 1981),

pp. 17–18. Collected as 'Making History' in *The World as Province: Selected Prose 1980–2008* (Belfast: Lagan Press, 2009) (pp. 72–92). See also Dawe, *The Proper Word*, p. 329, n. 16.

14   Dawe, *The Younger Irish Poets*, p. xi.

15   For example, Gerard Fanning's 'Waiting on Lemass', from his long-delayed first collection, *Easter Snow* (Dublin: Dedalus Press, 1992); Harry Clifton's 'Reasons of State', in *Comparative Lives* (Dublin: The Gallery Press, 1982); Dennis O' Driscoll's 'Death Duties', in *Kist* (Mountrath: Dolmen Press, 1982); and Aidan Mathews's 'Minding Ruth', in *Minding Ruth* (Dublin: The Gallery Press, 1983).

16   Colm Tóibín, *Walking Along the Border*, with photographs by Tony O'Shea (London: Queen Anne Press, 1987), p. 20. Subsequently published as *Bad Blood: A Walk Along the Irish Border* (London: Vintage Books, 1994).

17   Gerald Dawe, 'Child of the Revolution', *Of War and War's Alarms: Reflections on Modern Irish Writing* (Cork: Cork University Press, 2015), pp. 75–85.

18   Richard Ryan, *Ledges* (Dublin: The Dolmen Press, 1970), *Ravenswood* (Dublin: The Dolmen Press, 1973).

19   Fanning, in conversation with the author, 14 August 2007.

20   Tóibín, *Walking Along the Border*, p. 74.

21   Hugo Hamilton, *The Speckled People* (London: Fourth Estate, 2003). All further references, unless otherwise noted, are from this edition.

22   Elias Canetti, 'My Earliest Memory', *The Tongue Set Free* (London: Granta, 2011), p. 3.

23   Hugo Hamilton, 'Speaking to the Walls in English', publicity handout, n. p.

24   Hamilton, *The Speckled People*, p. 44.

25   Ibid. pp. 46–7.

26   Ibid. p. 132.

27   Ibid. p. 7.

28   Ibid. p. 295.

29   Ibid. p. 268.

CHAPTER 11

1   David Beresford, *Ten Men Dead: The Story of the 1981 Hunger Strike* (London: Grafton Books, 1987).

2   Ibid. p. 55.

3   Ibid.

4   Ibid. p. 88.

5   Ibid. pp. 98–9.

6   Ibid. p. 99.

7   Ethna Carbery, *The Four Winds of Eirinn: Poems* (Dublin: M.H. Gill, 1927), pp. 121–2.

8   Seamus MacManus, 'A Memoir of Ethna Carbery', *The Four Winds of Eirinn: Poems by Ethna Carbery. (Anna MacManus)* (Dublin: M.H. Gill & Son, 1927), p. xxi.

9   Louis de Paor, *Leabhar na hAthghabhála: Poems of repossession: 20th century poetry in Irish* (Hexham: Bloodaxe, 2016), pp. 160–3.

10   This line would provide the title to *The Same Age as The State: The Autobiography of Máire Cruise O'Brien* (Dublin: O'Brien Press, 2004).

11   Alice Milligan, *Poems* (Dublin: M.H. Gill, 1954), p. 139.

12   His papers are available at Trinity College Dublin Library.

13   Eileán Ní Chuilleanáin (ed.), *'As I was among the Captives': Joseph Campbell's Prison Diary, 1922–1923* (Cork: Cork University Press, 2001), p. 4.

14   Padraic Fiacc, *By the Black Stream: Selected Poems 1947–1967* (Dublin: The Dolmen Press, 1969).

15   A perennial outsider, Padraic Fiacc (real name, Patrick Joseph O'Connor) has remained outside the Northern republican pantheon and has also been much overlooked by the critical and literary establishment. See Gerald Dawe and Aodán MacPólin (eds), *Ruined Pages: New Selected Poems of Padraic Fiacc* (Belfast: Lagan Press, 2013).

16   Austin Clarke (ed. and intro.), *The Poems of Joseph Campbell* (Dublin: A. Figgis, 1963), p. 16.

17   Brian Moore, *The Lonely Passion of Judith Hearne* (London: André Deutsch, 1955), *The Emperor of Ice Cream* (London: Mayflower Books, 1970) and *Lies of Silence* (London: Vintage Books, 1992).

18 See Marianne Elliott, *The Catholics of Ulster: A History* (London: Allen Lane, 2000).

19 Clarke, *The Poems of Joseph Campbell*, p. 109.

20 Moore, *The Emperor of Ice Cream*, p. 36.

21 Ibid. pp. 36–7.

22 Ibid. p. 217.

23 Patricia Craig, *Brian Moore: A Biography* (London: Bloomsbury, 2002), p. 248.

24 Moore, *Lies of Silence*, p. 61.

25 Ibid. p. 62.

26 Ibid. pp. 69–70.

27 Ibid. pp. 79–80.

28 Ibid. p. 82.

29 Clifton Street, Brian Moore's family home, was situated across the road.

30 Moore, *Lies of Silence*, p. 82.

31 Ibid. p. 102.

32 Ibid. p. 135.

33 Gerry Moriarty, 'Gunman. Hunger Striker. Dramatist. Laurence McKeown', News Review, *The Irish Times* (13 August 2016), pp. 4–5.

34 Bobby Sands, *Writings from Prison* (Cork: Mercier Press, 1998), p. 43.

35 David McKittrick, Seamus Kelters, Brian Feeney, Chris Thornton and David McVea, *Lost Lives: the stories of men, women and children who died as a result of the Northern Ireland conflict* (Edinburgh: Mainstream Publishing, 2007), p. 1,526.

36 Sands, *Writings from Prison*, p. 46.

37 Ibid. pp. 103–4.

38 Ibid. p. 205.

39 Ibid. pp. 205–6.

40 Ibid. p. 185.

41 Milltown Cemetery, Belfast, would be Bobby Sands's final resting place. He was buried there on 7 May 1981, two days after his death in Long Kesh prison after sixty-six days on hunger strike. Sands was twenty-seven.

42   Sands, *Writings from Prison*, p. 186.

43   Terry Moylan (ed.), *The Indignant Muse: Poetry and Songs of the Irish Revolutions, 1887–1926* (Dublin: The Lilliput Press, 2016).

44   From Seamus Heaney, 'The Flight Path', *Opened Ground: Poems 1966–1996* (London: Faber and Faber, 1998), p. 413. See also 'Station Island: IX' *Opened Ground*, pp. 261–2. The encounter is recalled in Dennis O'Driscoll, *Stepping Stones: Interviews with Seamus Heaney* (London: Faber and Faber, 2008), pp. 257–61.

<h2 style="text-align:center">Chapter 12</h2>

1   Patrick Kavanagh, *Collected Poems*, ed. Antoinette Quinn (London: Allen Lane, 2004), p. 184.

2   Frank Ormsby (ed. and intro.), *Poets from the North of Ireland* (Belfast: Blackstaff Press, 1979).

3   I have in mind here recent monographs such as Guy Woodward, *Culture, Northern Ireland and the Second World War* (Oxford: Oxford University Press, 2015).

4   Hewitt, *A North Light*, edited by Frank Ferguson and Kathryn White (Dublin: Four Courts Press, 2013), p. 72.

5   Hewitt, *A North Light*, p. 20.

6   See Sandra O'Connell, *George Reavey (1907–1976): The Endless Chain, a literary biography* [Thesis 7783] (Dublin: School of English, Trinity College Dublin, 2006).

7   Samuel Putnam, 'Foreword to a Sunken Continent', in George Reavey, *Faust's Metamorphoses* (Fontenay-Aux-Roses: New Review, 1932), pp. 7–9.

8   Denis Devlin, *Selected Poems*, edited with a preface by Allen Tate and Robert Penn Warren (New York: Holt, Rinehart and Winston, 1963), p. 14.

9   J.C.C. Mays, 'Introductory Essay', *Irish University Review*, 5, 1 (Spring 1975), p. 12.

10   Derek Mahon, 'MacNeice in Ireland and England' in Terence Brown (ed.), *Journalism: Selected Prose 1970–1995* (Oldcastle: The Gallery Press, 1996), p. 21.

11   George Reavey, *Soviet Literature To-Day* (London: Lindsay Drummond, 1946).

12   I am indebted to Dr Sandra O'Connell for this reference from private correspondence with the poet Kathleen Raine (1908–2003).

13   Edna Longley, *Louis MacNeice: A Study* (London: Faber and Faber, 1988), p. 17.

14   Ibid. p. 40.

15   George Reavey, *Nostradam* (Paris: Europa Press, 1935).

16   Kay Donnelly and Gerald Dawe (eds), *Heroic Heart: A Charles Donnelly Reader* (Belfast: Lagan Press, 2012).

17   Dawe and MacPoilin, *Ruined Pages.*

18   Ormsby, *Poets from the North of Ireland*, p. 5.

19   Ibid. xi.

20   Lucy Collins, *Poetry by Women in Ireland 1870–1970, a critical anthology* (Liverpool: Liverpool University Press, 2014). See also Lucy Collins, *Contemporary Irish Women Poets: Memory and Estrangement* (Liverpool: Liverpool University Press, 2015). Readers might care to consult the included work of little-known women poets in the author's, *Earth Voices Whispering: an anthology of Irish war poetry 1918–1945* (Belfast: Blackstaff Press, 2008).

21   Frank Ormsby (ed. and intro.), *Poets from the North of Ireland: New Edition* (Belfast: Blackstaff Press, 1990).

22   Sinead Morrissey and Stephen Connolly (eds), *The Future always makes me so thirsty: New Poets from the North of Ireland* (Belfast: Blackstaff Press, 2016).

23   John Wilson Foster, *Forces and themes in Ulster Fiction* (Dublin: Gill & Macmillan, 1974).

24   Hewitt, *A North Light*, p. 171.

25   Frank Ormsby and Michael Longley (eds), *John Hewitt: Selected Poems* (Belfast: Blackstaff Press, 2007).

26   Seamus Heaney, 'The Poetry of John Hewitt', *Threshold*, 22 (Summer 1969), pp. 73–7, republished in *Preoccupations: Selected Prose 1968–1978* (London: Faber and Faber, 1980).

27   Sinead Morrissey, *Parallax* (Manchester: Carcanet Press, 2013).

28 Definition as shown in the Oxford English Dictionary.
29 Morrissey, 'Baltimore', *Parallax*, p. 12.

CHAPTER 13

1 *Hare Soup* (London: Faber and Faber, 2004), *Gethsemane Day* (London: Faber and Faber, 2006) and *Long-Distance Swimmer* (Cliffs of Moher; Salmon Poetry, 2010).
2 'Snow', *The Collected Poems of Louis MacNeice*, edited by Peter MacDonald (London: Faber and Faber, 2007), p. 24.
3 'The dream-world of my pillow', *Gethsemane Day*, p. 45.
4 'Waiting for Julio', *Long-Distance Swimmer*, p. 27.
5 'My Daddy's a Skeleton"', *Gethsemane Day*, p. 38.
6 'Ice Maiden', *Hare Soup*, p. 10.
7 *The Blue End of Stars* (Oldcastle: Gallery Press, 2012).
8 'Halcyon', *The Blue End of Stars*, p. 25.
9 Bashō, *The Narrow Road to the Deep North and Other Travel Pieces*, translated from the Japanese with an introduction by Nobuyuki Yuasa (London: Penguin Books, 1966), p. 116.
10 *The Flower and the Frozen Sea* (Oldcastle: Gallery Press, 2015).
11 Lucy Collins, *Biographical Entry: Michele O'Sullivan*, *Poetry International Web*: http://www.poetryinternationalweb.net/pi/site/poet/item/28852/Michelle-OSullivan
12 'From Moyview', *The Flower and the Frozen Sea*, p. 15.
13 'The Flower and the Frozen Sea', ibid. p. 59.
14 Ibid. p. 64.
15 'Kintsukuroi', ibid. p. 48.
16 Lucy Collins, *Biographical Entry: Michele O'Sullivan*, *Poetry International Web*: http://www.poetryinternationalweb.net/pi/site/poet/item/28852/Michelle-OSullivan
17 Leontia Flynn, *These Days* (2004), *Drives* (2008), *Profit and Loss* (2011)) and *The Radio* (2017) are published by Jonathan Cape, London. She has also published a monograph, *Reading Medbh McGuckian* (Dublin: Irish Academic Press, 2014).

18 For instance, 'Our Fathers' (*Drives*, pp. 53–5) and 'My Father's Language' (*Profit and Loss*, p. 28) among them.
19 'Barcelona' *Drives*, p. 16.
20 'Samuel Beckett', p. 11, 'Marcel Proust', p. 26; 'Elizabeth Bishop', p. 34, and 'George Orwell's Death', p. 43.
21 'April, 7 P.M.', *These Days*, p. 36.
22 'Mangles', ibid. p. 53, and 'this *Creda* cooker' ('The Oven', *Profit and Loss*, p. 4).
23 *Profit and Loss*, pp. 35–45.
24 *The Radio*, pp. 11 and 17.
25 Ibid. p. 21.
26 Ibid. p. 31–3.
27 Ibid. pp. 55–65.
28 'Drive', *Drives*, pp. 50–1.

Chapter 14

1 Thomas Kilroy, 'The Writers' Group in Galway', *Irish Times,* 8 April 1976, p. 10.
2 Michael Finlan, 'Ten-Week Course for Writers opens in U.C.G.', *Irish Times*, 19 January 1976, p. 11.
3 Kilroy, 'The Writers' Group in Galway', p. 10.
4 Ibid.
5 One such instance was the 'Group' of Northern poets at Queen's University Belfast, which met under moderator Philip Hobsbaum. See Heather Clarke, 'The Belfast Group', *The Ulster Renaissance: Poetry in Belfast 1962–1972* (Oxford: Oxford University Press, 2006), pp. 43–71.
6 In 1986, the School of English, Trinity College Dublin, in association with the Arts Council of Ireland established the Irish Writer Fellowship, with Derek Mahon as the inaugural Fellow.
7 See 'Fighting Words', http://www.fightingwords.ie
8 Louis Simpson, 'On the Neglect of Poetry in the United States', *Ships Going into the Blue: Essays and Notes on Poetry* (Ann Arbor, MI: University of Michigan Press, 1994), p. 88.

9   Even though the context is poetry in the United States, Simpson's remarks are worth quoting in full: 'Yes, many books of verse are published in the States every year, and many poetry readings are taking place, mostly on college campuses. On the other hand, the books are read by no one but poets and would-be poets, and the audiences at readings are composed of the same people, those who have a professional interest in poetry, that is, poetry as a means of getting a job … teaching "creative writing".' (Simpson, 'On the Neglect of Poetry in the United States', p. 85).

10   Simpson, 'On the Neglect of Poetry in the United States', p. 87.

11   See George Monteiro (ed.), *Conversations with Elizabeth Bishop* (Jackson, MS: University Press of Mississippi, 1996), p. 38.

12   Simpson, 'Theater business', *Ships Going into the Blue*, p. 41.

13   Elif Batuman, 'Get a real degree', *London Review of Books*, 32, 18 (2010), pp. 3–8.

14   Louis Menand, 'Show or Tell: Should Creative Writing be Taught?' *The New Yorker*, 8 and 15 June 2009.

15   Mark McGurl, *The Program Era: Postwar Fiction and the Role of Creative Writing* (Cambridge, MA: Harvard University Press, 2009).

16   Batuman, 'Get a real degree', p. 7.

17   Ibid.

18   Ibid. p. 11.

19   Ibid.

20   Ibid. p. 12.

21   Ibid. p. 15.

22   Louis Menand, 'Show or Tell', p. 111.

23   Ibid. p. 112.

24   Simpson, 'On the Neglect of Poetry in the United States', p. 91.

EPILOGUE

1   Oliver Goldsmith, *Selected Writings*, edited with an introduction and afterword by John Lucas (Manchester: Carcanet/Fyfield Books, 1988), p. 177.

2   Ibid. pp. 102–6.

3   Elizabeth Bowen, *Pictures and Conversation: Chapters of an Autobiography* (London: Allen Lane, 1975), pp. 22–3.

4   W.B. Yeats, *Explorations* (London, Macmillan, 1962), p. 293.

5   W.B. Yeats, *The Poems*, p. 241.

6   Thomas Kilroy, 'Anglo-Irish Playwrights and Comic Tradition', *The Crane Bag*, 3, 2 (1979), pp. 19–27.

7   Thomas Kilroy, 'The Anglo-Irish Theatrical Imagination', *Búllan*, 3.2 (Winter 1997/Spring 1998), pp. 5–12.

8   Thomas Kilroy, 'The Literary Tradition of Irish Drama', in W. Richleand and H. Kieper (eds), *Anglistentag Proceedings*, XVI (Tubingen: Max Niemeyer Verlag, 1995), pp. 7–15.

9   Thomas Kilroy, 'Two Playwrights: Yeats and Beckett', in Joseph Ronsley (ed.), *Myth and Reality in Irish Literature* (Waterloo, ON: Wilfrid Laurier University Press, 1977), pp. 183–95.

10   Kilroy, 'Anglo-Irish Playwrights and Comic Tradition', pp. 25–6.

11   Ibid. p. 26.

12   Ibid. pp. 20–1.

13   Goldsmith, *Selected Writings*, p. 104.

14   Ibid. p. 105.

15   Ibid.

16   Ibid. p. 106.

17   Michael Griffin, *Enlightenment in Ruins: The Geographies of Oliver Goldsmith* (Lewisburg, PA: Bucknell University Press, 2013).

18   Samuel Beckett, *Malone Dies* (London: Faber and Faber, 2010), p. 4.

19   Goldsmith, *Selected Writings*, p. 106.

BIBLIOGRAPHY

Armstrong, Gordon, *Samuel Beckett, W. B. Yeats and Jack Yeats: Images and Words* (Lewisburg,Pennsylvania: Pennsylvania University Press, 1990)

Atik, Anne, *How It Was: A Memoir of Samuel Beckett* (London:Thames and Hudson, 2001)

Bair, Deirdre, *Samuel Beckett: A Biography* (London: Picador, 1980)

Bardon, Jonathan, *A History of Belfast* (Belfast: Blackstaff Press, 1992)

Barry, Sebastian (ed.), *The Inherited Boundaries: The Younger Poets of the Republic of Ireland* (Dublin:The Dolmen Press, 1986)

Bashō, Matsuo, *The Narrow Road to the Deep North and Other Travel Sketches* (London: Penguin Books, 1966)

Batten, Guinn, 'Boland, McGuckian, Ní Chuilleanáin and the body of the nation', *The Cambridge Companion to Contemporary Irish Poetry*, ed. Matthew Campbell (Cambridge: Cambridge University Press, 2003)

Batuman, Elif, 'Get a real degree', *London Review of Books* 32:18 (23 September 2010)

Beckett, Samuel, *More Pricks than Kicks* (London: Calder Publications 1993 [London: Chatto & Windus, 1934])

—, *The Collected Poems*, ed. Seán Lawlor and John Pilling (London: Faber and Faber, 2012)

—, *The Complete Shorter Prose 1929–1989*, ed. S. E. Gontarski (New York: Grove Press, 1995)

—, *Disjecta: Miscellaneous Writings and a Dramatic Fragment*, ed. Ruby Cohn (London: Calder, 1983)

—, *Molloy* (London: Faber and Faber, 2009 [1951])

—, *Malone Dies* (London: Faber and Faber, 2010 [1951])

—, *Echo's Bones* edited with an introduction by Mark Nixon (London: Faber and Faber, 2015)

The Letters of Samuel Beckett, Vol.1: 1929–1940 ed. Martha Dow Fehsenfeld, Lois More Overleck, Dan Gunn, George Craig (Cambridge: Cambridge University Press, 2009)

Behan, Brendan, *Borstal Boy* (London: Arrow Books, [1958] 1990)

Bellow, Saul, *It All Adds Up: From the Dim Past to the Uncertain Future* (New York: Viking, 1994)

Beresford, David, *Ten Men Dead: The Story of the 1981 Hunger Strike* (London: Grafton Books, 1987)

Boland, Eavan, *After Every War: Twentieth-Century Women Poets*, translations from the German (New Jersey: Princeton University Press, 2004)

—, *A Journey with Two Maps: Becoming a Woman Poet* (Manchester: Carcanet Press, 2007)

—, *New Collected Poems* (Manchester: Carcanet Press, 2005)

—, 'A Final Thought', ed. Dan Sheehan, Joanne O'Leary, Eoin Nolan, Anna Kinsella, *Icarus: 60 Years of Creative Writing from Trinity College* (Dublin: Dublin University Publications, 2010)

—, *Object Lessons: The Life of the Woman and the Poet in Our Time* (Manchester: Carcanet Press, 1995)

Böll, Heinrich, *Irish Journal* (Chicago, Illinois: Northwestern University Press, 1967)

Bowen, Elizabeth, *Collected Impressions* (New York: Longmans Green, 1950)

—, *Pictures and Conversations: Chapters of an Autobiography* (London: Allen Lane, 1975)

Brown, John, *In the Chair: Interviews with Poets from the North of Ireland* (Cliffs of Moher, Co. Clare: Salmon Publishing, 2002)

Brown, Terence, *Ireland: A Social and Cultural History 1922 to 2002* (London: Harper Perennial 2004 [1985])

—, *The Life of W. B. Yeats* (London: Blackwell, 1999; Dublin: Gill & Macmillan, 2001)

Campbell, Joseph, *The Poems of Joseph Campbell,* edited with an introduction by Austin Clarke (Dublin: A. Figgis, 1963)

Campbell, Matthew (ed.), *The Cambridge Companion to Contemporary Irish Poetry* (Cambridge: Cambridge University Press, 2003)

Canetti, Elias, *The Tongue Set Free* (London: Granta, 2011 [1979])

Carbery, Ethna, *The Four Winds of Eirinn: Poems by Ethna Carbery (Anna MacManus),* new edition, with memoir and additional poems (Dublin: M. H. Gill & Son, 1918)

Carlson, Julia, *Banned in Ireland: Censorship & the Irish Writer* (London: Routledge, 1990)

Clare, Aingeal, http://www.theguardian.com/books/2015/may/29/the-boys-of-bluehill-eilean-ni-chuilleanain-review

Clark, Heather, *The Ulster Renaissance: Poetry in Belfast 1962–1972* (Oxford: Oxford University Press, 2006)

Collins, Lucy, *Contemporary Irish Women Poets: Memory and Estrangement* (Liverpool: Liverpool University Press, 2015)

—, *Poetry by Women in Ireland 1870–1970: A Critical Anthology* (Liverpool: Liverpool University Press, 2012)

Cooney, Helen, and Mark Sweetnam (eds), *Enigma and Revelation in Renaissance English Literature: Essays Presented to Eiléan Ní Chuilleanáin* (Dublin: Four Courts, 2012)

Cosgrove, Brian, *The Yew-Tree at the Head of the Strand* (Liverpool: Liverpool University Press, 2001)

Craig, Patricia, *Brian Moore: A Biography* (London: Bloomsbury, 2002)

Cronin, Anthony, *Heritage Now: Irish Literature in the English Language* (Dingle: Brandon Books, 1982)

—, *Dead as Doornails* (Dublin: The Lilliput Press, 1999 [Dublin: The Dolmen Press, 1976])

—, *Samuel Beckett: The Last Modernist* (London: HarperCollins, 1996)

Dawe, Gerald, *The Proper Word: Ireland, Poetry, Politics: Collected Criticism,* ed. Nicholas Allen (Nebraska: Creighton University Press, 2007)

—, *In Another World: Van Morrison & Belfast* (Newbridge, Co.Kildare: Merrion Press, 2017)

— (ed.), *The Younger Irish Poets* (Belfast: Blackstaff Press 1982; 1991)

—, *Of War and War's Alarms: Reflections on Modern Irish Writing* (Cork: Cork University Press, 2015)

Deane, Seamus, *Gradual Wars* (Shannon: Irish University Press, 1972)

—, *Rumours* (Dublin: The Dolmen Press, 1977)

—, *History Lessons* (Dublin: The Gallery Press, 1983)

—, *Selected Poems* (Oldcastle, Co.Meath: The Gallery Press, 1988)

—, *Reading in the Dark* (London: Vintage, 1996)

—, 'The Education of Seamus Heaney', *The New Yorker*, 20 March 2000

—, *Foreign Affections: Essays on Edmund Burke* (Cork: Cork University Press, 2005)

—, 'Walter Benjamin: The Construction of Hell', *Field Day Review*, 3, 2007

de Paor, Louis, *Leabhar na hAthghabhala: Poems of Repossession: 20th-Century Poetry in Irish* (Hexham, Northumberland: Bloodaxe, 2016)

Devlin, Denis, *Selected Poems*, edited with a preface by Allen Tate and Robert Penn Warren (New York: Holt, Rinehart and Winston, 1963)

Donleavy, J.P., *The Ginger Man* (London: Abacus, 1996 [1955])

Donnelly, Charles, *Heroic Heart: A Reader*, ed. Kay Donnelly with Gerald Dawe (Belfast: Lagan Press, 2012)

Dukes, Gerry, *Samuel Beckett: Penguin Illustrated Lives* (London: Penguin, 2001)

Elliott, Marianne, *The Catholics of Ulster: A History* (London: Allen Lane, 2000)

Ellmann, Richard, *Four Dubliners: Wilde, Yeats, Joyce, and Beckett* (London: Hamish Hamilton, 1986)

Fallon, Brian, *An Age of Innocence: Irish Culture 1930–1960* (Dublin: Gill & Macmillan, 1998)

Farrell, J.G., *Troubles* (London: Jonathan Cape, 1970)

Ferriter, Diarmuid, *The Transformation of Ireland* (New York: Overlook Press, 2005)

Fiacc, Padraic, *By the Black Stream: Selected Poems 1947–1967* (Dublin: The Dolmen Press, 1969)

—, *Ruined Pages: New Selected Poems* (Belfast: Lagan Press, 2012)

Bibliography

Fogarty, Anne (ed.), 'Eiléan Ní Chuilleanáin: Special Issue', *Irish University Review: A Journal of Irish Studies.* Spring/Summer 2007

Foster, Roy, *W. B. Yeats: A Life. Vol. II The Arch Poet* (Oxford: Oxford University Press, 2003)

Friel, Brian, *Philadelphia, Here I Come!* (London: Faber and Faber, 1965)

Garvin, Tom, *News from a New Republic: Ireland in the 1950s* (Dublin: Gill & Macmillan, 2010)

Goldsmith, Oliver, *Selected Writings*, edited with an introduction and afterword by John Lucas (Manchester: Carcanet/Fyfield Books, 1988)

Greacen, Lavinia, *J. G. Farrell: The Making of a Writer*, 2nd ed. (Cork: Cork University Press, 2012)

Grene, Nicholas, *Yeats's Poetic Codes* (Oxford: Oxford University Press, 2008)

Griffin, Michael, *Enlightenment in Ruins: The Geographies of Oliver Goldsmith* (Lewisburg, Pennsylvania: Bucknell University Press, 2013)

Haberstroh, Patricia Boyle. *The Female Figure in Eiléan Ní Chuilleanáin's Poetry* (Cork: Cork University Press, 2013)

Haffenden, John, *The Life of John Berryman* (London: Routledge & Kegan Paul, 1982)

Hamilton, Hugo, *The Speckled People* (London: Fourth Estate, 2003)

Hanna, Adam, *Northern Irish Poetry and Domestic Space* (Basingstoke: Palgrave Macmillan, 2015)

Heaney, Seamus, *Opened Ground: Poems 1966–1996* (London: Faber and Faber, 1998)

Hewitt, John, *A North Light: Twenty-five Years in a Municipal Gallery*, ed. Frank Ferguson and Kathryn White (Dublin: Four Courts, 2013)

—, *Loose Ends* (Belfast: Blackstaff Press, 1983)

—, *Collected Poems of John Hewitt*, edited with an introduction by Frank Ormsby (Belfast: Blackstaff Press, 1991)

Johnstone, Robert, 'Playing for Ireland', *Honest Ulsterman*, 96, Spring-Summer 1989

Jordan, Neil, *Night in Tunisia and Other Stories* (Dublin: Writers Co-Op, 1976)

Bibliography

Kavanagh, Patrick, *Collected Poems*, ed. Antoinette Quinn (London: Allen Lane, 2004)

—, *Self-Portrait* (Dublin: The Dolmen Press, 1964)

—, *Come Dance with Kitty Stobling & Other Poems* (London: Longmans, Green and Co. Ltd, 1960)

Keogh, Dermot (ed.), *The Lost Decade: Ireland in the 1950s* (Cork: Mercier Press, 2004)

Kiberd, Declan, *Inventing Ireland: The Literature of the Modern Nation* (London: Jonathan Cape, 1995)

Kilroy, Thomas, 'The Writers' Group in Galway', *Irish Times*, 8 April 1976

—, 'Anglo-Irish Playwrights and Comic Tradition', *The Crane Bag* (3:2, 1979)

—, 'The Anglo-Irish Theatrical Imagination', *Búllan* (3.2., Winter 1997/ Spring 1998)

—, 'The Literary Tradition of Irish Drama', *Anglistentag Proceedings* (Vol. XVI, Tubingen: Max Niemeyer Verlag, 1995)

—, 'Two Playwrights: Yeats and Beckett', *Myth and Reality in Irish Literature*, ed. Joseph Ronsley (Waterloo, Ontario: Wilfrid Laurier University Press, 1977)

Kinsella, Thomas, *Collected Poems 1956–2001* (Manchester: Carcanet Press, 2001)

Knowlson, James, *Damned to Fame: The Life of Samuel Beckett* (London: Bloomsbury, 1996)

Lee, Joseph, *Ireland 1912–1985: Politics and Society* (Cambridge: Cambridge University Press, 1990)

Longley, Edna, *Louis MacNeice* (London: Faber and Faber, 1988)

—, *From Cathleen to Anorexia: The Breakdowns of Irelands* (Dublin: Attic Press, 1990)

—, *The Living Stream: Literature and Revisionism in Ireland* (Newcastle upon Tyne: Bloodaxe Books, 1994)

—, 'Encryptions: Stephen Enniss, *After the Titanic: A Life of Derek Mahon*', *The Yellow Nib*, no.10, Spring 2015

Lowell, Robert, *Collected Poems* ed. Frank Bidart and David Gewanter (London: Faber and Faber, 2003)

—, *Collected Prose*, ed. Robert Giroux (London: Faber and Faber, 1987)

MacDonogh, Patrick, *Poems*, ed. Derek Mahon (Oldcastle, Co. Meath: The Gallery Press, 2001)

MacNeice, Louis, *The Strings are False: An Unfinished Autobiography* (London: Faber and Faber, 1965)

Maguire, W. A., *Belfast: A History* (Lancaster: Carnegie Publishing, 2009)

Mahon, Derek, *Poems 1962–1978* (Oxford: Oxford University Press, 1979)

—, *Collected Poems* (Oldcastle, Co. Meath: The Gallery Press, 1999)

—, *New Collected Poems* (Oldcastle, Co. Meath: The Gallery Press, 2011)

—, *Journalism: Selected Prose 1970–1995* (Oldcastle, Co. Meath: The Gallery Press, 1996)

—, *Selected Prose 1970–1995* (Oldcastle, Co. Meath: The Gallery Press, 2012)

—, *Harbour Lights* (Oldcastle, Co. Meath: The Gallery Press, 2005)

—, *Night-Crossing* (Oxford: Oxford University Press, 1968)

—, *New Collected Poems* (Oldcastle, Co. Meath: The Gallery Press, 2012)

Maxwell, D.E.S., *A Critical History of Modern Irish Drama, 1891–1980* (Cambridge: Cambridge University Press, 1984)

Mays, J.C.C. 'Introductory Essay', Brian Coffey Special Issue, *Irish University Review*, 5:1, Spring 1975

McConnell, Gail, *Northern Irish Poetry and Theology* (Basingstoke: Palgrave Macmillan, 2014)

McCormack, W. J., *From Burke to Beckett: Ascendancy, Tradition and Betrayal in Literary History* (Cork: Cork University Press, 1994)

—, *Blood Kindred: W. B. Yeats: The Life, the Death, the Politics* (London: Pimlico, 2005)

—, *Northman John Hewitt, 1907–87 An Irish Writer, His World, and His Times* (Oxford: Oxford University Press, 2015)

McGahern, John, *Love of the World: Essays* (London: Faber and Faber, 2009)

—, *The Collected Stories* (London: Faber and Faber, 1992)

—, *High Ground* (London: Faber and Faber, 1985)

—, *The Leavetaking* (London: Faber and Faber, 1984 [1974])

McGahern, John (ed.), *John Butler Yeats, Letters to his son William Butler Yeats and others 1869–1922* (London: Faber and Faber, 1999)

McGurl, Mark, *The Program Era: Postwar Fiction and the Role of Creative Writing* (Cambridge,Massachusetts: Harvard University Press, 2009)

McIntosh, Gillian, *The Force of Culture: Unionist Identities in Twentieth-Century Ireland* (Cork: Cork University Press, 1999)

McKittrick, David, Seamus Kelters, Brian Feeney, Chris Thornton and David Mc Vea, *Lost Lives: The Stories of Men, Women and Children who Died as a result of the Northern Ireland Conflict* (Edinburgh: Mainstream Publishing, 2007)

McMullan, Anna and S. E. Wilmer, *Reflections on Beckett: A Centenary Celebration* (Ann Arbor, Michigan: University of Michigan Press, 2009)

Menand, Louis, 'A Critic at Large: Show or Tell: Should Creative Writing be Taught?' *The New Yorker*, 8 and 15 June 2009

Milligan, Alice, *Poems* selected and edited with an Introduction by Henry Mangan (Dublin: M. H. Gill, 1954)

Montague, John, *The Figure in the Cave and Other Essays* (Dublin: The Lilliput Press, 1989)

— (ed.), *The Faber Book of Modern Irish Verse* (London: Faber and Faber, 1974)

—, *Company: A Chosen Life* (London: Duckworth, 2001)

—, *The Pear is Ripe: A Memoir* (Dublin: Liberties Press, 2007)

Monteiro, George (ed.), *Conversations with Elizabeth Bishop* (Jackson, Mississippi: University of Mississippi Press, 1996)

Moore, Brian, *The Lonely Passion of Judith Hearne* (London: André Deutsch, 1955)

—, *The Emperor of Ice Cream* (London: Mayflower Books, 1970)

—, *Lies of Silence* (London: Vintage, 1992)

Moriarty, Gerry, 'Gunman. Hunger Striker. Dramatist. Laurence McKeown', News Review, *The Irish Times* (13 August 2016)

Morrissey, Sinead and Stephen Connolly, *The Future Always Makes Me So Thirsty: New Poets from the North of Ireland* (Belfast: Blackstaff Press, 2016)

—, *Parallax* (Manchester: Carcanet Press, 2013)

Bibliography

Moylan, Terry, *The Indignant Muse: Poetry and Songs of the Irish Revolutions, 1887–1926* (Dublin: The Lilliput Press, 2016)

Muldoon, Paul, *Poems 1968–1998* (London: Faber and Faber, 2001)

Ní Anluain, Cliodhna (ed.), *Reading the Future: Irish Writers in Conversation with Mike Murphy* (Dublin: The Lilliput Press, 2000)

Ní Chuilleanáin, Eiléan, *Acts & Monuments* (Dublin: The Gallery Press, 1972)

—, *Selected Poems* (Oldcastle, Co. Meath: The Gallery Press, 2008; London: Faber and Faber, 2008)

—, *The Sun-Fish* (Oldcastle, Co. Meath: The Gallery Press, 2009)

—, *The Boys of Bluehill* (Oldcastle, Co. Meath: The Gallery Press, 2015)

—, 'Rousing the Reader: *One Thousand Things Worth Knowing* by Paul Muldoon'. *Dublin Review of Books* (Issue 66, April 2015)

— (ed.), *Irish Women: Image and Achievement: Women in Irish Culture from Ancient Times.* (Dublin: Arlen House, 1985)

— (ed.), *As I was among the Captives: Joseph Campbell's Prison Diary, 1922–23* (Cork: Cork University Press, 2001)

— (ed.), *The Wilde Legacy* (Dublin: Four Courts Press, 2003)

—, *Verbale / Minutes / Tuairisc / from the Italian of Michele Ranchetti* with Cormac Ó Cuilleanáin and Gabriel Rosenstock (Dublin: Instituto Italiano di Cultura, 2002)

—, Ní Dhomhnaill, Nuala, *The Water Horse* with translations into English by Eiléan Ní Chuilleanáin and Medbh McGuckian (Oldcastle, Co. Meath: The Gallery Press, 1999)

O'Brien, Máire Cruise, *The Same Age as the State: The Autobiography of Máire Cruise O'Brien* (Dublin: O'Brien Press, 2004)

O'Connell, Sandra, *George Reavey 1907–1976: The Endless Chain, a literary biography* (TCD Thesis, 2006)

O'Driscoll, Dennis, S*tepping Stones: Interviews with Seamus Heaney* (London: Faber and Faber, 2009)

O'Keeffe, Timothy, *Myles: Portraits of Brian O' Nolan* (London: Martin Brian & O'Keeffe, 1973)

Oppenheim, Lois (ed.), *Palgrave Advances in Samuel Beckett Studies* (New York: Palgrave, 2004)

O'Reilly, Caitríona, 'Notes to Self', *The Irish Times*, 4 June 2011

Ormsby, Frank, *Poets from the North of Ireland* (Belfast: Blackstaff Press, 1979)

—, *A Rage for Order: Poetry of the Northern Ireland Troubles* (Belfast: Blackstaff Press, 1992)

O'Sullivan, Michael, *Brendan Behan: A Life* (Dublin: Blackwater Press, 1997)

Parker, Stewart, *Plays 2* (London: Methuen, 2000)

—, *Television Plays*, ed. Clare Wallace (Prague: Litteraria Pragensia, 2008)

—, *Dramatis Personae & Other Writings*, ed. Gerald Dawe, Maria Johnston and Clare Wallace (Prague: Litteraria Pragensia, 2008)

—, *High Pop: The Irish Times Column 1970–1976*, ed. Gerald Dawe and Maria Johnston (Belfast: Lagan Press, 2008)

Pilling, John, *Samuel Beckett* (London: Routledge & Kegan Paul, 1976)

Plimpton, George, *Writers at Work: The Paris Review Interviews* (London: Secker & Warburg, 1977)

Plunkett, James, *Strumpet City* (Dublin: Gill & Macmillan, 2013 [1969])

Pound, Ezra, *ABC of Reading* (New York: New Directions, 1960)

—, *Selected Poems* (London: Faber and Faber, 1975)

Quinn, Antoinette, *Patrick Kavanagh: A Biography* (Dublin: Gill & Macmillan, 2001)

Quinn, Justin, *The Cambridge Introduction to Modern Irish Poetry 1800–2000* (Cambridge: Cambridge University Press, 2008)

Randolph, Jody Allen (ed.), *Eavan Boland: A Sourcebook* (Manchester: Carcanet Press, 2007)

Reavey, George, *Faust's Metamorphoses* (Fontenay-Aux-Roses: New Review, 1932)

—, *Soviet Literature Today* (London: Lindsay Drummond, 1946)

—, *Nostradam* (Paris: Europa Press, 1935)

Richtarik, Marilynn, *Stewart Parker: A Life* (Oxford: Oxford University Press, 2012)

Roche, Anthony, *Contemporary Irish Drama from Beckett to McGuinness* (Dublin: Gill & Macmillan, 1994)

Ryan, John, *Remembering How We Stood: Bohemian Dublin at the Mid-Century* (Dublin: Gill & Macmillan, 1975)

Sandbrook, Dominic, *Never Had it So Good: A History of Britain from Suez to The Beatles* (London: Abacus, 2006)

Sands, Bobby, *Writings from Prison* (Cork: Mercier Press, 1998)

Simpson, Eileen, *Poets in their Youth: A Memoir* (London: Faber and Faber, 1982)

Simpson, Louis, *Ships Going into the Blue: Essays and Notes on Poetry* (Ann Arbor, Michigan: 1994)

Swift, Patrick and David Wright (eds), *An Anthology from X* (Oxford: Oxford University Press, 1988)

Synge, J. M., *Collected Works: Vol. 1. Poems*, ed. Robin Skelton (London: Oxford University Press, 1962)

Thompson, Sam, *Over the Bridge*, edited with an introduction by Stewart Parker (Dublin: Gill and Macmillan, 1970)

—, *Over the Bridge & Other Plays*, ed. John Keyes (Belfast: Lagan Press, 1997)

Tóibín, Colm, *Bad Blood: A Walk Along the Irish Border* (London: Vintage, 1994 [1987])

Wills, Clair, *That Neutral Island: A Cultural History of Ireland during the Second World War* (London: Faber and Faber, 2007)

—, *The Best are Leaving: Emigration and Post-War Irish Culture* (Cambridge: Cambridge University Press, 2015)

Woodward, Guy, *Culture, Northern Ireland and the Second World War* (Oxford: Oxford University Press, 2015)

Worth, Katharine, *The Irish Drama of Europe from Yeats to Beckett* (London: Athlone Press, 1986 [1978])

—, *Samuel Beckett's Theatre: Life Journeys* (Oxford: Clarendon Press, 2001)

Yeats W.B., *The Poems, A New Edition*, edited by Richard J. Finneran (London: Macmillan, 1984)

—, *Autobiographies* (London: Macmillan, 1970)

—, *Explorations* (London, Macmillan, 1962)

—, *The Collected Plays* (London: Macmillan, 1966)

— (ed.), *Oxford Book of Modern Verse 1892–1935* (Oxford: Oxford University Press, 1936)

—, *Letters on Poetry from W.B. Yeats to Dorothy Wellesley* (Oxford: Oxford University Press, 1964 [1940])

INDEX

Index